Mirrored Minds
Søren Kierkegaard and Hans Christian Andersen

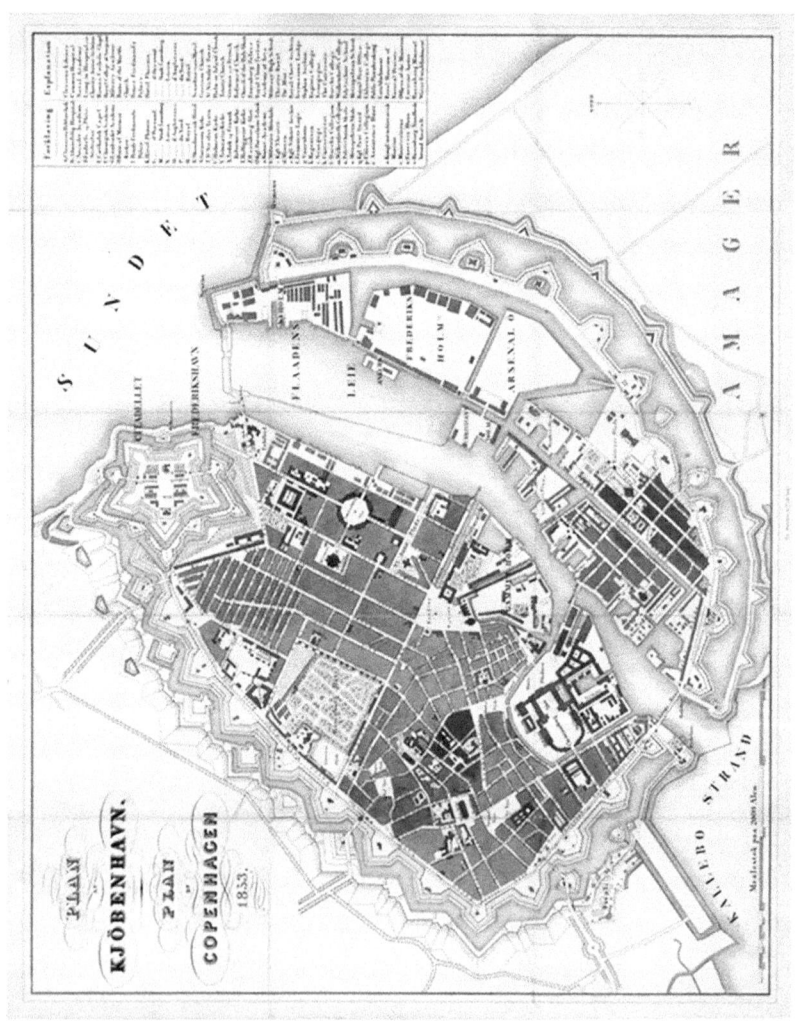

Map of Copenhagen 1853.

Mirrored Minds
Søren Kierkegaard and Hans Christian Andersen

Kate Ashton

The Lutterworth Press

The Lutterworth Press.

P.O. Box 60
Cambridge
CB1 2NT
United Kingdom
www.lutterworth.co
publishing@lutterworth.co

Paperback ISBN: 978 0 718 89751 2
PDF ISBN: 978 0 718 89752 9
ePub ISBN: 978 0 718 89753 6

British Library Cataloguing in Publication Data
A record is available from the British Library

Published by The Lutterworth Press, 2025

Copyright © Kate Ashton, 2025

All rights reserved. No part of this edition may be reproduced, stored electronically or in any retrieval system, or transmitted in any form or by any means, electronic, mechanical, photocopying, recording, or otherwise, without prior written permission from the Publisher (permissions@lutterworth.com).

'Half childish game, half God in your heart.'

—*Goethe,* Faust

'Explanation when there is nothing else.'

—*Marguerite Duras,* Hiroshima Mon Amour

'That is the road we all have to take – over the Bridge
of Sighs into eternity.'

—*Søren Kierkegaard,* Journals

*For Colin and Jo,
Elliott and Lochlan*

Contents

Acknowledgements ix
Acknowledgements for Images xii
Preface xiii

1. Divine Doubt — 1
2. A Lowland Habitat — 12
3. The Path of Perdition — 40
4. The Bridge of Sighs — 67
5. Lily of the Valley — 87
6. A Palace of Pretend — 114
7. Into the Silence — 131
8. Shadow Boxing — 156
9. Esquisse — 177
10. To Will One Thing — 197
11. Divine Folly — 223

Bibliography 251
Index 253

Acknowledgements

I am indebted to The Lutterworth Press, with special thanks to publisher Adrian Brink for his faith in the book, and the editorial team for realising the end product. My first editor, Samuel Fitzgerald, set me off on the right path, and his successor Sarah Algar-Hughes kept us carefully focused thereafter. I want to thank Georgina Melia for the perfect, greatly admired front cover. My irreplaceable agent, Wampe de Veer of The Blackbird Literary Agency, was and is an unfailing source of sound advice, perspective and encouragement – to say nothing of our rejuvenating cross-Channel phone conversations.

The Society of Authors again demonstrated its indispensability, and I am extremely grateful to Kate Pool for her guidance. A writer is only a writer and some of us are not much good at anything else, let alone the finer points of contractual arrangements and intellectual property rights, professional matters in which the SoA specialises. I was fortunate to find Sharon Rubin and the patient Emma Brown prepared to offer expert permissions assistance.

As libraries all over the country are being summarily closed, this might be an opportune moment to note their priceless value, particularly to a writer in a remote area. Nairn Library, under the auspices of Highland High Life Libraries, supplied the patient, highly specialised support of librarians Louise Sorrell, Dawn Allison, Helen Williamson and Laura Blaikie, while Andrina Gammie, library assistant at the High Life Highland Library Support Unit in Inverness tracked down and forwarded rarer titles, re-renewing on request. Thank you all.

During the writing I often enquired casually about people's feelings and childhood experience of Hans Christian Andersen's fairy tales, so gathering spontaneous adult reactions to the work. During such encounters I hid my project for fear of diverting attention from fresh and unadulterated response to the main topic; many a gratefully absorbed if unattributed remark enhanced my background sense of Andersen's lasting societal influence. Studiously avoided was any discourse relating to Kierkegaard, the man or his work. In the public arena this was easy, as he is comparatively little read, but neither did I seek expert input. The perils of a solitudinous approach to biography are obvious, but just as plain to me, thanks to Kierkegaard and Andersen, was the potentiating power of pure subjectivity in interpreting their story.

When it came to the technical skills of addressing a new audience, writing friends offered generous help. Janet Sutherland shared unwavering confidence in the project, along with advice on the more arcane aspects of annotation and footnoting; I continue to learn much from her as writer and poet. Lucy Hamilton's mastery of condensed form provided stylistic inspiration. Tony Frazer of Shearsman Books offered kind encouragement at exactly the right moments. Jude Welton went to great lengths to convey advice from a former colleague. Warm thanks to Cynthia Rogerson for our book-talks/dog-walks along the beach. My thanks to biographer Jennifer Morag Henderson, who unhesitatingly made time to help solve a technical dilemma.

Many others offered regular support: Cleo Welsh and Catriona Dutton drove us to Thursday yoga classes in Findhorn with the peerless Louise Simmons, thanks so much. Ally Macdonald amply proved the 'friend in need' maxim, and Alex Williamson shared many a refreshing literary lope along the byways. My thanks to Marc Marnie and Mandy Lawson; Tess Dennis, Elaine and Ian James, for all the unreturned hospitality. Ellen Maxwell kept her car at cosy five-star feline rating for a bitterly cold midwinter mid-book flit. Thank you, Sam and staff at Sky Delights, purveyors of culinary comfort and philosophy. Sally Ward spurred on the work whilst constantly tempting me, with Kay and Stella, to join them at the pub or out in a skiff on the Moray Firth. Long walks with Therese Muskus made space for Nature's true artistry, thank you. Debriefing over a glass of wine with Pam Bochel was a Friday treat. Tanera Bryden, Rhona MacDonald and Jean Godden showed endless interest; my special thanks to Jean as first reader of an (awful) early draft. Samantha Holland, thank you for The Nairn Bookshop. My thanks to all those

Acknowledgements

unnamed but unforgotten whose interest invigorated the writing process.

Without the financial support of The Highland Council, I would not have been able to retire from paid work at 65 to write full-time.

My deepest gratitude is reserved for family. Colin grew into the beautiful person he is alongside and despite the project; without him I should never have arrived at a premise and there would have been no book. Chloe King, treasured niece, has swum alongside no matter how choppy the waters. Ben Fowler is the best of stalwart brothers, boatbuilder and oarsman that he is. To you and yours, my thanks for all the tender troubles, joy and love we've shared, and times cherished over the past decade.

Areas of expertise touched on in this book, including theology, history, psychology, art and literature, are familiar to me only as a lay person. All errors and omissions, misunderstandings and misrepresentations in the book are mine alone.

Kate Ashton
Nairn, February 2025

Acknowledgements for Images

The following illustrations relating to Hans Christian Andersen are reproduced courtesy of the Museum Odense, Odense, Denmark. My thanks to Ejnar Stig Askgaard, senior researcher, for his help in accessing these: Hans Christian Andersen's birthplace, Odense; Vilhelm Pedersen's illustration for 'The Little Mermaid'; portrait of Edvard Collin; portrait of Henriette Wulff. Also, Andersen's sketches from his travels: 'The Simplon Road Across the Alps', 19 September 1833; 'Genoa', 2 October 1833; 'The dancing dervishes of Pera', from a letter to Henriette Wulff, 29 May 1841; 'Piazza del Trinita, Florence', 11 April 1834; portrait of Andersen from 'The Story of My Life', 1855.

Illustrations relating to Søren Kierkegaard are reproduced courtesy of the Royal Danish Library, with particular thanks to Laurids Nielsen: 'Unfinished sketch of Kierkegaard by his cousin Niels Christian Kierkegaard', circa.1840, in a private collection; 'Bishop Mynster', painting by C. A. Jensen (1792-1870); photographic portrait 'Regine Olsen Schlegel. 1855'. 'Letter to Regine: Kierkegaard sketches himself standing on the Knippelbro, peering through a spyglass'. Image of 'Regine Schlegel by photographer Niels Willumsen (1812-1870)' in juxtaposed portraits of her and Kierkegaard. Diamond ring given to Regine on their engagement, returned, refashioned by Kierkegaard into a cross to remind him of his decision to dedicate himself to his faith and writings and worn until his death in 1855. Image courtesy: The Museum of Copenhagen.

Preface

As any expert or lay reader will recognise from the bibliography, this account of the parallel lives of two great men does not pretend to present a fully researched biography of either. Two authoritative biographies have provided factual chronology and background, chosen for their accessibility and clarity, but most of all for authorial warmth toward their subject: Lowrie's *A Short Life of Kierkegaard*[1] and Wullschläger's *Hans Christian Andersen, The Life of a Storyteller*.[2] For the rest, I have relied on Kierkegaard's *Journals*[3] and Andersen's *Diaries*.[4] Rather than any unqualified attempt at academic rigour, my aim has been to offer some more subtle and intuitive insight into the emotional and spiritual kinship between Søren Kierkegaard and Hans Christian Andersen. This, thanks to many extraordinary biographical synchronicities, is perceptible in both their individual histories and writings, as well as in their often fractured and fractious personal relationship.

Like many another child, I came to Andersen as a six-year-old, when after a long hospital stay my parents arrived to collect me bearing a small volume of fairy tales as homecoming gift. Of the long taxi ride back

---

1. Walter Lowrie, *A Short Life of Kierkegaard* (Princeton NJ: Princeton University Press, 1974).
2. Jackie Wullschläger, *Hans Christian Andersen, The Life of a Storyteller* (London: Penguin Books, 2001).
3. Søren Kierkegaard, *The Journals of Søren Kierkegaard*, ed. and trans. by Alexander Dru (Oxford: Oxford University Press, 1938).
4. Hans Christian Andersen, *The Diaries of Hans Christian Andersen*, ed. and trans. by Patricia L. Conroy and Sven H. Rossel (Washington: University of Washington Press, 1990).

from London to Stevenage my salient memory concerns that book – its prince gazing out over cobalt waters from which arises a golden-tressed mermaid – how I clasped it close to my chest to keep it safe: the same 1950s edition I have used as source material here. Nearly half a century later, my son made me a birthday present of Andersen's complete diaries. Kierkegaard's ageless wisdom arrived at another moment of need, a lifechanging crisis in my thirties, when my late sister gave me his journals. I have been reading them alongside the works ever since.

The pattern and relevance of an unwritten literary and relational history between Kierkegaard and Andersen took longer to reveal itself, emerging gradually from the expanding worldview that came with many years living and travelling in mainland Europe. The more familiarised with the continent, the more aware I grew of how profoundly the strangely interrelated works of these two Danes had permeated European culture, fanning out from here to shape the spirit and imagination of the wider western world. At the same time came a dawning realisation of the transformational effect on my own life of this hidden vein.

Later still, I sensed a story seeking to be told, but how to find a form sympathetic and sinuous enough to convey the deep confluence of these two mighty rivers? Contemporary prodigious minds at work in the same small corner of nineteenth-century northern Europe, each recognising in the other their individual confrontation with the societal ambiance and stigmata of their day; sometimes a violent clash of words and temperament, more often an unspoken awareness each of the other following their particular personal and creative course. The streaming now toward the other, now apart, of these discrete creative currents revealing something of the mystery and majesty of solitary artistic effort in shaping meaning from random circumstance and contributing that cognisance to an all too often unreceptive world.

Each life demonstrates the paradoxical writerly yearning both to reach and remain hidden from others; every flawed striving toward love resounds with the same dread which invites divine inspiration. Each tentative moment of jubilation is a trembling on the edge of faith, each failure a rebirth. The incidental interplay between these two great men and minds creates a new conceptual space within which each is constantly reilluminated, reanimated and defined, offering infinite shifts in perception and perspective that reveal the sacred individuality reflected in the other and their work – even and especially when they lose sight of it themselves.

Chapter 1

Divine Doubt

There were moments in his life when the Danish poet and philosopher Søren Kierkegaard (1813-55) believed he was going mad. Famed for his Socratic irony and self-parody, in this matter, as in all others, he was deadly serious. Indeed, he consulted his doctors about the possibility on several occasions. If Jean-Paul Sartre was right in asserting a century later that 'Hell is other people', then there were grounds enough for Kierkegaard's concern. He was a tortured soul, having suffered a traumatic childhood and he carried the scars throughout his life. It was a background that predisposed him to an agonisingly lonely adulthood. Yet he also bore the mark of genius from his earliest days and even his uncomplicated, loving and rejected mother recognised in her youngest son the brilliance of his star.

The eminent Kierkegaard scholar and translator, Walter Lowrie, in a 'Background' to his brief biography *A Short Life of Kierkegaard* warns how problematic is any attempt to disentangle mental disarray from genius, of the perils of making 'observation upon a superior mind'.[1] He quotes Kierkegaard recalling Seneca, himself citing Aristotle: *nullum unquam exstetit magnum ingenium sine aliqua ementia*, ('There never was great genius without some madness'), to which Kierkegaard adds, 'For this dementia is the suffering allotted to genius, it is the expression if I may say so, of the divine jealousy, whereas the gift of genius is the expression of the divine favour.'[2] So

---

1. Lowrie, *Short Life of Kierkegaard*, p. 28.
2. Ibid., pp. 27-28.

Unfinished sketch of Kierkegaard by his cousin Niels Christian Kierkegaard, circa. 1840, in a private collection.

Kierkegaard introduces the idea of an equivocal element in genius, present from the outset but maintained and amplified with the experience of living out of kilter with the universal: a form of intrinsic 'madness' registered as an insoluble paradox. Faced with this inner conundrum, the sufferer – for it is a suffering – may either reject the sense of impotence it imposes upon him by denying all his limitations and so stray into the realm of hubris, or else seek refuge in religion. Either way, genius uniquely and definitively isolates the bearer.

How then is any critic or commentator to go about remarking on the origin of genius? Who dare tread such hallowed ground? The poet, the philosopher, a great artist of any kind pays dear for his gift. The doctors having failed him, Søren Kierkegaard became his own physician, and no professional could have been more rigorous a seeker after psychopathology, diagnosis and cure. Central to Kierkegaard's search for existential truth was a thorough and remorseless mining of his childhood for clues to his later experience and response to life. No aspect of parental or sibling influence on his own psyche escaped him, with one exception, to be discussed. His self-examination extended to interrogation of the strengths and weaknesses of the wider society into which he had been born, and to the established Danish Church which had played so prominent a part in his upbringing and which, far from escaping his forensic eye, became its ultimate focus.

He loved the land of his birth and its people and held in his heart very real affection for the city of Copenhagen, revelling in its commonplaces and modesty in relation to other grander European cities. He revered and championed the Danish language, even at its most parochial, and delighted in engaging in conversation with all and sundry on the streets during his daily walks. A gifted listener, he humbly adopted ideas gleaned in such encounters, recognising and valuing the wisdom of the 'Everyman'; preoccupied always with the individual rather the body politic, he had no time for specious, showy argument. Yet, as Lowrie insists, despite such pragmatism, Kierkegaard would recoil from any analysis of his works and life predicated purely upon his personal history; for him the individual was capable of absolute transcendence over hereditary and material circumstance and the individual stood above the race.

Although his own character and the background factors Kierkegaard unearthed in exploring his response to life might easily have led such a man to conclude insanity to be his unavoidable fate, there was another variable. He was also a poet, in the original sense of being a maker, a writer, or at least of possessing a poetic imagination; and, given that psychology may be described as an inexact science, the same must be said of art. According to the psychiatrist and psychologist Carl Gustav Jung (1875-1961) 'both these spheres of the mind have something in reserve that is peculiar to them and can be explained only in its own terms'.[3]

* * *

If Kierkegaard spent his life commuting self-knowledge into the fathoming of humankind's relationship to God, an absolute

---

3. Carl Gustav Jung, 'On the Relation of Analytical Psychology to Poetry', a lecture first delivered to the Society for German Language and Literature, Zurich, May 1922, in C.G. Jung, *The Spirit in Man, Art, and Literature* (Collected Works of C.G. Jung, Volume 15) (Princeton, NJ: Princeton University Press, 1972), p. 66.

methodological antithesis may be found in his contemporary, friend and literary sparring partner, the storyteller Hans Christian Andersen (1805-75). Kierkegaard's senior by eight years and a month, almost to the day, Andersen was as tall, gauche, ugly and awkward a figure as his younger counterpart was slight, delicate, charismatic and handsome. The two men were youthful drinking companions. They followed one another's career and at least spasmodically read each other's work, reviewing and/or commenting on it. Each went through life noting their differing philosophical and literary paths, and where they converged. The strange spiky attraction between the two surely rested upon something close to filial love, or at least a measure of unspoken mutual compassion.

Andersen too dreaded losing his mind. He also knew himself marked by catastrophic childhood and sexual trauma, but Andersen found his salvation lay in evasion. His escapism was radical and took many forms, from travel to sexual fantasy to fairy tale. It was not that Andersen denied the devastation of his early experience; often, as his circumstances improved, he boasted of and capitalised on it. He knew how damaged he was and was haunted by an awareness of mental derangement which had plagued him from early childhood, a thread of insanity which ran through both sides of his family. His father had lost his mind, and a paternal grandfather earned the taunt of 'Mad Anders' from the Odense village louts for wandering the forest, laurelled with a coronet of wild flowers, as he whittled strange creatures from bits of wood. Andersen's alcoholic mother would die in the madhouse.

There was no length to which Andersen would not go to avoid the same fate, and if this involved some deep repudiation of his background and the lifelong cultivation of those he considered his social betters, so be it. However, just beneath the surface of this enervating daily effort lurked always truths as lurid and threatening as those of a fairy tale. Andersen's compulsion to mythologise his own life is epitomised in what he considered his definitive autobiography, in which he sublimates and embroiders reality to a quite extraordinary degree. This in marked contrast to the realism of his stories, which always ring true. In composing the fairy tales he never loses sight of the bald facts of human existence or shrinks from exposing us, often brutally, to our weaknesses. It is this purity that lies at the heart of his oeuvre and which renders it so universal, compelling and consoling, however swathed in sentimentality, however consciously we absorb or resist his message.

Writing at the age of 30 to his closest friend, Edvard Collin, the first man with whom he fell deeply and hopelessly in love, Andersen pleads for compassion; if Edvard could look into the depths of his soul he would understand 'the source of my longing'.[4] The waters of the clearest lake had unknown depths to which no diver had descended. This letter coincides with the first stories to come from his pen. It was Edvard's marriage plans which precipitated the vengeful agony that animates *The Little Mermaid*, the most famous, macabre and lauded of Andersen's stories. It is a parable that perfectly embodies the ferocious power of its author to distance himself from painful reality by walking us slowly through the darkness.

* * *

Both Andersen and Kierkegaard recognised their own genius. While one embraced his tortured truth and the other found ways of evading it, each endowed the world with literary works that would shape the soul of modern Europe and spread their influence far beyond it. Their private interchange sprang from mutual recognition of extraordinary literary effort and output, fuelled by a life of agonising loneliness and alienation, the impossibility for each of 'realising the universal'.[5] It was this suffering that drove each individually to the brink and which underpinned their unspoken kinship. The contact between the two might shift from fraught to tenuous, but it was no less real for that. Each recognised the other's response to their time as Europe emerged from the 'age of reason'. The early years of the nineteenth century saw the ousting of old order, radical review and replacement of personal and social values. The arrival of German Romanticism led on from the *Sturm und Drang* of the inner man, matched by turbulent external change as the country and continent moved towards modernity.

The relationship between genius and madness has been much debated and never resolved. Genius is an equally contested central theme in European Romanticism, and a salient feature of its characterisation. Jung surely came closest to the truth in admitting

---

4. Wullschläger, *Hans Christian Andersen*, p. 2.
5. Kierkegaard's term, used throughout his writings to indicate the normal course of events leading to marriage and the founding of a family.

the deep ambiguities and difficulties involved in dissecting psychology free of art. There being no consanguinity between art and science, he confined himself and his entire discipline to treating only that aspect of art which may be 'submitted to psychological scrutiny without violating its nature' by moving beyond the process of artistic creation to probe its 'innermost essence'.[6] This essence could no more be explained by the psychologist than feeling might be grasped or described by the intellect.[7] Jung goes on to stress the discrete nature of art as opposed to science, expressed in fundamental differences which long ago impressed themselves upon the human mind and led to their separation. He was concerned about reductive scientific attitudes, specifically an oversimplification of highly developed states of mind, such as the creative, by eliminating its more nebulous nature in trying to trace it back to an underlying undifferentiated state. In thus disallowing unification between disparate areas, science sought to tether them to a simple causal link and so subordinate them to a general but more elementary principle.[8]

Jung could identify no fundamental unifying principle that justified so reductive a step, be that the undifferentiated chaos of the primeval or infant mind, or magical mentality, or the absence of demonstrable 'mind' in animals.[9] He expands on the similarity between this and another then current reductive tendency, that of applying the same technique to art and literary criticism, particularly poetry. To dissect and generalise a poem, said Jung, not only turns it into nothing more than a crude psychological pen-portrait of the poet but renders it susceptible to confusion with psychopathology. Such distraction does disservice to both the artist and the work but succeeds in disarming and rendering it safely distanced from the viewer or reader, who may now take cover from any challenge or threat posed to their peace of mind – an easy but deeply flawed approach. The material and treatment in a poet's work is easily traced back to seminal formative experience and primal relationships, but so are neuroses and psychoses: everyone has been a child, has good and bad habits, preferences, passions, etc, but common aetiology stops there:

---

6. Jung, 'On the relation…' in *The Spirit in Man*, p. 66.
7. Ibid.
8. Ibid.
9. Ibid.

'If a work of art is explained in the same way as a neurosis, then either the work of art is a neurosis or a neurosis is a work of art. This explanation is all very well as a play on words, but sound common sense rebels against putting a work of art on the same level as a neurosis.'[10]

As Jung points out, all of us have had parents, the nervy intellectual, the poet, or the bricklayer, all take into adult life a father- or a mother-complex, all experience the common difficulties associated with knowing about sex. In the work of one may be detected the overriding influence of the father, in another that of the mother, and a poet may show obvious signs of sexual repression in their poetry. These traits being universal and so shared by the neurotic and every other person, nothing is gained by applying the criteria to a work of art. So, Jung concluded, by studying the artist we may at most improve our understanding of the psychological antecedents of a work of art, but not much else.[11]

This observation marks yet another of the small and greater fractures and differences which led to his final departure from the path laid out for him by his former mentor, Sigmund Freud, whom Jung felt 'encouraged the literary historian to bring certain peculiarities of a work of art into relation with the intimate, personal life of the poet.'[12] It was an attitude Jung deplored, an indelicacy he attributed particularly to the medical psychologist and one which led to flagrant abuses. 'A slight whiff' of scandal might spice up a biography, but a pinch more amounted to prurient curiosity – 'bad taste masquerading as science'; the poet becomes a clinical case, very likely yet another addition to 'the curiosa of *psychopathia sexualis* …',[13] and the psychoanalysis of art turns aside from its proper objective into a province as broad as mankind, not in the least specific to the artist and of even less relevance to his art. This may be easily recognised for the ubiquitous trait it is today, in a western society insatiably hungry for sex and scandal, where boundaries have been jettisoned and individual understanding of the human body, mind and spirit is regressed to the point of totemic response to symbol and image. Here

---

10. Ibid., p. 67.
11. Ibid.
12. Ibid.
13. Ibid., p. 68.

the beauty and profundity of a work of art may be either elevated or entirely subsumed beneath transitory moral judgement of its creator: the mindless culture of celebrity and pariah.

A work of art, then, is not born of disease. Yet Jung gave full credit to the biographies of great artists in attesting to the tyrannical character of the creative urge, which may take hostage the entire personality of the artist, subjecting their very humanity to the work and casting aside along the way every pleasurable distraction, health, and even ordinary human happiness. The unborn work of art, Jung suggests, may be seen as a force of nature, so insistent in its need to be realised that it renders the personal fate of the artist immaterial, a mere vehicle, and makes of the creative process a living entity implanted in the human psyche. Jung termed this in the language of analytical psychology 'an *autonomous complex*: a split-off portion of the psyche which leads a life of its own outside the hierarchy of consciousness.'[14] Imagine how it might feel to the artist to sense this mysterious dichotomy at work beyond their conscious control but within the context of day-to-day reality. The struggle to reconcile the demands of everyday life with an overriding compulsion to mould meaning from it. The constant and exhaustive search demanded by their chosen medium – or the medium which has chosen them – for the means and energy to do so. Most of all, the conflict between external and interior worlds which might impede progress in either, so suggesting or proving to the artist's rationale their own hopelessly inadequate, flawed and fragmented personality. It is not hard to conjure up moments in which this conviction triumphs and they sense the nearness of the madhouse.

The clandestine nature of an autonomous complex such as the creative urge is described by Jung as being incapable of open expression unless and until it 'outs' itself in the nascent work of art, during which process 'the divine frenzy of the artist comes perilously close to a pathological state, though the two things are not identical.'[15] Meanwhile, it gathers the strength and momentum within the psyche with which to carry itself over the threshold into consciousness. Up until this point it is not susceptible to control, but independent of the will. In this it imitates pathological processes, as these too are characterised by the presence of such complexes, especially in the case

---

14. Ibid., p. 75.
15. Ibid., p. 78.

of mental disturbance, but they also present from time to time in the normal individual. Such a complex develops by withdrawing energy from the conscious control of the personality. It deals not in ordered reason but in an extraordinary blind search for representation, for some *symbol* to exhibit, to make manifest for the benefit of cognition. These symbols are what carry the meaning that we sense moves us in a work of art. In the absence of the perceived presence of a symbol, the work remains simply what it is: a thing, incapable of moving us. Whereas the archetypes (symbols) deliver some message from a world of shared primordial significance which we recognise, and which transports us out of ourselves and away from the convolutions of everyday life into a sphere of common human heritage or mythology Jung termed the *collective unconscious*.[16] There are two sorts of poet: one immediately identifies with the creative process and acquiesces to the prompting of the unconscious imperative, the other experiences the creative force as alien, cannot surrender and is caught unawares. The work of the former is shaped for effect and will be readily understood. The latter, born not of human consciousness, wilfully defies it, following its own path and producing effects that may only be apprehended intuitively as meaning mysteriously emanating from the work: powerful, unknown messages, 'bridges thrown out towards an unseen shore'.[17]

The nebulous nature of the collective unconscious makes it unavailable via any analytical technique, according to Jung, (at least, not any available to him at his time of writing). As he described it, it is not to be considered 'a self-subsistent entity' but rather a mere '*potentiality*', a mnemonic we inherit from primordial times in the form of *archetypes*, images or figures which constantly recur throughout history, reappearing as a result of the creative imagination at work.[18] Each archetype embodies a recognisable fragment of human fate, emotion or human psychology – a remnant of the whole human history of joys and sorrows that have been repeated since time immemorial. Whenever one of these images becomes apparent to us it is accompanied by a surge of particular emotional intensity and suddenly we are no longer engaged in the everyday struggle with input from the world around us, but find foothold in something utterly

---

16. Ibid., p. 80.
17. Ibid., p. 76.
18. Ibid., pp. 80-81.

familiar which offers sanctuary, for it speaks in a voice stronger than our own or the random cacophony of the world: it has authority. We are captivated, enthralled at an idea lifted out of the everyday into the realm of the everlasting. In such a transportive moment our personal destiny becomes the destiny of all mankind, so that we are no longer alone, but offered refuge from ourselves and so enabled 'to outlive the longest night'.[19]

This then is what Jung felt was the secret of great art, and its effect on us. The creative process unconsciously activates an archetypal image and shapes it into the finished work. The work translates image into current language, bringing it into alignment with conscious values so that it may be apprehended by the contemporary mind and in seeing or reading we may find our way back to our true origins. Whereas an essential feature of every age is exclusion of many aspects of the past as simply anachronistic – incompatible with current reality, the *zeitgeist* – and most people go along with the general trend without coming to harm, there will always be those who cannot endure the main thoroughfare and will be first to discover in the back streets psychic elements waiting to contribute to the collective. Thus a comparative lack of adaptation in the artist leads them to follow their own feral path, to stumble upon 'what it is that would meet the unconscious needs of their age.'[20]

In the mind of a child there is no differentiation between the conscious and unconscious, and it is this state of sacred chaos that allows its uninhibited cascading upon us of its pure joys and sorrows, the mimicry and emotional intensity that powers its free expression. This is the child who miraculously survives in every great artist and cannot be suppressed or grow old. Somewhere within him persists the innocence, the delight and childlike wisdom of the 'holy fool', and he cherishes and relishes it. The outer signs of the active inner child are impassioned empathy and identification, attitudes instantly recognised and responded to by the young. Inwardly, the inner child is characterised by uninhibited imagination and readiness to let go of rationality, to run away from home in the adult world, to wander wilder woods and meadows and bring back the wisdom they still hold. Surely no genius was ever born who did not carry this trait. Søren

---

19. Ibid., p. 82.
20. Ibid., p. 83.

Kierkegaard preserved the mischievous soul of a child throughout his life and his most profound philosophical works are leavened with the same slant view. Hans Christian Andersen never grew up. His childlike persona was seen, remarked upon and generally loved by all who met him. Most never guessed the struggles that went on beneath the surface of his gregarious persona, but his stories are drenched equally in their author's guileless luminosity and inner darkness.

Chapter 2

A Lowland Habitat

The name Copenhagen derives, via the Low German 'Kopenhagen', from the Danish words for 'merchant' and 'harbour'. Originally a small fishing community named 'Havn', it grew from Viking roots to trade in herring, in particular, the provision of Lenten salted herring for the majority of Catholic Europe. This was trade encouraged by Absalon, the then bishop of Roskilde, into whose possession the settlement had come in the middle of the twelfth century. From this moment the stature of the small fishing port grew and in 1343, influenced by the latest bishop of Roskilde, Jens Nyborg, King Valdemar IV Atterdag made the city the capital of Denmark. It remains to the present day the seat of the Danish royal family.[1]

As its economy expanded so the population of Copenhagen increased, and numerous churches and abbeys were founded. Prosperity also attracted unwanted attention and, although this coast had always been subject to raids by marauding pirates, Valdemar now began actively building defences, including a large fort outside the city. Increased trade with the northern German merchant towns of the Hanseatic League soon gave rise to Danish ambitions for a Baltic empire, leading to power struggles and wars. The city was repeatedly besieged by the German traders; and yet it continued to thrive and increase in wealth. The growing power of the Lutheran

---

1. https://www.kongehuset.dk/en/palaces-and-the-royal-yacht/amalienborg/#.

Church in Germany led to widespread disaffection with Catholicism, and in 1536 the Danish Church split from Rome and Lutheranism became, as it remains, the official religion. The late sixteenth and seventeenth centuries saw Danish territory lost to Sweden, but it was the plague of 1711, followed by two catastrophic fires (1728 and 1795) that ravaged Copenhagen, which marked the start of a series of disasters to befall the city. Copenhagen's castle was almost totally destroyed by fire in 1794 and a year later a second fire reduced by a third the largely timber-built city. The destruction necessitated a huge rebuilding initiative, funded by wealth accumulated mainly during the early French Revolutionary Wars. The nascent nineteenth century saw Danish naval skirmishes with British forces in the Battle of Copenhagen, followed by a second marine encounter in 1807 during which Copenhagen came under heavy bombardment. The city ramparts and fort, having proven useless as a defence, were now dismantled, allowing new housing development around the city's lakes.

War had by now bankrupted Denmark, and in response it ceded Norway to Sweden and began a slow but steady period of recovery. Central to the reconstruction of Copenhagen was King Frederick VI's personal appointment of the architect Christian Frederik Hansen to the role of Chief Building Director, a function he took extremely seriously. Attentive to every detail of town planning, Hansen began radically regenerating Copenhagen, including its institutional buildings, and from this refashioning there emerged a truly modern city, the unique backdrop against which would be born and flourish a completely refreshed and vibrantly diverse urban culture. The elegance of the new Copenhagen was epitomised in its neoclassical streets and thoroughfares; the Royal

Copenhagen, late 19th century... Chief Building Director Christian Frederik Hansen's 'truly modern city' with (left) Vor Frue Kirke.

Theatre and Christiansborg Palace, Hansen's town hall and the subdued splendour of its cathedral, Vor Frue Kirke (Church of Our Lady). Maritime trade continued to thrive, and the harbour area was busy with the disembarking and loading of triple-rigged sailing barques. Tall town houses graced the city's crescents, squares and watersides. Innovative features began to appear. Expressive of the first 'modern city' were the development of entertainment and recreational facilities; the fantastically ambitious Tivoli Gardens opened in 1843.

It was not long before the powerfully nurturing effect on the creative imagination of a beautiful and harmonious built environment became evident. Along with new trade and commerce the nineteenth century also brought fresh external influence. Denmark soon absorbed German Romanticism and began to cast off the stifling creative restraints of Enlightenment rationalism. Here in Copenhagen, August Bournonville was inspired to create his ballets, Bertel Thorvaldsen, his sculpture, Adam Gottlob Oehlenschläger and Andersen, their poems and stories. Hans Christian Ørsted developed his innovative science of optics and physics, and Kierkegaard his equally revolutionary synthesis of psychology, theology and philosophy. The cultural contribution of the creative mind is always more clearly evaluated in the case of utilitarian outcomes; Hansen's architectural resurrection of Copenhagen is a most eloquent statement of the city's Golden Age status and ambition. Stone speaks more loudly than canvas and paint or pen and paper, and so does functionality in a time of burgeoning trade and industry, while the work of the dissenting artist is often masked or deliberately erased by commerce. Resistant to commodification and monetarisation and at its best subversive of the status quo, the worth of such a work of art cannot be easily or immediately quantified; either it falls foul of the noise and turmoil of political and social upheaval or is lost in it. The questions it poses are ignored; its challenges overridden. Just as resistant to measurement and so overlooked are the intuitive insights of the artistic mind; what might be the true significance, for example, of its uncanny prescience? What silent clandestine catalysis for change might such exercise of the human spirit bring to bear upon a doggedly materialistic society? Considered in all its aspects, it was largely the extraordinary blossoming of art from the ashes of nineteenth-century turbulence that provided the lasting legacy of Denmark's Golden Age.

At the core of this creative ferment lay the most liberating tenet of Romanticism, the potential power of the individual over the crowd and conservatism, and the figure behind it was the man who in 1839 would ascend the throne as King Christian VIII. He was a person of great personal charm and physical attraction, which entranced his subjects, but it was Christian's love of science and the arts, inherited from his gifted, short-lived mother, which changed the cultural climate of his country forever. Denmark, in a symbolic marrying of its pragmatic and creative nature, was to acquire a lasting reputation for a very particular functional aesthetic, becoming renowned for the lovely elemental elegance of its furniture and interior design, jewellery and glass. It is an aesthetic still recognised today by both citizen consumer and connoisseur. During the 1814 dispute surrounding the sovereignty and governance of Norway, Christian, then heir presumptive to the kingdoms of Denmark and Norway, had done all in his power, despite opposition by the so-called Swedish Party, to strengthen bonds between Norway and Denmark. His subsequent reputation for democracy tarnished his political image, estranging him from all the reactionary courts of Europe, including his own. Having married his second wife Caroline Amalie of Augustenburg in 1815 he virtually retired from public life. Between then and 1839 the royal couple devoted all their energy to supporting cultural endeavour on all fronts, founding a valuable prize for astronomy and championing scientific research in general. The king did not apparently miss the pomp and circumstance of absolute monarchy; he read widely and throughout his reign sought out and cultivated warm personal relationships with many artists and writers, including both Kierkegaard and Andersen.

Christian VIII, King of Denmark (1839-1848).

* * *

Hans Christian Andersen was an instantly recognisable figure on Copenhagen's streets and in its fashionable salons. Immensely tall and thin and shambling, he always dressed as though his clothes belonged to someone else: coat too short in the arm, collar ragged, cuffs torn, trousers too short. It was as though he was unable to shake

Andersen, portrait from *The Story of My Life*, 1855.

off the poverty of his background and in appearance constantly betrayed it. His enormous feet were clad in ancient boots. He wore a musty old top hat, but, even without it, he was half a head taller than any other man. His eyes were small and hooded and he always seemed to be looking down his huge nose at people. His odd appearance made him the subject of much gossip and, despite the extremely respectable family of his benefactor into which he had been adopted as a teenage schoolboy, it was soon common knowledge that his father was a poor provincial shoemaker and his mother a drunkard. By the time he finally managed to leave school and had written some poems and a couple of plays, one or two staged at the Royal Theatre, he was also known to regular audience members for hanging around the stage door. It was said he kept bad company. Kierkegaard, too, cut a rather strange figure in the city. Reputedly, a childhood fall from a tree had caused him to walk lopsidedly with a marked limp which made one trouser leg look shorter than the other. Unlike Andersen, however, he dressed expensively, evidence of his privileged background. Everyone knew him from his daily strolls around the streets of Copenhagen, leaning lightly on a rolled umbrella or cane, his mass of fair curls crammed beneath a fine, glossy, silk top hat which he doffed to all. His habit was to stop and speak to anyone who returned his bright and enigmatic smile, so he was well liked and popular. He had a ripening reputation as a charming and witty salon conversationalist. Occasionally he would be glimpsed in a carriage on his way out of town to get a breath of fresh air, driving out into the countryside that began just beyond the city ramparts.

Copenhagen had a famous literary circle and glittering salons, foremost among them that of the poet, playwright and literary critic, Johan Ludvig Heiberg (1791-1860), and his wife, the actress Johanne Luise Heiberg (née Pätges), whose stage debut at the Royal

Theatre would by chance coincide with that of Andersen. However, alongside cultured drawing-rooms the city also had its less salubrious venues – like the backroom bar behind a so-called boarding house or hostel that served cheap meals for students, the meeting place for a group of young reprobate literati who dubbed themselves 'The Unholy Alliance'. They included Andersen, who drank there most days when he was not putting himself on show in people's drawing-rooms and begging an audience for his verses and short plays. He loved to declaim and endlessly craved praise. Companion to the budding playwright in the Unholy Alliance was another aspiring author, Søren Kierkegaard, whose caricatures of members of the club would later feature famously as 'The Seducer' and 'The Judge' in his works *Either/Or* (1843) and *Stages on Life's Way* (1845). Another, Emil Boesen, became dean of Aarhus and Kierkegaard's closest lifelong friend and only confidant.

The young boarding-house drinkers entertained themselves with pontificating on politics, particularly the current liberal agenda. Their ideas would feed into Kierkegaard's early writings and were satirised in Henrik Hertz's novel *Moods and Conditions*, in which Kierkegaard appears supercilious and self-confident as 'The Translator' and Andersen as 'Amadis', whose constant failures are shored up by boundless ambition. Already unappeasably hungry for fame, Andersen soon identified his direction and in spring 1837 rushed into print with his first collection of fairy tales, convinced it would bring the recognition he thought belonged to genius. In his story *The Shoes of Fortune* he parried Kierkegaard's discursive virtuosity by satirising him as a parrot with a sharp beak and intellectual pretensions, flattered and praised by Johan Heiberg (who saw nothing in Andersen)[2] at the expense of the canary. Answering Andersen's assertion that genius could only develop in the warmth of admiration, Kierkegaard scoffed that the spirit of man was not an egg; he would never lose sight of the role played by sheer hard work in 'genius' and never mistook it for a God-given free lunch. The artistic and intellectual comrades of the Unholy

---

2. Andersen caricatured the critic Heiberg in a later story, *The Nightingale*, as the court musician, who could write about music using all the longest Chinese words (Hegelian expressions) but preferred the mechanical singing bird to the real nightingale.

Alliance were as rowdy and argumentative a bunch as any of their age in any era, and they were not shy of the brothel. Neither did their exploits go unremarked. The city of Copenhagen had at the time fewer than 200,000 inhabitants: a small, close-knit and pious enough community to maintain a thriving grapevine. Everyone gossiped and knew everybody else's business.

* * *

In 1830, the seventeen-year-old Kierkegaard had already entered university and, thanks in great part to endless lively childhood dialogue with his father, was firmly set on the path of exploring his lifelong love of dialectics. From the start he showed unmistakable signs of the able student determined to find his own way, and while welcoming the liberal opportunities for academic enrichment offered by the university, he could be capricious, frivolous and immature. There was an acerbic side to his nature, and he was rapier sharp. Frail and sickly as a child, he had once been rebuked at home for shovelling food greedily into his mouth and called 'Fork', to which he had retorted: 'I *am* a fork, and I will stick you.' A fellow schoolboy later described him as 'a regular little wild cat'[3].In his many writings on his childhood, Kierkegaard goes over and over the close bond he experienced with his father, an attachment which was coupled with deep inner unhappiness and extreme independence of spirit. By his late teens he was already engaged in an inarticulate interior battle with Michael Pedersen's ambition for him to become a cleric, though the son was not yet suffering from the cyclic high moods and melancholy inherited from his father. Meanwhile, the aesthetic life beckoned; the young Kierkegaard was a regular at Royal Theatre performances and loved music. His interests were diverse and eclectic; as well as theology, and despite academic brilliance in the classics and physics, mathematics and philosophy, his natural metier was not the lecture hall but the debating society.

It suited him best to absorb knowledge in the daily round of student life and simply by watching and listening during everyday conversation. This was a methodology that would become his lifelong habit, despite having been most strongly condemned and cause of early estrangement from his censorious elder brother, Peter, already a lecturer in the university. If his father had taught him his first

---

3. Lowrie, *A Short Life of Kierkegaard*, pp. 38-39.

A Lowland Habitat

lessons in dialectics, Kierkegaard the younger had also inherited from him his passionate nature. Søren was constitutionally incapable of deviating from his own path, and this applied as much to his intellectual development as to the deeper process of personal maturation. In his nineteenth year and third at university, carefree student life was suddenly and cruelly disrupted by a series of close family bereavements which were to concentrate and monopolise the young Kierkegaard's mind for the next two years. In 1832 he lost a sister at the age of only thirty-three; a year later a brother of just twenty-four. Then July 1834 brought the death of his mother, with whom Kierkegaard had never bonded and, far more devastatingly, in December of the same year that of Petrea Severine, the sister who had actually mothered the little Søren throughout his childhood. The loss of this greatly beloved sister must have shaken him to the core. Altogether, it was a catalogue of grief which culminated in convincing Kierkegaard that his own life would not extend beyond his mid-thirties.

Petrea Lund, Søren's most beloved sister (1801-1834).

This sudden early confrontation with mortality may also have precipitated him into jotting down thoughts and daily activity, a record-keeping begun in 1833 and kept up much more seriously from August 1834, to be maintained until just before his death on 11 November 1855. These notes became the now famous *Journals*, documenting the most significant turning points and elaborating on decisions taken in his life. As such, they offer a complete and comprehensive map to the religious route taken by Kierkegaard from childhood to his final destination, providing even the most obtuse writings with all the candour, clarity and context needed for understanding them. The journal entries differ markedly in style and tone from the works, being openly autobiographical, tender, funny and delicately self-deprecating as well as profoundly wise. They show us the man in all his vulnerability and humility, and read alongside the polemical works lend them a welcome immediacy, warmth and humanity.

Kierkegaard at his desk by artist Luplau Janssen (1869-1927).

His had been a childhood haunted by his father's evocations of his own early youth and the mark it left upon him. Michael Pederson Kierkegaard was born of peasant stock in a tiny, scattered settlement, Sædding, on the bleak and infertile West Jutland heath. The ancient settlement dating back to Viking times possesses a few ancient runic stones and the remnants of a little old two-part stone church, renovated in the 1970s and now porched and lacking its steeple. In Kierkegaard's time there were a couple of farms and a hundred or so inhabitants. The current parish of around 12,000 inhabitants is centred on the busy Esbjerg harbour, and despite its sandy beach is not a place that features prominently on today's tourist trail of Denmark. Of the few humble dwellings there in the mid-nineteenth century, one, the 'Red House', Michael Kierkegaard had built for his mother and sisters to live in on the condition that after their demise it become a schoolhouse. It was still occupied by an elderly aunt with whom his youngest son stayed for three days during his pilgrimage to Jutland as a new theological graduate. On this visit Søren fell half in love with the romance of the simple dwelling, committing to memory how he had stood in the doorway in late afternoon light, while the sheep drifted home beneath dark clouds broken by strong beams of light, the heath rising in the distance.

Nothing grows on the moors but moss, heather and other crouching bog flora and a few stunted trees which bow before the prevailing north-easterly wind. In winter the landscape is petrified, cold, sodden with rain and snow. As a small boy Michael had been tasked with shepherding the sheep, a lonely and comfortless existence he led until released from his hardship by a benevolent uncle, his mother's brother, who suddenly removed the twelve-year-old to Copenhagen and started him on the road to a prosperous future in retail business. Memories of his harsh childhood never faded and the father's stories of his heathland misery became etched in turn into the vividly intelligent and imaginative mind of the youngest of his seven children. They were impressions which grew in intensity, finding sustenance in the strange melancholy which emanated from his father and pervaded life under his roof. They would be further strengthened by the visit made to his father's birthplace after his death, and most dramatically by a deathbed confession which threw new light on one of the dark secrets of his life. Søren's elder brother, Peter (1857-75), by now Bishop of Aalborg, in great old age related how their father Michael Pedersen had confessed to his beloved Bishop Mynster that as an eleven-year-old suffering cold, hunger and solitude on the moors he had once cursed God and lived all the remainder of his life with the resulting guilt. It had driven him to extreme piety and to despair, for he could never feel forgiven.

The more his God seemed to pour worldly blessings upon him, success in business, a fine house, the respect of his fellow citizens and a beloved first wife, the less deserving the poor man felt. So that finding himself widowed and childless just two years into this marriage broke him completely. He felt the curse inevitable. Within a year of his wife's death, he was compelled to marry his housekeeper, twelve years his junior and a distant relative from Jutland. Their first child was born five months into the marriage. Abruptly abandoning life as one of the most successful and prosperous retailers in Copenhagen, a 'hosier' whose actual business was the manufacture and supply of ready-to-wear men's suiting, he sold up and became almost a recluse, spending all day in his study among his books. Michael Pedersen's former housekeeper and now second spouse, Ane Sørendatter Lund, was described by her granddaughter as: 'a nice little woman of even and cheerful disposition'[4], to whom her children's education was something

Ane Sørendatter Lund, Søren Kierkegaard's mother (1768-1834).

---

4. Ibid., p. 24.

of an enigma. She left to her husband areas of their lives that were above her head and cherished her brood in other ways, never happier than when they were off colour, when she could put them to bed and keep them snug as a mother hen her chicks. Lowrie comments on the 'amazing and ominous' fact that throughout his journal and works S.K. speaks endlessly of his father and nowhere refers to his mother:

> It is evident that morally she had no influence upon him, or only a negative influence. S.K. seems to have divined in early childhood, perhaps as an inference from his father's treatment of the mother of his seven children, that she was not in the highest sense a wife.[5]

In old age Bishop Mynster, formerly pastor to Michael Kierkegaard, recalled him turning up in great agitation to see him one day after the man was already married to his second wife. Mynster recorded his parishioner's guilt-ridden words: "Good God, I have been thinking so much today of my blessed wife… I thought of her so long…" and holding out a wad of notes, he asked that they be donated to the poor. Ane, simple and good-hearted as she was, never emerged from beneath the shadow of her predecessor. After her marriage she continued to work as housekeeper for her husband, doing exactly what she had done while his first wife lived, and all under his strict supervision, for he arranged everything, failing to delegate to her even the authority to buy food. She was 45 by the time her last child came into the world, and had been pregnant or feeding a child almost continually since her marriage. She was worn out, not least by her husband's moods. At the cathedral church on Sunday, trooping in behind her husband with the brood of which she was so quietly proud, she must also have felt the nudges and scorn of the gentlefolk of the congregation, all of whom knew her history. Lowrie observes that something impeded Kierkegaard from honouring and loving his mother 'as a son ought', venturing to suggest that this might also account 'in part for the particular misfortune'[6] of Kierkegaard's inability to realise the universal in marrying the woman he loved. It is a strangely neglected remark, surely the most eloquent, poignant and under-explored ever made regarding Kierkegaard in all the extensive literature concerning him.

---

5. Ibid.
6. Ibid., p. 25.

A Lowland Habitat

Vor Frue Kirke (Cathedral Church of Our Lady), Copenhagen, 1520.

Vor Frue Kirke interior by C.F. Hansen with Thorvaldsen's Christ on the altar, and his apostles along the nave.

His most devout biographer and translator seems perplexed by the glaring omission amidst all Kierkegaard's obfuscation, noting how capable he was of depicting woman spiritually, while his tendency was always to see her only in relation to man, and rarely if ever mentioning the 'noblest and tenderest aspect of woman as mother.'[7]

Kierkegaard on at least one occasion refers to woman's 'heart', meaning her enhanced capacity for compassionate love (comparing it with a lesser capacity in men) and, more often and reverentially, to the immediacy of female being which he placed in the category of the religious. Sisterly love seems, however, to have been inadequate compensation for some fundamental lack of primary female attachment. Echoing throughout his works is the unheard voice of the unmothered child: fierce grief-engendered pride palpable just beneath the surface of his lonely struggle to survive, a fighting back of tears. A repeat pattern of approach, retreat, self-sabotage, relived abandonment; the strange stubborn resilience of the orphan continually reaching for faith in an inaccessible tomorrow. To grow up deprived of mother love is to feel no firm ground beneath the feet and incoherent terror of all that consciously or subconsciously evokes what has been missed; to be filled with unspeakable fear,

---

7. Ibid., p. 25.

disseminated, nameless fear for which there are no words. This is the only darkness Søren Kierkegaard dared not explore in himself and, however deep, it still does not define him.

In his case, lasting estrangement from the mother would seem to have been entirely self-imposed, but no less catastrophic for that. It would deprive him in adulthood of the woman he loved, force him to face and transmute worldly lost love into its eternal religious reality, and make him the writer he became. Whatever fastidious fancy or traumatic truth involving the father prompted him to disown his mother, it was not she who deliberately cast him aside. By all family accounts, Ane was devoted to her many children and offered them her daily care and concern. If nothing else, she was an experienced and constant maternal presence. She feared for her youngest, as in her simple way she watched him fall under the spell of her husband's to her unfathomable mind. Maybe she smothered her precious last-born boy, arousing jealousy in his father. She would not live to see her son grow into the most tortured, the tenderest of men. Despite his rejection, it seems this unsophisticated, middle-aged and exhausted woman managed at the very least not to douse in her last-born his immense inborn capacity for love. Possibly, she ignited it, necessitating filial distance. His was a precocious soul; perhaps his growing needs were far more complex and profound than she could ever have imagined or provided for. This is the tragic truth of many a childhood, let alone that of the genius.

A century and a half later, in his seminal report on 'Maternal Care and Mental Health' published in 1951, and in the later book based on it, the psychiatrist John Bowlby would detail the devastating effects on a child of maternal deprivation, while confirming the capability of the 'normal mother' to 'rely on the prompting of her instincts in the happy knowledge that the tenderness they prompt is what her baby wants. "This little pig went to market" is a first textbook on child care'.[8] Ane Lund must have been capable of the rudiments of such instinctive maternal nurture, but her youngest son found more succour in the paternal. Søren shuttled continually between the two poles of Michael's character: a child alternately enchanted by his father's wonderful gift for storytelling and playing pretend, then bewildered and fearful of dark moods during which the father became remote and preoccupied, unreachable however hard his son tried to make him laugh. His mother was to claim that she had done

---

8. John Bowlby, *Child Care and the Growth of Love* (London: Penguin Books, 1965 and (Part III) Mary Salter Ainsworth, 1965), p. 20.

her best to encourage merriment and self-mockery in her youngest boy, for he was so very serious and tender a child at heart and so terribly susceptible to his father's dark stories that she feared he must inherit the melancholy. Perhaps she receives too little credit for S.K.'s delicious sense of humour. Her youngest, by nature preternaturally acute, serious and impressionable, watched and guessed something of his mother's position and her humiliation and from it gleaned his father's shame. The shattering deduction, arrived at carefully over boyhood's long lonely hours of rumination, was that his father must have seduced his mother and taken her virginity. Furthermore, because Michael had married late in life, this had perhaps not been his first lapse. It is difficult to overestimate the emotional, spiritual and physical effect of this deposition on the ultra-sensitive youngest son.

Uncertainty surrounds what prompted the crisis described by Kierkegaard in his *Journals* as 'The Great Earthquake', but it befell him on or around his twenty-second birthday. There are few dates for the journal entries, and Kierkegaard is deliberately misleading in his attribution of their timing. Many an assiduous attempt by academic and biographer to unravel events leading up to this mysterious epiphany have been defeated by the indefatigable Kierkegaard, whose skill in hiding his secrets in his writings is legendary. What is certain is that this experience marked for him a definitive loss of innocence and end to childhood. It may have been occasioned by some sort of partial confession by his father, so deeply drowned in grief at recent bereavements that he confided in his favourite son, his Benjamin. In any case, the effect was to awaken in the boy an agonising awareness of original or inherited sin. On 31 December 1838 he mapped his new trajectory, transcribing:

CHILDHOOD

> *Halb Kinderspiele, Halb Gott im Herzen*
>
> *Goethe*

YOUTH

> Begging – that's not for us!
> Youth on the road of life
> Forcefully seizes the prize.
>
> *Christian Winter*

> ...and at 25 YEARS OLD: 'And take upon's the mystery of things,' *King Lear.*

The subsequent two journal entries are perhaps the most tumultuous. They document the 'terrible revolution' which forced him to reinterpret the facts surrounding his father: that his great age was not divine blessing but in fact a curse and the intellectual gifts in the family conferred only for the purpose of tearing each other to pieces. He records how he experienced 'the stillness of death' when looking at his father, an unhappy man outliving them all. There must be some terrible guilt involving the whole family, the punishment of God upon them all, and the only thought that consoled to any degree was the idea that his father had tried to soften the fate of the family with religion. They might be deprived of everything in this world, be wiped out completely here... but a better world awaited them. So, the youngest son explains, small wonder that he had sought refuge in the gifts of the mind. Stripped of any expectation of a happy earthy life 'as it naturally springs from and lies in the natural historical continuity of family life'[9] he had grasped and clung to the intellectual, his only joy being thoughts of his own great powers of mind in the presence of mankind's indifference to him. At the start of the previous year, Kierkegaard had recorded an episode which occurred between himself and his father and which planted in the boy the seed of his lifelong preoccupation with the nature of fear and faith; it also laid bare the unbearable inner conflict in Kierkegaard between love and terror of his father. Almost palpable in the recording of this incident is new outrage against the inculcation of unmitigated dread. Michael Pedersen had repeatedly introduced his youngest child, as intermission to some wondrous dialogue or story of enchantment, to the crucified Christ, so that the young mind was thrown into confusion as to why so good and loving a Saviour should meet such a fate.

Mikael Pedersen Kierkegaard, Søren's father (1756-1838).

Now Søren saw his early defence-lessness in the face of his father's

---

9. Kierkegaard, *Journals*, p. 67.

religious zeal, that terrible irreducible piety; dread. That fear of his God which led him into order, regulation, autocracy, control; the antithesis of faith. Evident to the son at last was how childhood innocence had been stolen from him when as a trusting boy he had rushed to his father and flushed with romantic enthusiasm for the story of a *master-thief* declared that his crime was only misuse of powers, he might easily be saved by conversion. Kierkegaard shuddered at recollection of his father's dismissal, the solemn warning that there were some offences only fought off 'with God's continual help', recalling how he had rushed away to scrutinise himself in the mirror in his room.[10] They were words before which the son's soul shrank. Of what could his father be guilty that he felt it necessary to issue such a warning? Some terrible foreboding stirred in the boy; perhaps he too was guilty. He must have running in his blood the same dark stain of sin. Yes, he too was tainted. When his father declared how good it would be to have a venerable confessor 'to whom one could open one's heart',[11] the growing boy discerned in himself the same pernicious piety, the same ghastly morbidity. Suddenly the full horror of his situation struck home; this was too terrible a fate to share with his father, however beloved. In the son's soul rose insurrection. He began to rebel against the idea of taking a degree in theology, a direction that was becoming more and more of an enigma and scandal to him, the more terror he sensed lay at the root of his father's faith. He, Søren Kierkegaard, would not be reduced to fear. If Christ condemned, if we were to be cowed into goodness, if there was no mercy, then let us revel in evil, for it is a great relief to indulge our so-human humanity, our boundless propensity for badness. Yes, let us be embodied!

So at the dawning of his own manhood the young Kierkegaard discovered in Michael Pedersen and in their family circumstances his father's true nature. Poised on the threshold, the son glimpsed his father's feet of clay; saw in him a masculine creature broken in his being, his God affording him no comfort, bestowing no forgiveness. A God who dealt out due deserts; a deity appeased by no surfeit of prayer. This father was a damned soul and his sin was his very corporeal mortal reality, his manhood. There was no divine mercy. It

---

10. Noted in body text of *Journals*: (cf. F. Schlegel's Works, Vol. VII, p. 15). Karl Friedrich Wilhelm Schlegel (1772-1829), German poet, critic and philosopher.
11. Kierkegaard, *Journals*, p. 41.

was as it was with him, and his suffering was fathomless. What pathos! In 1848 Kierkegaard summarised his childhood and the feelings it evoked in the Point of View: he had been, 'humanly speaking, crazily brought up'.[12] No wonder that he had sometimes perceived Christianity as the most inhuman cruelty, despite never losing his reverence for it. He had sworn to himself on such occasions that he would never divulge the difficulties he had encountered and which he had never yet heard or read described. Thus, repelled by his father and all his famous Christianity, the child of his old age (Michael was 55 when Søren was born) reacted with characteristic vigour. Revealed to him now was an entire emasculating religion. The image elaborated itself before his inner eye: everyone marching off to church, dressed up as though it were the Royal Theatre. Sitting down hard in their hard pews – penance in plenty! Falling sound asleep during the sermon; the very presiding minister hard pressed to stay awake to the end of his own deathly diatribe. At last, the cleric forces open his drooping eyelids, ceases droning, peers about the congregation from his high eyrie, spies a pretty face here, a yawn at the back there, an averted gaze of guilt and shame – ha, bravo, his words hit home! Then, full of smug self-satisfaction and the grace of God, he descends to receive the reverence of his flock.

The young Kierkegaard swore he should not be found among them. Christ himself abhorred the hypocrite. It all began with fear and fear was inimical to faith. Fear, like the fear of illness which infallibly brings on symptoms of the disease. Yet, he reflected, the first man did not suffer from fear, merely from curiosity – and curiosity does not kill. In that case there was *no* original sin, so he should not be subject to it. Henceforth he would not fear evil or retribution, but found his manhood in forgiveness, however meek, however ludicrous it made him; however he was mocked and however complete must be this rift with his father. One holy son must suffice. Michael Pedersen would have to content himself with Peter's vocation, hatching a single priest from his sad brood of seven prayed-over and preyed-upon progeny. Søren decided he would not sit the theology exam. Yet still something troubled him. Should he not find another way to gainsay silence, to let the Christian world into which he had been born know what he really

---

12. Lowrie, *A Short Life of Kierkegaard*, p. 50-51.

thought of its castrated catechism, its quivering, its quaking and its best Sunday suits? A way to delineate in full detail how oppressive was its dry insistence on human misery, punishment, mortification of the flesh; how utterly alienating it all was to the true follower, the pilgrim prepared to stand and fall on faith alone, to question and receive response not from the frocked and frigid ministry but from his Lord alone. Ah, how the churchman shrank from such an encounter! How he insisted upon tribulation, spiritual trial by cleric, and then wallowed in power over the prostrated. How deep was his hatred of joy, the demystified face-to-face meeting between Man and his God, all intimacy, close proximity.

Truly, Denmark was a nation of neutered spirituality: sterile, stabled stallions. This little land, this flat hinterland of Europe with its treeless islands and heaths – a landscape of brutal hardship civilised by trite town-dwellers and smug cities. Such sudden and profound disillusionment with his father's religion spread to colour the younger Kierkegaard's whole worldview, including that of his countrymen. Warm affection tinged with irony now gave way to stern disapprobation. He saw a people formed by the barren character of this northern European landscape and clothed in its chill climate of impoverishment, subservience, and survival. As fearful of their own warring Nordic nature and history as of Catholic self-regulation, they had fully embraced Reformed Christianity, welcoming a vernacular religion stripped of harsh demands upon their conscience. Here was no requirement for renunciation, no rule that could not be kept as easily as the law of commerce. And now its followers were free to make good as they pleased. Told to love their neighbour, they closed ranks and censured the outsider; cast the first stone and denied themselves nothing. Humility formerly forced upon them by the hardships of agrarian life on the land and the Roman Catholic sacrament of confession was gratefully forsworn, replaced by proud adherence to scriptural critique, self-satisfaction and a hardened heart.

Turning his attention to the new clergy, Kierkegaard saw their creed as that of clan, conformity, and safety in the crowd. Now that the old religion had been rooted out, its sacraments denounced, holy scripture belonged to the clerics and they dressed themselves in its authority. From their pulpits they declaimed the old stories in a new guise: the Christ as cherubic new-born gurgling in a trough; his mother a smiling gentlewoman presiding over her salon of a stable. It was all so cosy and sociable, nearly as nice coming to church for an hour or two of a Sunday as staying at home beside the stove. It seemed to Søren Kierkegaard a desecration and disgrace. He saw sentimentalisation of the sacred as nothing less than sacrilege, and deplored the smug assumption that this was the practise of Christianity rather than realpolitik. Christ was a purist, yet here was an hybrid affinity he recognised, the perfect match between Protestantism and the contemporary political viewpoint: they shared the same struggle for sovereignty over the people, and he observed how the real unalloyed royalists among them leant towards Catholicism. It all added up to gelding by Christianity; a sterile form of the faith which instead of empowering its adherents bound them to their weaknesses and 'sin', trampling on their manhood. His new sense of emancipation was transferred to the page with all the fervency of fresh conversion: Christianity had turned from the 'imposing figure'[13] it had been when once it had vigorously spoken its mind, into an old man who wants to control everyone with scripture, rules and priestly sovereignty and in his dotage feels he has lived too long and wants to retire from the world.

So now, Kierkegaard felt, Christianity had passed into its second childhood. All it wanted was fairy tales.

* * *

Hans Christian Andersen arrived in Copenhagen, the great city of his dreams, on the morning of 6 September 1819. He was a lad of fourteen and had travelled for two days from the small provincial town of Odense on Funen island, first sailing the two-hour crossing over the Baltic (an experience he found terrifying) and then in a swaying carriage over rough mainland roads to the city ramparts and the heights of Frederiksberg hill. Here he was set down outside his lodgings for the night. He would make the remainder of his journey to the city centre on foot, carrying his little bundle of belongings. He records how the streets were in uproar, but he was unsurprised at the noise and crowds. He had always imagined Copenhagen like this, as the centre of a bustling universe. The evening before his arrival Copenhagen had seen the start of the Danish Jew baiting, following that experienced by many European countries as the 'Hep-Hep riots' after the chant used to incite them. It was unrest that had begun in Würzburg and was by now widespread throughout the German

---

13. Kierkegaard, *Journals*, p. 21.

Confederation and beyond in response to Jewish emancipation. Given his familiarity with Judaism from schooldays, Andersen's lack of further comment is surprising. He had attended the Jewish school in Odense, placed there by his outraged mother in an extraordinarily enlightened move following on a beating at his first Dame school. He seems to have very happy at his new school, as he stayed in touch for decades with his old teacher there, Fedder Carstens. Sympathetic treatment of Jewish protagonists would become a consistent and marked feature in Andersen's work.

This description of his arrival in Copenhagen does not, however, omit the ominous details of his introduction to the Royal Theatre. After walking all around the building which had appeared in so many of his childish dreams, he was approached by a ticket tout who asked if he wanted a seat. Thinking in his innocence that he was being offered free entrance, Andersen accepted with profuse thanks, a response the man angrily misinterpreted as insolence, so that the confused boy fled in terror from the very place he called the dearest to him in the city. He makes no mention of the decade of scornful rejections which was to precede production of his first drama there, but he does proudly note in the final version of his memoir the fact that the Royal Theatre was venue for his debut bow to the Danish public. The storyteller allowed himself huge poetic licence in his heavily romanticised definitive autobiography: in 1805 there had dwelt, he began, in a small humble room in Odense a young couple who were very fond of each other. He was a shoemaker, a 'remarkably gifted man of truly poetic bent', while his slightly older wife knew nothing of the world but was 'kind to the bottom of her heart.'[14] The husband, he elaborated, had become a cobbler and built his own workshop, as well as the bridal bed. He continues with well-honed pedantry that this last was fashioned from the frame which had supported the coffin of the late Count Trampe as he lay in state, and while remnants of the black crepe that had adorned the woodwork still clung to the timber, come the morning of 2 April was found lying there not a nobleman corpse but... 'a living, crying child... I, Hans Christian Andersen.'[15]

He was born at one o'clock in the morning on that date and christened at home the same day, a usual procedure in the days

---

14. Hans Christian Andersen, *My Fairy-tale Life*, trans. W. Glyn Jones (Dedalus Limited, 2013,) p. 11.
15. Ibid.

Cottage of Andersen's birth, Odense, lithograph by P. Nordahl Grove, 1868.

when neonatal death was common. The two names Hans and Christian were to be used together in referring to the child and man; sometimes he was called 'Christian', but never simply 'Hans'. At the time of their wedding at St Knud's Church in Odense the 22-year-old shoemaker and his 8 years older wife had both been registered as homeless. The shoemaker's baby was blessed two weeks later on Easter Monday at St Hans Church, where the vicar complained that he 'screamed like a kitten',[16] prophesied by the French emigrant godfather to auger a fine singing voice, which indeed it did. When Andersen was two the little family moved into a rented cottage where they would live for the next twelve years. It was a humble, half-timbered, yellow-washed dwelling at number 3, Munkemøllestræde (Monk's Mill Street) with an L-shaped room containing a stove and windows at either end. The shoemaker's bench, a bed and a crib comprised the furniture, but there was a cupboard above the workbench containing books and songs. Via a ladder one could clamber up into the attic, and from there out onto the roof. Here Andersen's mother found purchase for pots of flowers and herbs in what would become her son's setting for Gerda and Kay's meeting and the forging of their childhood love in his unforgettable story of *The Snow Queen*.

Andersen was to hear often from his mother, Anne Marie, how much luckier he was than she had been, for he was being brought up like a nobleman's son. He was certainly surrounded by much grandiose fantasising. His mother's mother, Anne Catherine, claimed to be daughter of a noblewoman in Kassel, northern Germany, who had run away with an actor and so lost her fortune. In fact, her father had been a glove-maker who ended up in the workhouse. Hans Christian's

---

16. Wullschläger, *Hans Christian Andersen*, p. 7.

mother inherited the day-dreaming gene, apparently nurturing a fantasy about her boy having been placed in her safekeeping by the king himself, whose illegitimate son he was. As for Andersen's paternal grandmother, she maintained she was descended from rich farming aristocracy, an imaginary history constantly denounced and derided by her daughter-in-law. By the time the adult Andersen was fraternising with European aristocracy and royalty such notions, however apocryphal, had hardened into myth in his mind and formed the unstable bedrock for his fragile sense of entitlement. The truth was that his maternal grandmother had sent his mother out to beg. Anne Marie, born around 1774 near the ancient town of Bogense on Funen, was the first of her mother's three pre-marriage illegitimate children. Poverty and promiscuity were to drive Anne Marie's younger sister, Christiane, to open a brothel in Copenhagen – to the horror and mortification of her storyteller nephew. His mother went into service and, while there, had her own illegitimate daughter, Karen-Marie, who lived with her maternal grandmother and became another source of embarrassment to Andersen for her ignorance and promiscuity. His greatest fear as he strove to improve his position in the world was that she would appear and drag him back down again. To his huge consternation, she did indeed eventually seek him out in the city; he had to pay her to leave him alone.

Odense may have been a small provincial town (at the start of the nineteenth century it had 8,000 inhabitants) but it was the capital of Funen and second in civic status only to Copenhagen; the crown prince had a residence there. Far from lacking sophistication, the town offered many cultural opportunities. Here in 1795 was built the only theatre outside the capital, where touring companies of actors from the capital's Royal Theatre came to perform. The town also had a garrison, a jail and a royal summer residence. There were cloisters for noblewomen, a bishop, and a cathedral, the attached school of which was staffed by 'professors'. However, Odense remained essentially a rural community and its culture retained cognisance of agrarian values and respect for country traditions. Folklore was alive and well, while rich merchants and an elite bourgeoisie lived in their grand houses on the main streets, cheek by jowl with the utterly poverty-stricken peasantry in their cottages. It is a world evoked and inhabited by the protagonists of Andersen's stories, where rich and poor, the vagaries of their lives and possibilities for transition between the two states are constantly explored and extrapolated.

The imagination of the young Hans Christian, already thriving on his father's constant story-telling and literary encouragement, was further enriched from the age of seven by his parents taking him to the theatre. His father built him a little wooden proscenium, complete with wooden puppet actors. Hans Christian quickly learnt from his mother how to sew clothes for these little figures and spent hours making them enact plays on the miniature stage. Quite often he accompanied his beloved maternal grandmother to the asylum where she worked in the gardens and where his poor mad paternal grandfather had been incarcerated. Here the young Andersen spent time eavesdropping on the stories and anecdotes of the women in the spinning room and learned much, from Danish and Nordic folk tales to legends about the terrifying 'bell deep' of the Odense river, where his mother scrubbed sheets for a living. In turn, he regaled the pauper women with his own chalk-drawing illustrated lessons in human anatomy, a cause of much hilarity among them. But the stories of trolls and witches, soldiers and fairies that he heard in the asylum, as well as encounters with some disturbed inmates, would turn Andersen into a very frightened child. These experiences, coupled with his father's stories and stage dramas, all contributed to the rich humus from which his literary oeuvre grew. Alongside Andersen's developing powers of creative transposition, though, was a far less benign tendency to link sex with poverty, debasement and social stigma, an association that would prove ineradicable and have tragic effects in adult life.

He was meanwhile forming an embryonic self-image based on compensatory self-aggrandisement: that he was special and different from everyone around him and that he must escape from what he called his roots as 'a swamp plant'. Bullied throughout childhood by the Odense street-urchins, a situation made worse by his mother's over-protection and the odd clothing she stitched for him from his father's cast-offs, Andersen began to cover his timidity and terror with a veneer of aloofness that was never to leave him. This trait of *hauteur*, so at variance with the charming naïvety and social awkwardness of the grown man, was to perplex and alienate many on first meeting him. By the time of his father's death when he was eleven, Andersen was set on life as an actor or poet in the big city. Hans the elder, while wandering reflectively in the woods, had decided to enhance his prospects by enlisting as a musketeer in the Napoleonic war against

A Lowland Habitat

Germany. Having previously been a flautist in the Odense regiment, he dreamt of money, prestige and personal pride in fighting as a foot soldier, and joined up in spring 1812. By 1814 the 33-year-old Hans was home again, his hopes dashed and his health fatally undermined by the harsh rigours of regimental life. In April 1816, three days after an interlude of delirium during which his mother ill-advisedly sent her son to beg for help from a 'wise woman', Hans died. His son was inconsolable. His father's body lay on the bed, while Hans Christian and his mother slept on the floor. All night a cricket chirruped, and his mother replied to it not to call her husband because 'He *is* dead already, the Ice Maiden has taken him'.[17] Her son knew what she meant, for his father had shown him how the ice figures on the winter windowpanes resembled a girl holding out both arms, adding in fun that she had come to collect him. From this desperate experience and his father's joke arose Andersen's fairy tales of *The Snow Queen* and *The Ice Maiden*, both featuring an archetypal female sorceress/seductress who abducts an innocent boy-child.

The loss of his father was an unspeakable blow just as Hans Christian was entering adolescence. This was also the moment his mother chose first to take her son into her bed, and then to marry another shoemaker, a much younger man. The three shared a single room. During her first marriage Anne Marie had exhibited great resourcefulness in contributing to the home and family finances, never too proud to beg for bread when needed or take in a foster child, but now their fortunes changed, and not for the better. The washerwoman worked hard, but she had begun drinking to keep warm as she scrubbed sheets in the icy waters of the River Odense. The stepfather proved irrelevant to Hans Christian; he took no part in the child's further upbringing. Anne Marie was eventually committed to the lunatic asylum, where she would die of alcoholism in December 1833. Andersen had acquired only the most rudimentary skills in reading, writing and arithmetic, gleaned at the Poor School attached to the workhouse after Carsten's closed in 1811. By his own account he had never done his homework at home, 'but managed it more or less on my way to school',[18] a feat interpreted by his mother as a mark of his genius. Well into maturity he was to revile all things factual and

---

17. Andersen, *My Fairy-tale Life*, p. 24.
18. Ibid., p. 30.

'scientific', preferring to rely on his prolific imagination to guide him through life in a rapidly industrialising world. As a child he had hated working in a cloth-mill, and a brief spell after his father's death when he was bullied by other child workers in a tobacco factory had bred in him a loathing of such environments.

Now his heart was set on an artistic career and, adopting the pose of gifted rural innocence that was to be his lifelong trademark, the young Andersen embarked energetically on his mission, cultivating one local personage after another in the attempt to gain foothold on the way to the big city and fame. Presented to the crown prince at the castle in Odense by the local chemist, whom he had impressed with his singing voice, the young prodigy told the prince that he wished to go to the grammar school and become a singer or actor; he rejected the royal offer of trade apprenticeship which the king must have thought a more realistic aspiration for a boy so little interested in learning. Undeterred, Andersen moved on to one of the town's top printers, whom he begged to write a letter of recommendation to a prominent ballerina at the Royal Theatre, Anna Margrethe Schall; the printer eventually agreed to this request while protesting that he did not actually know the lady. Finally, via another contact, Andersen introduced himself on 2 September 1819 to the bishop of Odense, from whom he begged his fare money for the journey to Copenhagen. He was asked to return in the evening and put on a little show. However, he had managed by now to save a few coins from the pocket money his mother gave him. Anguished at the thought of his leaving her for the city, she implored him not to go, to which her son replied pleadingly, 'First you go through an awful lot, and then you become famous.'[19] She knew when she was beaten and, hoping her son's timidity would return him to her sooner rather than later, she procured the special travel pass required for the journey and bribed the postillion to take him to Copenhagen as cheap passenger on the mail-coach for three *Rigsdalers*. She came to see him off, along with his beloved blue-eyed grandmother who wept with wordless grief at their parting, surmising, correctly as it turned out, that she would never see him again.

* * *

---

19. Wullschläger, *The Life of a Storyteller*, p. 30.

On his first morning in Copenhagen Andersen got up and dressed in his Confirmation suit to call on Miss Schall, the famous ballerina to whom he had a letter of introduction. Declaring she had never heard of the printer, the ballerina nevertheless listened as her visitor expressed his longing to go on the stage. She then stared in astonishment as he removed his boots to strengthen his petition by dancing the part of Cinderella, a role that had captivated him when the Royal Theatre touring company had brought it to Odense. He took off his huge hat and turned it into a tambourine, prancing and singing to the beat, "what do riches mean to me? What is pomp and pageantry?" As she would later frequently remind him, Miss Schall thought she had a madman in her drawing-room, flinging his long limbs wildly around in all directions, and she threw him out as quickly and politely as she could.

Nothing if not persistent, Andersen moved on directly to Mr Holstein, the theatre manager, and asked to be engaged. Looking the applicant up and down, the manager objected that he was too thin, to which Andersen replied that if only he would give him a salary of a hundred *Rigsdalers* he should soon put on weight. The manager took his own role seriously enough to dismiss this boy applicant, explaining that he only employed educated people. Hans Christian left and bought a ticket for the evening's opera. Here, he could not contain himself and wailed so loudly at the lovers' separation that a couple of women nearby in the audience comforted him with a sausage sandwich and sat with him for the rest of the evening. His faith in mankind restored, he was soon back on the long hunt for lodgings and sponsorship which would lead at last, via the kindness of various prominent figures, to the most distinguished of them all. At sixteen Hans Christian was still a penniless provincial boy, playing with his toy theatre, dressing puppets with samples of cloth and ribbons begged from the textile shops on Copenhagen's smart streets. He had begun writing poems to recite, as well as little plays, and had been admitted to the Chorus and Ballet School and given small parts in the chorus. In 1822 the school expelled him for unsuitability, but his fortunes were about to improve. He had introduced himself to the eminent translator of Shakespeare, Admiral Peter Wulff, and to the scientist Hans Christian Ørsted, beginning lifelong friendships with both. He was then introduced to Privy Councillor Jonas Collin, director of the Royal Theatre.

Jonas Collin, 'The Father', Andersen's patron and protector, by Constantin Hansen.

On first acquaintance, Andersen took this stern and serious personage to be simply a businessman: it was a gross underestimation. Collin would become the father-figure and advocate for whom Andersen had yearned, and his new patron's first act was to send the boy off for a sadly belated education at Slagelse grammar school, nearly sixty miles away in Zealand. This was to prove a salutary experience. On visits home to Odense his mother wept with pride, but back in Slagelse her son had to work harder than he had ever imagined to catch up with everything he had so far refused to learn. One day he was allowed as a pupil in the top class to travel in an open carriage overnight to view a hanging in the town of Skælskør. The incident was deeply traumatising and would later form the basis of his first fairy tale, *The Tinder-Box*. While hangings were a popular public spectacle at the time, this treat made a ghastly impression on Andersen, who watched with horror as the condemned girl and her lover were driven up to the scaffold, her face so pale, her head on his breast. Andersen's embryonic poet's soul was further stricken by an itinerant bard who went round selling a 'mourning song' meant for the criminals to sing. There the couple stood beside their coffins, the girl's voice rising higher in a hymn than anyone else's. Andersen's legs could hardly carry him, he found this sight 'more dreadful than the moment of death'.[20] To make things worse, some superstitious parents presented their sick son with a bowl of blood from the executed to cure him of a stroke.

Andersen's time at the Slagelse grammar school ended abruptly at just the moment when his hated headmaster, Meisling, was writing a positive report on his pupil, stating that if he kept up his hard work and dedication to study the boy would be ready to go on to the academy in October 1828. Andersen knew nothing of this report and had by now been bullied, maligned and humiliated in so sustained

---

20. Andersen, *My Fairy-tale Life*, p. 69.

a manner by the head that he was completely drained of faith or confidence in himself. He wrote openly of his sorrows and shame to his benefactor, just as Collin had asked him to do, and received a few affectionate lines back inciting him not to lose courage; to be calm and steady and then he'd see that everything would turn out all right. Hans Christian had found solace throughout these grim grammar-school days in the short annual respite he was given to spend in Copenhagen during which he often stayed with the Wulff family, whose hunchback daughter, Henriette (known to her friends as Jette), was to become his close friend and confidant. A few poems had come from his pen in Slagelse, including *The Dying Child*, which became his most widely known and translated early work. The poem arose directly from the frantic unhappiness Andersen experienced in the Meisling household, where his rent was considered too meagre and his appetite too great. Meisling never ceased bullying his pupil, while insisting that he stay under his charge, and his wife flirted with Andersen, adding to his huge confusion and disquiet. Writing miserably to Collin and the Wulffs with his woes, he was rebuffed with platitudinous promises that the headmaster did not mean to upset him, and perhaps he should try to be less egotistical.

It so happened that Meisling had heard from the poet Oehlenschläger how Andersen had read *The Dying Child* in Copenhagen, and the result was a vicious verbal attack by the headmaster on his pupil, dismissing the poem as sentimental claptrap and its author as a hopeless case. The long-standing mental anguish visited on the young Andersen had been witnessed by Hans Christian's one friend at the school, a young teacher named Christian Werliin. At Easter 1827 Werliin accompanied Andersen on the journey home to Copenhagen for the holidays and, unable to persuade him to speak to his protector about the headmaster, the teacher took it upon himself to go and see Jonas Collin. His report was so disturbing that Andersen was instantly removed from the grammar school and provided with a private tutor in Copenhagen. The Slagelse headmaster's parting shot was a prediction that his pupil would never pass his final examination. Once back in Copenhagen and under his patron's watchful eye, Andersen did so. He also published a first slim volume of poems and, in 1830, planned the first of his travels, across Denmark to the Jutland heaths and on to the North Sea coast, ending in a full exploration of his home territory of Funen.

Chapter 3

The Path of Perdition

As in the aftermath of the French Revolution and Napoleonic Wars Denmark lost its territories and empire, so the small city of Copenhagen, often referred to merely as a market town, had gathered all its institutional power and centred it on the castle. However, now the concept of the 'nation' began to emerge as distinct from centralised state, which led to discussion of linguistic and territorial aspects of the transition. Culturally, this came to be expressed as schism between centre and periphery, and re-organisational attempts by the state to converge and centralise local administrations were resisted. Even the idea of the 'centre' itself became a topic of serious controversy, symptomatic of the deeper nineteenth-century upsetting of the status quo between individual, community and state. Henriette Steiner describes developments in the Denmark of the time as the birth of a new social class comprising white-collar workers, including academics, in tandem with wider societal realignment of artists, writers and intellectuals. Referencing sources indicating censorship of written material, she reports that only certain genres are allowed and voices heard, although many newspapers and periodicals are founded during this time, as well as political writings disseminated in pamphlet form. All was not well in Copenhagen. Beautiful and increasingly beneficial as the city might have become for the creative mind and soul, it could also be claustrophobic. Like Edinburgh, its Scottish counterpart (the 'Athens of the North'), Golden Age Copenhagen was a Jekyll and Hyde of a city, its dual nature manifested both socially and topologically between the prosperous grandiose monumentalism of Hansen's city reconstruction and the diversity and impoverished domestic circumstances of the many who inhabited the old timber tenements and cottages of the periphery and inner-city slums. Here lived the artisans, craftsmen, shipwrights, journeymen and labourers who had rebuilt the city, a population almost entirely estranged from the well-to-do merchant class. A remarkable exception to this rule was the privileged Søren Kierkegaard, who on his daily strolls made it his business to stop and chat to everyone, thus endlessly enriching his understanding of those of lower social status.

A rare autobiography of a 'common child' came from the pen of actor, playwright and theatre historian Thomas Overskou (1798-1873), who lived through the bombardments of Copenhagen. Published in Danish in 1868, his book *Of My Life and My Time* describes being born and brought up in a revitalised Golden Age city dipping its toe into a new era of industrialisation while still lacking the most basic amenities of such, e.g. a sewerage system, streetlighting and railway. A vivid picture emerges of childhood in a Copenhagen slum tenement and how the 'brats' of his age (he does not count himself among them, proudly recording how careful and caring a housekeeper his mother was) might be found rummaging in the gutter for whatever could be found there, playing on the street and deserted fire-sites. They were a noisy and troublesome horde, hurling things at walls and bawling insults and jokes at anyone within earshot. A drunk was good game, and they chased staggerers, jeering at their state, and joined the cheering mob as nightwatchmen transported inebriated destitute women on ladders to the police station. 'A common child was very well dressed',[1] even if wearing only well-darned and patched clothes with holed stockings and clogs. As in Andersen's case, the absorption of petty bourgeois values cultivated by his mother fed into Overskou's growing aspirations towards a better life, and he particularly credits the domestic milieu she created for the later improvement in his social status.[2] Unlike his peer, Andersen seems to have lacked insight enough to arrive at a similar conclusion.

---

1. Henriette Steiner, *The Emergence of a Modern City: Golden Age Copenhagen 1800-1850* (Aldershot: Ashgate, 2014), pp. 27-29.
2. Thomas Overskou, *Of My Life and My Time*, (1868) re-released with notes by Robert Neiiendam (1915-16). Publisher unknown. https://en.wikipedia.org/wiki/Thomas_Overskou.

In sharp contrast, Kierkegaard was born in and later inherited a fine four-storey residence on the city's finest square, between Hansen's town hall and the city's apothecary. A courtyard lay behind the building. Every morning the square swarmed with local farmers bringing their vegetables and poultry to market, but the house at Nytorv 2 provided Kierkegaard with almost an entire lifetime of peaceful comfort and refuge, only towards the end becoming a millstone of which he was glad to rid himself. Here he lived for years with a manservant and secretary who saw to all his needs. He ate and drank well – some thought him excessively lavish – while maintaining a punishing work routine. From this tranquil and secure base, he sallied forth to explore the city and its people, not infrequently expressing his ironic loathing of it all: 'the residence of prostituted philistinism, my dearest Copenhagen'.[3] A 23-year-old Kierkegaard was to note the view from his window on 10 June 1836:

> An ambulant musician played the minuet from Don Giovanni on some kind of reed-pipe (I couldn't see what it was as he was in the next courtyard), and the druggist was pounding medicine with his pestle, and the maid was scouring in the yard, and the groom curried his horse and beat off the curry-comb against the curb, and from another part of town came the distant cry of a shrimp vendor, and they noticed nothing, and maybe the piper didn't either, and I felt such well-being.[4]

The very notion of a 'Golden Age' belongs to the bourgeoise, whose intellectual romanticism subsequently leads them to credit themselves with realising it. It is these claimants to the creativity and attainments of an era who eventually become the ruling class in 'democratic' politics, to the detriment of the less privileged whose reality is lost along with their own aspiration to belong to an age of renewal. Like many another European metropolis, Copenhagen entered a modern age yearning towards engineering and philosophy, imagination and idealism with much of its population both blindsided and sidelined by the change. Andersen and Kierkegaard illuminate both sides of this reality; their respective backgrounds and oeuvres situated at the crux

---

3. Henriette Steiner, *The Emergence of a Modern City*, p. 71.
4. Ibid., p. 72.

of a question addressed not least by the scientist Ørsted, who dismissed talk of a contemporary Golden Age as conceit. The works and diaries of the two authors reveal another truth concerning Copenhagen as a place of continuing petty persecution and frustration for a writer, and one in which personal suffering counted for very little in the public arena. Representing diametrically opposed social strata, each took as the basis of his work the two extremes of social experience during the so-called Golden Age and between them paint a less than gilded portrait of it: the former sentimental nostalgia for simpler times and modest striving after social justice, juxtaposed with the latter's violently repulsed aspirations towards more elevated betterment of the human condition through individual responsibility.

Their common ground was contemporary Danish Protestant Christianity, but from this sprang on the one hand morality tales derived from shared myth and folklore and, on the other, a theology of individual relationship to and with the Godhead. Of central concern to both writers are virtue and love. In Andersen's work the struggle between light and darkness is played out on the grand stage by archetypal characters in stories derived from his childhood puppet plays; he mythologises in order to arrive at commonly held Christian values. Kierkegaard takes his personal experience as the departure point for rejecting Christianity as generally understood and practised, focusing instead on the potential of the unique individual soul to follow Christ's example of divine love. Yet the two men were and remained oddly faithful friends. We may imagine the sort of bruising verbal exchange between them as young and driven writers in their encounters at the boarding-house bar.

The dichotomy between Kierkegaard and Andersen and their literary attitudes may also be discerned from a comparison of their treatment of the same subject: the famous Langebro (the 'Long Bridge'). This thoroughfare leading to Amager, along with its companion Knippelsbro, connects Copenhagen city centre with the enclosed island of reclaimed land named Christianshavn, established in the seventeenth century by Christian IV as exclusive rural retreat for rich merchants after the economic crisis, and site of endless augmentative city fortifications. Once Denmark's seafaring centre, it fell into disuse and is, at the time of writing, a thriving bohemian tourist attraction. In 1828 Andersen, newly liberated from his frightful Slagelse schooldays, had eighteen months to prepare for his matriculation exams. This meant a walk twice daily from the city centre across the inner harbour, via two bridges, to his tutor on Amager. The return journey, freed from preparation for his lesson, allowed his mind to roam, and so some six years before trying his hand at a first novel Andersen dreamt up the outline for his initial attempt at prose writing, a venture he hoped would mark his literary debut. This was *Fodrejse fra Holmens Kanal til Østpynten af Amager i aarene 1828 og 1829* (A Walking Tour from the Holmen Canal to the Eastern Point of Amager, in the years 1828 to 1829). The title was jocular, implying a long journey whereas everyone knew it took only about an hour to walk the distance. Andersen was enjoying himself: 'On New Year's Eve I sat quite alone in my little room and looked out across the snow-covered roofs of the neighbouring houses; then came the evil spirit, whom people call Satan, who encouraged my sinful thoughts about becoming a writer,'[5] and his narrative spans New Year's night 1828-1829. It is, according to Wullschläger, a jittery experiment in fantasy realism, a prototype of the fairy tale for which the author would become famous, and one that already quietly embodies a barely suppressed lifelong terror of failure. Published by Reitzel as a short book on 2 January 1829, *A Walking Tour* was enthusiastically received and, to Andersen's great joy and pride, favourably reviewed by the critic Heiberg.

There is no known full English translation,[6] but partial renderings of the self-referential Danish text reveal Andersen's hero confronted by a female entity guarding each bridge: the first seductive and most loquacious of the two trying to tempt him away from serious literature with threats of failure thanks to undereducation. In contrast the tragedienne fairy guardian of the Langbro persuades him of the corrupting influence upon the world of inferior and superficial writing. Our hero chooses to follow the latter. Written in the high-flown style of German fairy tale writer and musician Ernst Theodore Amadeus Hoffmann (1776-1822), under whose influence Andersen had fallen (along with that of Scott, Shakespeare, and Heine), the narrative pirouettes from one fantastical arabesque to the next before returning the hero to his starting point. It was a mildly witty, hysterical but ominous first foray. Andersen's entire and prolific literary oeuvre would be built on re-enactment of childhood trauma and attempts to outmanoeuvre it.

---

5. Wullschläger, *Hans Christian Andersen*, p. 80.
6. My thanks to Ane Grum-Schwensen, H.C.A. Andersen Centret, Syddansk Universiteit Campus (SDA), Denmark.

Kierkegaard's treatment of the Long Bridge reflects the very different trajectory taken by his literary imagination. Writing on the same subject nearly twenty years after Andersen, in *Concluding Non-Scientific Postscript to the Philosophical Fragments* (1846), he describes crossing the bridge as analogous to the dialectical tension between the busyness of the city and the serene emptiness of Christianshavn. He sees the latter as a mirror image of the capital, though placed in the middle of it, and contrasts the feeling of being in each location, the noise and traffic of the city with the distinctive rural peace of Christianhavn's streets which dispels all notion of what it is that keeps urban inhabitants so busy. Here on Amager, where vegetables are cultivated for the city's markets, there is nothing inconsequential to join in with; no distractions or 'diverters'. One feels abandoned to an isolating silence, surrounded on all sides by non-diverters. He is emphasising the essential silence of transcendence banished by the endless chatter and superficial activity of a city crowd and epitomised by mindless modern entertainments such as that offered by the Tivoli Gardens.

* * *

By 1833 the 28-year-old Andersen had been forging his literary way in the city for fourteen years and gained a considerable reputation for his readings and plays. The previous year he had helplessly witnessed his mother's pathetic decline towards death, having failed in his own eyes to earn or do enough to alleviate her sufferings, and had written the first of his many attempts at autobiography. This he offered as courtship gift, met with stony silence by Louise Collin, daughter of the protector he now called 'The Father', with whom he had fallen in love on the rebound from his first love, Riborg Voigt. Ricocheting from one immature infatuation to another would come to typify Andersen's relationships with women, but these first attempts were both anguished and tenuous. His truest orientation had already been found in the first and most long-lasting of his

Edvard Collin, photograph by Michael Mang & Co. Rome, 1863.

deep attachments, and it was to Louise's brother, Edvard Collin. The pattern was in place for all his romantic adventures from now on: tumultuous erotic feelings for a man inexpertly camouflaged by sentimental displays of affection towards a generally inaccessible woman.

Each early rejection was followed by rescue by his patron, who set him on the path to recovery by advising travel and arranging stipends. After the break with Riborg there had been a first foreign trip to Germany and Berlin. Two years of tours followed, most notably to Italy. The era had begun of the Grand Tour, when the Continent opened up to travellers, not least through the advent of the railway train. The Tour was considered the 'finishing school' for privileged young men with a classical education and as such it greatly appealed to Andersen's voracious appetite for social advancement, as well as serving as emotional emollient and escape. A subsidiary factor concerned Andersen's extreme temperamental volatility, which had begun to try the patience of the sober Collin family, deluged as they were with his agonised letters. At last, driven to despair by the cool insistence of Edvard on a formal form of address denoting calm, fraternal relations, Andersen wrote begging for more intimate terms and was gently refused adoption of the more familiar nomenclature. It was the last straw. Unable to cope with his emerging sexuality or contain his frantic need for affection and response, he left for Italy on 22 April 1833. Many came to see him board ship, including Louise and Edvard, around whose shoulders he placed an arm as they walked the quay towards the ship. As he sailed along the south coast a letter was delivered by the captain. It was from Edvard: 'I shall miss you dreadfully ... and yet, you will miss us even more, I know, because you are alone.'[7] Softened by the prospect of distance, Edvard's heart reverted to its genteel but genuine habit of kindness.

* * *

Søren Kierkegaard's twenty-second year was to be momentous even given the normal turbulence of every young man's heart, body and mind at this time of life. The recent years of bereavements had left his father shocked and stumbling, convinced that it was his dire fate to outlive all his children. Still deeply under Michael Pedersen's influence, his son too believed he would die young. He

---

7. Wullschläger, *Hans Christian Andersen*, p. 117.

was struggling with doubts about his university studies, and now he wrestled with even more painful conflict concerning his father, lasting reverberations from the 'master-thief' exchange, from which the son had been unable to recover a sense of his father's previously firm moral stature. Precipitated into dread as to his own inherited proclivities, it is possible that the 'The Great Earthquake' led young Kierkegaard to some terrible, irreparable sense of shame in relation to his mother, and later towards women and children in general. In any case, he could not escape his father's guilt. He was simultaneously struck by the story of Solomon's Dream, in which the son inherits both his father David's intellect and his sensual nature. The horror of this dream lies in its contradictory conclusion that only the ungodly become the chosen; that all David's majesty and grace are proof of nothing but his deeply flawed nature.

Kierkegaard saw his own propensity for sin entirely through his father's eyes. He made good Wordsworth's truth that the child is father of the man. He found simple solutions to what he understood to be his shortcomings, taking refuge in physical frailty, isolation and a sort of assumed pride. At sixteen he had been made to transcribe a letter from his 73-year-old father to his elder brother, Peter, who was studying abroad. At the end of this letter the father incited his younger son to add the following self-reproof:

> I do not know what is the matter with Søren. I cannot make him write to you. I wonder whether it is intellectual poverty that prevents him from thinking of something to write about or childish vanity that keeps him from writing anything except that for which he will be praised, and, inasmuch as he is unsure about it in this case, whether that is why he will write nothing.[8]

Now, understanding that he was of his father's blood and had inherited all its freight of sin, he repeated it. Try as he might to repent, to turn away from the world, he could not. This paralysing sense of inevitability he called 'foreboding', and issued admonishment:

---

8. Søren Kierkegaard, *Kierkegaard's Writings, XXV: Letters and Documents*, intro and trans. by Henrik Rosenmeier with Notes (Princeton, NJ: Princeton University Press, 1978); further details available at: https://www.jstor.org/stable/j.ctt1d2dm59.

> One must be very careful with children, never believe the worst, or, as the result of ill-timed suspicion, or a chance remark (the infernal machine which sets fire to the tinder in every soul) induce that sense of anxiety in which innocent but weak souls are easily tempted to believe themselves guilty, to despair, and so to take the first step towards the goal foreshadowed by the alarming foreboding – a remark which gives the kingdom of evil, with its stupefying snake-like eye, an opportunity of reducing them to a state of spiritual impotence.[9]

He comments on the profundity of the idea, the view of life of knowing all evil, warning that one must remain suggestible, for the unbaptised see things which others do not see. He himself understood and believed that he could give himself over entirely to Satan so as to be shown every abomination, every sin in its most frightful form – 'it is this inclination, this taste for the mystery of sin.'[10] Then there was foreboding, which might work in one of two ways upon the soul: as temptation or deterrent. Perhaps it indicated predestination. One acts as though moved by something outside oneself, and the consequences of this act are equally beyond the acting self. The arrival of foreboding in the midst of good fortune is one of its most prescient features, so that one is not aware of anything much wrong but then something happens to reveal the power of original sin as it has manifested in the family history, leading to a sense of foreboding and then despair. Thus Kierkegaard felt his soul ever in retreat from action; from the present moment, from now, from immediacy. He recognised his own as the soul of a poet, but one that recoiled from romantic response and yearned to turn inwards towards reflection. How was he to act in the world, tempted towards poetry and arrested in the same moment by intellect? Melancholy. It was the stasis of foreboding; the dead hand of the past upon his shoulder. He felt in himself empathy for the very depths of depravity. In the absence or abeyance of harmony between body and soul the entire being fell under the spell of the demoniacal, and this provided a sort of supreme comfort in the boundlessness of the fall from which one could fall no further. Kierkegaard recognised the unspeakable relief of letting go

---

9. Kierkegaard, *Journals*, p. 40.
10. Ibid., p. 41.

of the good in an ultimate relinquishment of guilt and dread. Never able to fuse the two aspects within himself of the spiritual and the sensual, this is also the explanation he gives in *The Concept of Dread* in relation to his youth. From this the critic Heiberg deduced an association between Kierkegaard's 'thorn in the flesh' with 'a wounded bashfulness' relating to a youthful drunken visit to a prostitute, the memory of which is ignited by the thought of marriage… then comes dread. The possibility of being a father tortures him night and day… as Kierkegaard would one day confess, 'The fact that religion enters into marriage is my misfortune':

> The real meaning of bashfulness (*Scham*)[11] is that the spirit cannot acknowledge as its own the extreme point of the synthesis (of the body and soul). That is why the dread belonging to bashfulness is so equivocal. Without the least sensual desire there is shame; about what? About nothing. And nevertheless an individual can die of shame, and a wounded bashfulness is the deepest suffering because it is the most inexplicable of all.[12]

* * *

From Hamburg, Andersen travelled down through the Alps towards Italy. *En route* through the Jura mountains he paused at the little clock-making town of Le Locle to complete and dispatch to Copenhagen a new reworking of his poem *Agnete and the Merman*, based on an old Danish ballad. Accompanying the script was a tremulous covering letter addressed to Edvard, expressing his longing for warm acceptance and recognition for the piece, which lay very close to its author's heart. He was devastated to hear back from Edvard that the poem was overblown, overlong and overwritten, self-referential and generally self-indulgent. It was mauled by the Danish critics as ill-conceived, mongrelised and pedestrian work, and the author was widely accused of imitating Oehlenschläger, who had also written a poem based on the ballad and sent it home from abroad. Andersen was distraught. He remained deeply committed to *Agnete*, which was in fact a thinly veiled parable of erotic love for a brother and sister in

---

11. Shame.
12. Ibid., p. xxxvii.

which the sexual identity of the protagonists is curiously melded in a way that would have been deeply offensive to its first reader: a strange and disturbing transmogrification of Louise and Edvard Collin. Weeks of agonising over the rejection followed, culminating by 31 January 1834 in Andersen railing in his diary against Edvard 'and the others' and accusing them of destroying him. He continued over the subsequent decade to revisit and work on *Agnete*, rewriting it as a play which was eventually staged in Copenhagen and again flopped, despite fine acting and some lovely musical accompaniment; Agnete's lullaby is the most familiar and admired surviving component of the doomed project. Andersen would later defend the piece as a creative crossroads in transition towards more mature poetical work: 'Despite all its faults, my play *Agnete* was a step forward, my purely subjective poetical nature was trying here to reveal itself in a more objective form… and this play rounded off what can be called my purely lyrical period.'[13]

But before him now lay the glories of Italy and he greeted them with rapture. From Milan cathedral, through the beautiful, flat and fertile Lombardy landscape to Genoa and the sea. The slopes were covered in blue-green olive groves, the sun shone, and soon they arrived in Carrera. Andersen knew nothing of sculpture. As a young boy in Copenhagen in 1819 he had briefly encountered Denmark's renowned sculptor, Bertel Thorvaldsen, in the street, but had seen little statuary in his homeland and hardly noticed such in Paris. Now he was overwhelmed by the sight of marble quarries glittering with quartz and mica, other-worldly enough for the old metaphor of antique gods and goddesses awaiting liberation by the sculptor, a Thorvaldsen or Canova, from their incarceration in blocks of stone. The awestruck traveller nevertheless retained his Danish pragmatism; its beauty was moderated by the trials of journeying through *bella* Italy, a degree of chaos which included cheating innkeepers, endless passport checks and such poor navigation skills on the part of the *veturrino* ('coachman') that, instead of arriving in Pisa in daylight he and his travelling companions got there only at midnight. Meanwhile Andersen's sketchbook filled with exquisite little line drawings: from pine-covered outcrops of the Jura mountains to the Simplon Road across the Alps to glaciers from his window at Brig in the Swiss canton of Valais.

---

13. Andersen, *My Fairy-tale Life*, p. 129.

The Path of Perdition

In Florence his eyes were opened on a dazzling new world of art. The works of Michelangelo took his breath away. Entering Rome on 18 October, the day of Raphael's second burial, Andersen found himself swept up in events of pomp and solemnity; the coffin draped in gold cloth, priests singing the *Miserere* and processing around the church. Behind them came high-ranking men and artists of the day, including Thorvaldsen himself bearing a wax candle. Soon Andersen was introduced to the great sculptor, who was living at his old home in Via Felice and working on a bas-relief of Raphael. Thorvaldsen talked with great verve and excitement about the previous day's ceremony and spoke of Raphael, Camuccini and Vernet. He showed his compatriot paintings by living masters, purchased by the sculptor and which he planned to bequeath to Denmark on his death. Here in the warm autumn sunshine Andersen met and fell half in love with a young painter, Albert Küchler (1803-1886), whom he was to find greatly changed on a later visit; ten years after Andersen first met him, the painter had shocked all his friends by converting to Roman Catholicism and becoming a Friar under the name Peter of Copenhagen. At the time of Andersen's first encountering him Küchler belonged to the bohemian circle surrounding Thorvaldsen, a group who, swiftly sensing Andersen's vital but impounded libido were soon teasing the painter about seducing him, along with scheming his induction

The Simplon Road Across the Alps, 19 September 1833, from Andersen's travel sketchbook.

Piazza del Trinità, Florence, with Michelangelo's house, Andersen's diary 11 April 1834.

into the delights of the bordello. Victim as ever of his own naïvety, Andersen's first impression of Küchler had been of someone 'so jovial and kind-hearted, and as far as I could see such an intellectually vigorous young man who painted those beautiful Italian pictures which always contained a roguish touch of the erotic'.[14]

In January 1834, Küchler painted a deeply sensitive portrait of Andersen, reproduced as frontispiece to the book about him by Kjeld Heltoft,[15] in which the high forehead surmounts softened facial features and the sitter's direct gaze conveys quiet confidence, kindliness and intelligence. Considering the anger and anguish Andersen was expressing in his diary at the time over the fate of his play *Agnete and the Merman*, the image radiates restoration and a rare state of relaxation. Contact in Italy with other artists, an ambiance of overt physical, spiritual and emotional creative expression, the irreverent fun and relish with which lecherous anecdotes were swapped – all had a transformative and liberating effect not only on Andersen's cramped attitude to sexuality, but on himself in relation to his own craft – the whole experience fostered by his friendship with the empathetic and unpatronising Thorvaldsen, a bond sealed in Rome. It was at the sculptor's studio that Andersen had been comforted after receiving the letter from Jonas Collin telling him of his mother's death on 16 December 1833, an event to which he briefly alludes in the diary entry for that day:

> My first reaction was Thanks be to God! Now there is an end to her sufferings, which I haven't been able to allay. But even so, I cannot get used to the thought that I am so utterly alone without a single person who *must* love me because of the bond of blood. I also received some critical commentary from Heiberg about my two singspiels – I am just an improvisator![16]

This time he managed to turn reaction into response and fuelled by new and furious energy on 27 December began working on a

---

14. Andersen, *My Fairy-tale Life*, p. 129.
15. Kjeld Heltoft, *Hans Christian Andersen as an Artist*, (Copenhagen: The Royal Danish Ministry for of Foreign Affairs, Press and Cultural Relations Department, 1977) frontispiece.
16. Wullschläger, *Hans Christian Andersen*, p. 127.

new novel, *The Improvisatore*, basing the story on his travels in Italy and describing in its opening pages a gentle, loving mother, a sentimentalised portrayal of his relationship with Anne Marie.

Meanwhile, his enthusiasm for Italian art took him from church to private palazzo to public gallery, viewing paintings by Rubens, Caravaggio and Titian. Stunned by the voluptuousness of Italian marbles, he felt for the first time the nature of real art; works informed not just by the head but by heart and soul. He sketched obsessively from his window in Rome, including a funeral procession. Other drawings include the Scala di Spagna, and the tender outline of 'a Jesuit' from the back. He sketched the River Tiber and Thorvaldsen's house, his Rome bedroom and balcony, as well as outlying villages. He recorded Egeria's Grotto and statuesque cacti. He drew the dome of St Peter's from Monte Mario and made line drawings of Vesuvius, where snow lay between the chasms and which he had climbed, suffering miserable after-effects from the cold. There are sketches of Pompeii, Naples and Florence, a palazzo in Verona, and sailing ships at the harbour of Genoa. These drawings are simple and untaught but bursting with the energy and intensity of fresh impressions. Here Andersen seems free with his pencil in a way he does not always appear with a pen, as in an energetic depiction, again from the back, of a peasant woman walking a high path bearing on her head a huge burden, perhaps a bale of hay. You can smell the warmth of

Genoa, 2 October 1833, from sketchbook.

Italian rock in these drawings, feel beneath your feet its treacherous mountain passes, scent the pines, glimpse a lizard sunbathing motionless on a stone wall, feel around you the bustle of city streets, a black-aproned mama watching from a curtained village doorway, get the whiff from within of carbonade, freshly baked bread, taste on your tongue the local earthy rich red wine and coffee. The beauty of Italian women was a revelation to Andersen; the men drove his imagination wild. Italy awoke all his dormant senses, most especially his long-suppressed sexual appetite. Excitedly, extravagantly, half fearfully he confided to his diary:

> If it really is a sin to satisfy this powerful urge, then let me fight it. I am still innocent, but my blood is burning. In my dreams I am boiling inside. The south will have its way![17]

In his anguish and agitation he envied the engaged, the married; and finding himself tempted by the sight of a half-naked girl felt with shame the danger of lechery. Everything set him on fire – the glowing colours, the ravishing light of Italy and the warm sensuality of this people and landscape made Andersen yearn unbearably for the nearness of another human body. And it was not the mere quickening of his blood that he found so intoxicating, these artists knew how to animate their work with a quality he clearly recognised as religious love. Immersed in the glory of the Italian Renaissance, he saw and felt for the first time how a work of art could convey the divine inspiration behind its creation. In allowing classical antiquity to challenge its rigid rule over sacred imagery the Church of Rome, so vilified at home, had relaxed its insistence on sentimentality in theological aesthetics, gifting Italian artists freedom to explore realism in form, proportion and spiritual expression, so that their work might breathe and weep and leave no soul unmoved. Shocked and enthralled, Andersen took in the glowing flesh of fresco figures – even limbs of marble seemed suffused with vitality, so that he recoiled from their coolness beneath his palm! Surely these figures sensed his touch, felt his warmth, returned his gaze? At some deep level he saw how classical simplicity thus infused with Christian spirituality lent the human body new dignity, and the effect was transformative. Andersen felt reconciled with himself, released from guilt and shame,

---

17. Andersen, *Diaries*, p. 80.

reinvigorated in the possibility of imbuing his own work with the same incarnated truth. If the spirit could move stone, surely his pen too could convey creative energy, his stories enshrine the sacred spark? He knew he had to garner strength to import this newly perceived power into his work, that it would be difficult to preserve this feeling and make lasting use of it in the chill northern climate of Copenhagen. And yet he must preserve and master it. If his little pencil doodlings could be admired by his new Italian friends, then he must be capable of similarly spontaneous writing? Suddenly the old narratives of the north and his homeland seemed mundane, dead-handed to him. He must come alive at last, cast off the past; he would no longer accept the 'improving' offered by his benefactor and family. His newly awoken spirit rebelled against the constant ostracism, the jibes, the cold and the small-mindedness of Denmark.

Thus, full of fresh knowledge and feeling rejuvenated, he contemplated the return home. It was not a welcome thought. These two years of travel had changed Andersen: a sliver of ice had entered his heart, just enough to turn him into something like a man, accepting of his own need for love. He vowed no longer to allow this to be reviled. He would not be bullied, forever so inhibited, submissive, grateful and compliant. He recalled Thorvaldsen's words to him when, in his studio, he had set a consoling meal of bread and cheese at the fireside after reading the letter telling him of his mother's death. The sculptor had warned that no artist could live under a cloud of condemnation; Andersen must not let that sort of criticism touch him, but keep to his own path, try to ignore popular opinion. Peace of mind, according to Thorvaldsen, was essential for creative work. These words came back to Andersen now and he determined to find the artist in himself, to dispense with the singing, dancing clown.

He would finish his new novel, *The Improvisitore*, and begin serious work on fairy stories for children, inspired during his travels by the work of the Brothers Grimm, who had resurrected national folk tales and retold them as fables for children. Andersen's novel would feature a poet son of Naples, who frees himself from fatherlessness, youthful suffering, brutality and shameful lusts to find true love at last. For years Andersen had tinkered with the fairy tale, but with this new start and output he would tell his countrymen what he thought of them, show them fire and blood! Throw off the shackles of fear. If even the pimps of Italy could see past his timidity and gaucheness to appreciate his talent… well…! The first of his new stories would be based on Aladdin and his lamp – but decidedly for adult consumption. Away with traditional pedagogic form! the new narratives would be radically contemporary in style, far from the improving tone adopted for children up until now. His scenery might be classically bucolic, but the new plots would carry the shock of the new.

In *The Tinder-Box* Andersen processes the trauma of his long-ago school outing from Slagelse to witness the hanging, ensuring his soldier hero is saved from the gallows by the last-minute intervention of three successively huge and terrifying dogs so that he can have the soldier marry the princess and invite the dogs along as special guests to the wedding. *The Tinder-Box* set the tone for Andersen's mature work. His early saccharine is soured, replaced by a definite hint of vengeful spite. Still, far from the feral settings and savagery of Grimm's fairy tales, these stories spring from the soothingly familiar social background of his fatherland, entirely recognisable to a Danish readership of the time. They are sentimental and homely enough for domestic consumption, if rather too coarsely presumptuous. The adult reader of these tales was confronted with no direct challenge, although their moral ambiguity definitely perturbed those accustomed to more conservative adherence to scriptural instruction. At most, the first readers of the fairy tales were left with an elusive but uncomfortable sense of injustice, cruel oversight or entirely unearned suffering.

* * *

Back in Copenhagen, Andersen subjected himself once more to the jibes of the young Kierkegaard during 'Unholy Alliance' drinking sessions. Susceptible as ever to superior social status, the storyteller made a ready victim despite the hardening effects of his recent travels. In response to the younger man's provocation, Andersen sought gently to placate, flatter and nurture their friendship, especially on grounds of their writing. Perhaps he was also a little disconcerted by the beauty in Kierkegaard's face and being, the seductive charm of one who knew so well how to crush a weaker personality. The young Kierkegaard was admired for his wit and his prodigious knowledge, but he was also feared, especially by those who were the butt of his terrible sarcasm. Andersen's naïve 'gentle giant' persona made him an irresistible target. But Kierkegaard's attention was now diverted to some extent by a life-or-death battle with his own nature. He fought his compulsions, but continued to drink heavily, producing in himself not only self-loathing, but persistent horror at having perhaps unconsciously fathered a child. This hidden fear was never conquered, and it produced the tenderest concern for every child he met. He could not stop himself from falling, but meanwhile made superhuman efforts to get his life back on track. Self-disgust led him to the most extreme conclusions, recording such in his journal:

> One went out and thought of committing suicide – at the same instant a stone fell down and killed him, and he ended with the words, 'God be praised!' ... I have just come from a party of which I was the life and soul; wit poured from my lips, everyone laughed and admired me – but I went away – and the dash should be as long as the earth's orbit _____ and wanted to shoot myself.[18]

His self-reproach was so deep, so nihilistic and so intractable that he could imagine no other state; the more frantic he felt, the wittier and wilder his demeanour, so that none at the world's party noticed his despair. Nobody but one. His revered, beloved teacher Poul Møller perceived the truth and witnessing Kierkegaard's mood warned his equally loved former pupil with the utmost gravity: 'You are so polemicalised through and through that it is perfectly terrible.'[19] The shock of what he would call this trumpet blast of awakening reverberated throughout the remainder of Kierkegaard's life, and probably saved it.

When later, in the first part of *Either/Or* (1843), he asserted that Christianity brought sensuality into the world he was 'reflecting seriously upon the grievous wounds he had received in childhood from his father's stern repression of the sexual instinct'.[20] The impression of this period of his life is one of desolation. He confided in no one, felt himself an 'observer' and in 1845 produced the following retrospective analogy: say a child was told that to break its leg was a sin, he would probably break it often, or come near to doing so, thinking that even to contemplate breaking it was a sin. Suppose it could not get that idea out of its mind, then out of love for its parents and so that their blunder would not result in his own ruin he would

---

18. Kierkegaard, *Journals*, p. 27.
19. Lowrie, *A Short Life of Kierkegaard*, p. 107.
20. Ibid., p. 98.

endure it as long as possible. A horse that is harnessed to too heavy a load pulls with all its might, and then collapses. The loyalty of this son to his father in so sensitive an area of experience is absolute. Gently, Kierkegaard goes on to expound the possibility of our being misled in our very understanding of the nature of sin; perhaps due to a very well-meaning person, for example a man who has been extremely dissolute might want to frighten his son from following in his footsteps and so imply the sinfulness of sexual desire itself, forgetting the difference between himself and the child, who is innocent and thus bound to misunderstand him. Here is the child who grows into the man who all his life remains harnessed to this unbearable burden. The state of social isolation despite company; the sense he describes of living 'as spirit' among men is both agonising and heartrending, as paraphrased by Lowrie from Kierkegaard's *The Point of View for my Life as an Author* from 1848. For long periods the writer had been preoccupied with his performative imagination, testing his mind as a musician tries his instrument, but he was not really living. Thrown from pillar to post by life, he faced endless temptations, including wrongful ones, and those of the worst kind that led to the path of perdition. He was twenty-five when he finally concluded that his life would be best spent doing penance. Then his father died, and the shift occurred: 'The powerful religious impression of my childhood acquired a renewed power over me, now softened by reflection.'[21]

* * *

Andersen's focus was upon fame. 'My name is gradually starting to shine', he wrote in 1837, 'and that is the only thing I live for.'[22] He drew a fascinating picture of his life for a visiting French journalist, Xavier Marmier, charming him into writing a little biography, *La vie d'un poète*, which appeared in the *Revue de Paris* of June 1837. Marmier also made a translation of *The Dying Child*. The biographical sketch was widely read; and Andersen wrote to his friend Henriette Hanck that Lady Byron had done so, adding 'and you know, le poète c'est moi!'[23] Intent on claiming wider fame within Scandinavia, he set out for Sweden in the summer of 1837 and made a happy trip of it. On the boat to Stockholm, he met a Swedish novelist and gave her a copy

---

21. Ibid., p. 105.
22. Wullschläger, *Hans Christian Andersen*, p. 172.
23. Ibid., p. 173.

of *The Improvisatore*, which she read overnight and admired. Once home, he finished his third novel, *Only a Fiddler*, for publication in November. As in the writing of *The Little Mermaid*, he was deeply emotionally invested in this sentimental story of two children who grow up in different worlds. Here is the poor boy, Christian, and his rich friend, a little Jewish girl called Naomi, and, like *The Snow Queen*, it is a retelling of the struggle to overcome humble origins, but this time incorporates outsider status, most significantly that of the Jew. Here at last is a full and compelling description of the pogrom a manifestation of which Andersen had witnessed on his first arrival in Copenhagen. In a brief but daring exposition of cross-dressing and sexual ambiguity, Andersen also allows Naomi, dressed as a boy, to exchange a kiss with Christian onboard ship. Edvard was by now married, and Andersen will never again explore sex so overtly in his work. His heroine eventually makes a disastrous marriage but remains haughty and spoiled. At last, she rides as a noble lady in a grand carriage through Funen, bowing her head as she passes Christian's funeral and the book ends on a note of bathos, after all: He was only a poor man they bore to the grave… only a fiddler!

Illustration from *The Little Mermaid*, by Wilhelm Pedersen, circa. 1848.

Andersen could sometimes choose precisely the wrong moment to approach his prickly counterpart for encouragement. Having promised the 25-year-old theological student a review copy of his new work, he delivered the same and Kierkegaard duly read and trashed it. *Only A Fiddler* is treated by Kierkegaard to an entire book of his own, his first, in which he goes for thorough dismemberment. *From the Papers of a Person Still Living, Published Against His Will*, subtitled *On Andersen as a Novelist*, may have been a laborious and turgid debut which Copenhageners joked had earned only two readers, Andersen and Kierkegaard himself, but it displays considerable insight into Andersen and his work. The title of his venomous little treatise may indicate one of two sentiments, or both: Kierkegaard's bemusement at his own life continuing in the light of so much premature death in the family and/or snide commentary on what he considered Andersen's incapacity to make of himself any sort of authentic human being. The novelist's only talent, wrote Kierkegaard, was an ability to capitalise on his own hardships by succumbing to and writing of them, creating alter egos of extraordinary pathos and self-indulgence. He accused Andersen of drowning his own unformed personality in self-pity.

Nonetheless, much of this pamphlet is actually devoted to developing the germ of Kierkegaard's central thesis of the potentiating self-realising individual. In criticising his contemporary, he condemns sentimental Romanticism and the supremacy of circumstantial life experience in nurturing or destroying genius. Already Kierkegaard is insisting on the nature of existential truth being found only within the context of the individual. It may be that Andersen's novel touched a raw nerve in describing the suffering of genius, for at the time of reading the novel Kierkegaard was struggling with his own lack of self-definition and direction, lamenting the lack of the idea for which he might live. By the time his pamphlet was published a year later, Kierkegaard had been reconciled with his father and lost him; there had been a transformational conversion experience, and the young critic had determined to continue his theological studies and enter the clergy. The ground felt firm beneath his feet, and perhaps he needed to consolidate this with a self-validating attack. Andersen's response was a valiant attempt to rise above it. In his definitive memoir he contrasts this novel with his first, which he now admits might perhaps indeed deserve the charge of improvisation, whereas *Only a Fiddler* was struggle and suffering as he understood them. He defends the third book as having been carefully planned, every detail derived from his own experience and describes the rebellious moods he experienced during the writing as arising from the injustice, triviality and pressure surrounding him, and how this is manifested in his central characters.

Andersen goes on to complain that despite its success at home, the book brought him neither thanks nor encouragement. He is further infuriated by the inference that the work was produced not by genius but through the lucky cooperation of some primitive natural propensity in its author. The critics suggested that he was 'often guided in some strangely fortunate manner by *my instinct*. They chose the expression used of animals'[24] raged Andersen, whereas the relevant term in the world of human beings and poetry is genius. His memory flowing on from this outburst, he reports retrospectively on how for a little while *Only a Fiddler* occupied the mind of one of the country's most highly gifted young men: Søren Kierkegaard. One day when they met in the street the student theologian had promised Andersen he would write a criticism of the new novel that would satisfy its author more than previous ones had done for, Kierkegaard confessed, people badly misunderstood him. Poor Andersen was to wait a whole year for the approval he craved, and then be forced to forfeit it. Modestly enough, having hoped that the age that seemed to pass before he heard from his friend would bring relief, he finally had to submit to the truth that upon close reading Kierkegaard had found the novel very full of faults. All Andersen said he had gleaned from the pages of Kierkegaard's critique was that he was sorely lacking as a poet and some future versifier should bring him back into the fold as a better version of himself. The sweetness that ran like a red thread through Andersen's character allowed him humbly to add to his recall of this incident that he would later come to better understand this Kierkegaard, 'who has shown me kindness and discretion as I progressed.'[25] Still, he mourned the lack of appreciation for his novels in Denmark, and sought comfort instead in Heiberg's enthusiastic endorsement of his fairy tales or 'Everyday Stories', edited by the great critic himself.

In fact, the third novel should never have been written, but if Andersen claimed later to have come better to know Kierkegaard, reading the book had certainly led the latter to understand Andersen in many, various and subtle ways. Noting how the joylessness of the author's life reveals itself in the novel, Kierkegaard goes on to say the work 'should rather be compared with those flowers which have male and female placed on the same stalk'.[26] He recognised sexual anguish when he encountered it; the dread and fear such struggles could engender. He had closely read and pondered Andersen's story of the mermaid: a girl entering maidenhood crowned and enflowered by the storyteller's macabre imagination. Noted the elements of crudity and

---

24. Andersen, *My Fairy-tale Life*, pp. 186-87.
25. Ibid., p. 187.
26. Wullschläger, *Hans Christian Andersen*, p. 175.

cruelty that pervade the fairy tale: bleeding feet, a severed tongue, agony at the place where her tail must come. Kierkegaard senses in the mermaid her creator's fear of sex and the vulnerability of innocence, his insistence that in recompense she be stripped of chastity and grace, and of her song. So he reduces her to silence and to stilts, and renders sterile her sacrifice: no redemption for this very Protestant heroine. Kierkegaard may also have perceived, despite Andersen's adherence to the values and tenets of the Church, some deep-seated ambiguity in his attitude towards it, particularly in regard to the then ubiquitous Christian antisemitism and deliberate ignorance and lack of understanding concerning 'Mohammedanism'. Further, Kierkegaard empathised with Andersen's rejection of Golden Age bourgeois values, his championing of the poor and downtrodden. Most significantly, both writers must have sensed in the other their attempt to address the state of existential isolation imposed on man by modernity; both chose celibacy and were concerned with the possibility and impossibility of meaningful love. Where their paths diverged was in examining the wider moral morass of their Age. While the timid and conventional Andersen dared only test the waters artistically, Kierkegaard struck out for the depths with his view that the aim of genius was pursuit of the Idea(l), so endowing finite life with meaning and becoming all one could become in relation to God.

On and on they sparred, Andersen feinting, Kierkegaard on the attack – as in 1838 he mocks the storyteller's ineffectuality in surrounding himself with a bunch of weedy aesthetes and acolytes who existed merely to eternally protest their honesty, and little else. They certainly could not be accused of equivocating minds, quipped Kierkegaard, for they had nothing whatsoever in mind. As for Andersen's accusation that Kierkegaard's witticisms were recherché, well, the latter considered Andersen's plain absent… But the storyteller bore no lasting grudge regarding his friend's critique of the early novel, although ten years would pass before he could respond directly in a wry note accompanying a new edition of his fairy tales in 1848: 'Dear Mr Kirkegaard [sic], *Either* [i.e. whether] you like my little ones, *Or* you do not like them, they come without *Fear and Trembling*, and that is in itself something. Sincerely, the Author.'[27]

* * *

---

27. Ibid. footnote, p. 175-76.

To Kierkegaard, his recidivism felt like the enchantment wrought by a fairy king, only to be undone when one succeeded in playing backwards without a single mistake the same piece of music by which one was enthralled. Returning each time from his revels to his father's house, he felt the need to approach him as Solomon approached David 'with back turned and with averted eyes in order not to witness his dishonour.'[28] As though this were not burden enough, there was the virtuous elder brother hanging around there too, forever quoting the 'Good Book' and creeping about cloaked in piety. Fine specimens of manhood, one and all! Kierkegaard found a room in town from which he could carry on taking meals at the hostel and for which his father would pay. The son was thankful. He took a job teaching Latin, an easy way to earn money and redeem some dignity. His self-respect was at an extremely low ebb.

Drinking heavily and deeply disillusioned as he was with Christianity, his studies in philosophy were a frantic search for meaning, a new template by which to live. All his efforts at self-reform, in terms of synchronising the physical and spiritual sides to his being, were stymied by Christian intolerance of sensuality. If this were not true of the Eastern Orthodox Christian tradition, it was certainly central to post-schism teachings espoused across the West. So long as sensuality was counterposed with spirituality it presented human reality with an impossible conundrum, yet the core Christian concept of incarnation unequivocally demanded resolution, synthesis. The more Kierkegaard encountered the lack of an ethical framework for incarnation within the teachings as they had been passed on to him, the less he loved them. The more he enumerated the ways in which the western Church corralled, controlled and demeaned bodily experience, the more he rejected this tainting of the natural state with unnatural disapprobation and constraints. The more vitriolic the Church, the less viable any lasting reconciliation between the apparently disparate aspects of human nature, until any attempt at imbuing the body with grace and accepting its status as a temple for the soul became insuperable. Even the pagans had managed to bridge the divide, but Kierkegaard knew that his own final choice, if such had to be made, must be spirit.

In his struggle to find harmony, or at least some degree of compatibility between Christianity and other constructions, he read

---

28. Kierkegaard, *Journals*, p. 565.

and rejected Hegel, at the time the most popular philosopher in Denmark. Kierkegaard's main objection to Hegel's worldview was what he saw as the distortions of 'mediation' imposed by systematisation. In the end, his admiration for the philosopher was confined to the intellectual brilliance of his thinking and stopped short of Hegel's passion for *explaining* religion. Such did not, in Kierkegaard's view, constitute a right approach to or appreciation of *reality*, which could not exclude the ineffable. A new formative influence was Johann Georg Hamann (1730-88), the German thinker who on a business trip to London had undergone radical conversion from secular Enlightenment ideology to more conventional Protestant orthodoxy while reading the Scottish sceptic and anti-rationalist writer David Hume. Kierkegaard was drawn both to Hamann's Counter-Enlightenment sympathies and his manner of communication; Hamann's writing style was elliptical, mercurial and opaque, making free use of Socratic irony. He loved the natural fluidity of language and held it higher than reason. In his writings context is designed to counter the notion of universal reason in the interest of refuting fixed knowledge and tying his reader down to a particular (anonymous) author in a particular time and place: an emphasis on the unnamed singular, the individual. Hamann's insistence on the impossibility of subjection of the religious to reason was the pivotal point at which his thinking converged with that of Kierkegaard, and he convinced the Dane of Christianity's capability in fact to provide the framework he needed for delineating reality. The discovery was decisive.

Kierkegaard could move on. His preoccupation with original, in Danish 'inherited', sin now assumed a wider, more secular significance. No longer dissociated from their individual, social and emotional context, body and spirit found common ground. The old myth of 'the sins of the fathers' suddenly stood firm. Repentance, Kierkegaard now saw, must mean repenting himself back to God via his own world, clan and family, for his fall was commensurate with his father's guilt. It was *the* essential sense of solidarity which lent reality to traditional doctrine. If philosophy and Christianity were on a collision course, thought Kierkegaard, then it was philosophy that had to go. The task before him now was to liberate himself from the need for any map. If Christ had been a purist, this must be the starting point. What was needed was a newly conceived Christianity, one founded on the incarnated Christ and his humanity, sweeping away the detritus of dogma and superstition with which the Church had swathed him. Perhaps in exploring this approach Kierkegaard intuited the possibility of self-integration; so crucial, priceless and remote a horizon he hardly dared contemplate it. Kierkegaard believed himself to be 'uncommonly erotic', but Lowrie disputes this, quoting the many who knew and thought him a most pure man. Indeed, Kierkegaard effectively describes himself thus in speaking of a particular situation known to him as requiring 'an extraordinary combination of purity and impurity.' Lowrie's contention is that Kierkegaard possessed a rare sense of shame and was possibly more distressed by 'the impure suggestions of sensuality'[29] than most men are.

Preoccupied as Kierkegaard was with the flaws in his own nature, his worries embraced the wider world. In spring 1837 he was lamenting in his journal the utter bankruptcy towards which the whole of Europe seemed to be sliding, including unavoidable spiritual bankruptcy. He saw confusion in language itself, rebellion of words among themselves which, dislocated from human mastery, hurtled one upon another in despair, so that everyone reached randomly for the first word that came to mind in some confused attempt to express their presumed thoughts... and nothing sensible was said. The predominant idea of the whole age seemed to be to 'get ahead', whatever that meant, so that everyone spent their whole time leapfrogging over the one in front. He saw it all: the whole misconceived notion of 'progress'; the terrible sloth, the laziness with language and its corruption – in a word, popularism. In his journal he bemoaned a leap of lemmings for whom speed was everything and brevity paramount, even in reflection. The result was a sort of attenuated but bloated discourse employing short-cut expressions and abbreviation; codified communication to the point where a kind of weird long-windedness had deprived language of its truly concise and pregnant phrases, in the place of which was pompous oratorical twaddle devoid of meaning. We could only hope for better times, he drily observed, if this economy bred enough prodigal sons among words. As for philosophy, it began and ended with moving with the times: 'that's the idea nowadays – wonderful, how profound!'[30] Then there was the nature of democracy, when a majority of votes decided a matter was one not subject to the masses? So his journal plunged

---

29. Lowrie, *A Short Life of Kierkegaard*, p. 98.
30. Kierkegaard, *Journals*, p. 37.

onwards, as though his own thought processes had undergone the same exaggerated acceleration, and he had hardly time to catch and write one idea down before it was rushed upon by another… until he felt he really was going mad! and then a quiet reflection came along and calmed him: 'Most of all I like to talk with old women who retail family gossip, after them with lunatics – least of all with very sensible people.'[31]

The close of 1837 found Kierkegaard in quietly pensive mood, noting on 26 December some rare reflections on the healing capacities of distraction:

> Why is the soul so rested and strengthened by reading fairy stories? When I am bored with everything and 'tired of life' fairy stories are always a rejuvenating bath and do me so much good. There all mundane and finite cares are banished, joy and sorrow are infinite (and for that very reason they are unconsciously beneficial).[32]

Off goes the reader's imagination in search of the bluebird, just like the Princess who goes to look for her unfortunate beloved. Such sorrow in the girl's heart! Dressed as a peasant she meets an old woman and tells her, "I am not lonely, my good mother, a great bird of Grief, Sorrow and Suffering accompanies me." So that all our private sorrows are forgotten, dissolved in shared sorrow, and we long to meet an old woman whom we could call "Good Mother", or join the young girl in her quest, or meet the royal couple who have only one daughter, and there is never any mention of money or politicians…

Such unfamiliar wistful longing for escape! Such perfect correlation with Jung's consolation of the archetype. Just seven months earlier there had occurred the most sudden, disorientating and irrevocably life-changing event of Kierkegaard's life.

---

31. Ibid., p. 38.
32. Ibid., pp. 54-55.

Chapter 4

The Bridge of Sighs

It was not until after her husband's death in 1896 that Regine Olsen Schlegel spoke openly at last of her relationship with Søren Kierkegaard. After almost half a century as a loyal wife, she was suddenly free to break her silence and, as though transported back to girlhood, to relive her first encounter at fifteen with the love of her life. Her memory of him was as fresh as though it were yesterday: his beauty, his lovely trepidation, his shy, fleeting smile, the blue light in his eyes, the torrents of witticism and wisdom. She was a child, he almost ten years her senior and as gentle as she imagined an older brother might be. She felt in that instant the strange sense of remembrance known to all true love, that she had known him forever and knew what he would always be to her, knew in her innocence that this was no fraternal friendship. After that day she had waited and after a few days he returned to see her, just as she had known he would, as though it were his right always to seek out and find her. It felt to her as though this was indeed his absolute entitlement and that they would never be parted.

He had entered the drawing-room that first afternoon at the house of friends of Regine's father: a party to celebrate the birthday of Bolette, the widow Rørdam's daughter. Søren Kierkegaard had come for Bolette's sake, to see her in particular. She was just over twenty, near his own age, and they were friends. Perhaps each felt towards the other a little more friendship; later he would recall a measure of 'responsibility' towards her, while insisting that their relationship had been 'innocent', purely intellectual. In any case, that day eight young people were gathered to enjoy each other's company. Happy noise and chatter filled the room, rising to its high moulded ceiling. Spring sunshine flooded in through high casement windows, sparkling in crystal chandeliers. Regine had retreated to a window-seat to rest a moment. She recalled his arrival with great clarity. He stood in the doorway, a slight figure leaning on a rolled umbrella. Sunlight in his halo of fair hair, a mass of dark blond curls above a high clear brow. Sunlight sheened the silk velvet high hat he held. His face was exquisite; perfectly spaced expressive eyes beneath delicately winged eyebrows, full, softly curved mouth. Like an icon, his image took immediate possession of her soul. He in turn immediately found her face and returned her gaze with gentleness and grace, the faintest softening in his demeanour. They were introduced; he must have crossed the room during the secret meeting of their eyes, but Regine already knew his name. Bolette had spoken of him. Anyway, she did not need names. She knew him by heart. She felt her whole being suddenly on high alert. People, friends, clothes, gaiety, laughter, they disappeared, and she watched the whole room turn towards the same point. He was talking and the air buzzed with shared attention and laughter. What was he expounding? What were the words that so captivated each listener. He had simply enchanted everyone, and all the time sent secret smiles her way.

   Now, all these decades later, her own drawing-room was constantly full of enquirers asking about him. How could she begin to convey anything of his reality? Her lover's truth was then as now ineffable, a kingfisher that flits beneath the bridge, an azure glimpse of God. The flash of quicksilver that leaps to sip at air and plunges back into the river's spate – a twist, a pirouette of light. His was the most vital presence, and yet he possessed supreme stillness; an inner being that seemed to exist in utter peace and steadfastness, silent and unseen. It was in that quiet truth that they had met and, until now, she had never spoken of it – or of anything that followed.

* * *

May 1837 had found Kierkegaard once more out looking for diversion, doing his best to forget his (better) self, breaking his resolution to remain a penitent. He nevertheless decided in his loneliness to seek out the 'intellectual' friendship of a girl he knew, daughter of a deceased clergyman and herself engaged to a theology student, to try to talk to her. He knew he was turning back to the world again, succumbing to temptation, but it was not the bustle that he sought, but quiet conversation with Bolette. He had vowed to leave at home his 'demoniacal wit', which he felt stood with a sword of fire between himself and every innocent girl. Returning to the Rørdams in Frederiksberg on subsequent days and recording these visits in his journal, he seems bemused and disconcerted by this new pattern of behaviour, throwing him from his usual habit of proud solitude. He cannot trust or welcome the new inclination for company and feels belittled by it. There is fervency in his prayer for divine support at this moment when he senses imminent breach in his integrity. As the visits to Frederiksberg continue there appear in the journal several extraordinarily passionate outbursts of anguish and dread, in one of which he curses his 'arrogant satisfaction' in standing alone and declares that all will despise him now. He asks God to stand by him, to let him live and better himself. These were the entries that Regine Olsen believed alluded to their first meeting and the effect they had had upon each other. He agonises over the ambiguity of his situation and the effort required to suppress the emotions aroused, and again resorts to fairy tale to remind himself of his life task and restore some sort of balance: 'The early Christian dogmatic terminology is like a magic castle where the most beautiful princes and princesses lie in a deep sleep – it only needs to be awakened in order to appear in all its glory.'[1] It is more human enchantment, though, that still holds him hostage, and about two months later comes a very deliberately dated passage written on a Sunday in the gardens of the Frederiksberg after a visit to the Rørdams:

> *July 9.* I stand like a lonely pine tree egotistically shut off, pointing to the skies and casting no shadow, and only the turtledove builds its nest in my branches.[2]

There follows a short vignette describing someone wishing to write a novel about a character who goes insane; while working on it, the writer gradually succumbs to madness and finishes his book in the first person. In 1849 Kierkegaard was to record his first meeting with her, just as in old age Regine recalled how she had seen him when he turned up unexpectedly at the party and the impression he

---

1. Kierkegaard, *Journals*, p. 46.
2. Ibid.

had made on her with his liveliness of mind, although she could no longer recall all he had said. In any case, he was fighting now for his very existence as he knew it, and intellectually exhausting himself in the process. How, he reasoned, could he find himself thus tempted? Six years later, in *The Diary of a Seducer*, which concludes the first part of *Either/Or*, he would vividly describe this scene in which a young man, finding himself in the company of eight pretty women, captivates them with his conversation. Yet in truth, a few days after his twenty-fourth birthday he had fallen in love for the first time with a girl of fifteen. Moreover, this was no passing infatuation but a love that would endure for a lifetime and, he believed, beyond.

How was this reality to be reconciled with loyalty to his father, the curse that lay upon his family? A sacred marriage vow demanded absolute transparency. It could not be compromised by secrets, hidden vice and duplicity. He knew that many marriages involved such little or greater falsities and omissions, but could not imagine either hiding from or confiding in a woman the extent of his own depravity and lost virtue. He felt utterly debarred from any fully committed relationship with a woman. Yet, driven by desolate loneliness, he now found himself using his prodigious powers of espionage to discover when this girl would be at the Rørdams and contriving somehow to be there himself, visits that would become the couple's alibi. Scandalised by his own behaviour, he felt deserving of the world's derision and worse, that despite his conviction of forgiveness at the heart of Christianity he was not released from his fallen state. Thoughts of both the absolute need for candour in marriage and confession in entry to the ministry were paralysing. His current state left him drained, unable to summons energy for anything at all. Walking tired him; if he lay down, he feared he'd never get up again. The thought of riding was too violent to contemplate. He felt only slightly tempted to take a carriage out of town to linger amidst nature and so surrender to his languor.

His own ideas and conceits repelled him, and even the pithy language of the Middle Ages failed to work its usual magic in banishing his ennui… Driven again to the edge of madness, drinking and overthinking, he despaired: 'All the flowers of my heart turn to ice-flowers.'[3] He could do nothing, not retain a single serious idea. His dissertation eluded and reflection deserted him. The only occasion

---

3. Ibid.

which allowed him to keep a mental grip was in a room full of chatter; then he hung on grimly to his precious thought, determined to preserve it through the hubbub. He felt himself a lunatic, a Janus who laughed with one face and wept with the other. December came and cast its own darkness on his spirit, so that he sat one day ruinously sunken in himself, losing himself and his ego in pantheism. He was reading an old folk song about a girl who waits fruitlessly for her lover, until she goes to bed and weeps, and awakens weeping… and suddenly Sædding came to Kierkegaard's mind's eye, his father's birthplace, its lonely larches and desolate moors, and one generation after another arose before him, their girls singing and piteously tearfully sinking back into the grave, and he wept with them.

The old year passed into a new, and March 1838 brought news of the death of his most loved and esteemed teacher, Professor Poul Møller, he who had warned his pupil against his monstrous wit and love of refutation. The memory of Møller, and perhaps particularly of his admonishment, now returned with startling clarity, concentrating his pupil's mind, shaking him out of his apathy and precipitating a solemn vow to make something of his life for his teacher's sake. It was five years since Kierkegaard had passed the first two parts of his theological examinations with honours. Having studied Greek, Latin, Hebrew and history, mathematics, philosophy and physics, he began again to reflect seriously on what might constitute his life's work. Among his contemporaries only one man had penetrated Kierkegaard's incognito. Poul Martin Møller, academic and poet, recognised in him the manifestation of a rare prodigious intellect and typecast him fatefully enough as Ahasuerus, mythological archetype of the Wandering Jew.[4] The friendship between mentor and pupil had been instrumental in liberating Kierkegaard from the thraldom of Hegelian logic and Kierkegaard had in turn enriched Møller's poetical and philosophical endeavours; Möller would become more widely recognised as poet than philosopher.

It was a meeting of 'the younger and older philosopher of personality', as acknowledged by Kierkegaard in his most important philosophical work, *Concluding Unscientific Postscript to the Philosophical Fragments*. Apart from his father and Regine Olsen, writes Dru in his Introduction to the Journals, only one man influenced Søren Kierkegaard, and that man was Møller; he is also the

---

4. Kierkegaard, *Journals*, p. xxxi.

only one to whom his pupil officially dedicated a work. *The Concept of Dread*, in which Kierkegaard expands on his youth, is inscribed: "To the late Professor... The happy lover of Greece, the admirer of Homer, the confidante of Socrates, the interpreter of Aristotle – Denmark's joy... the enthusiasm of my youth, the mighty trumpet of my awakening, the desired companion of my moods, the confidant of my beginnings, my departed friend, my missing reader..." Here, 'the mighty trumpet of my awakening' refers to Møller's warning Kierkegaard of his terrible capacity for polemics, which shocked the younger man into awareness of his powers of (self-)destruction. These were the words which recalled the then 25-year-old from wandering the path to perdition and set him firmly on another that may not merely be said to be 'running into uncertainty, but going to certain destruction – in confidence in God that means victory'.[5]

Møller had been well acquainted with the youthful Kierkegaard's ambitious plan for a comprehensive philosophical exposition of certain neglected aspects of the Middle Ages: "Life outside religion in its three typical aspects – doubt, sensuality and despair", as he had outlined it. Now Kierkegaard learnt of Møller's deathbed plea: 'Tell little Kierkegaard not to undertake too big a task, for that was injurious also to me.'[6] His pupil was stunned, not only at so personal an admonition, but the sudden removal from his life of so great a bulwark. He felt bereft, robbed of all direction. How was he to tackle any serious work, especially in his current state of ennui? Was this the reason why his mentor's words had been passed on so faithfully – as (yet another) warning and reminder? In any case, he resolved to abandon the original large-scale project. Then, just when he was at his lowest ebb, his twenty-fifth birthday dawned and with it came a solemn summons from his father. Søren recoiled. His father always sensed precisely the right moment and seized it. What kind of birthday gift had he prepared for his youngest son? It was bound to be a lecture! Had his boy got his thesis planned? Had he seen how well his dear brother was doing? He who with a tragic air murmured of his own inadequacy even as he clambered up the greasy spire. A small slithering slide from grace was nothing to Peter, he always found his way upright again. They were so very upright those two, father and

---

5. Ibid., p. xxxii.
6. Lowrie, *A Short Life of Kierkegaard*, p. 95.

elder son, they bobbed back to the surface like a couple of ducks. The youngest Kierkegaard could hardly meet their eyes.

Nonetheless, duty called and like Isaac he answered his father's summons. It had seemed to Søren lately that the old man had long perceived him thus, as sacrificial lamb. So, in deepening dread he entered his father's presence, and to his astonishment found tenderness awaiting him. Michael Pedersen greeted his youngest child with open face and mind; no harsh word, rather his eyes were moist with tears.

Peter Christian Kierkegaard, Søren's brother (1805-1888).

As though for the first time, the son saw before him a gentleman in great old age, one humbled and reduced by the griefs of his 82 years. The dying father gestured for his youngest boy to take a seat. In the silence that followed, every busy thought was stilled and Søren discovered his derision fled. The father began to speak, to tell his son everything, pouring forth a cataract of sufferings; a torrent, a cascade of repentance that cleansed the air between them of all but grace. Listening, the son watched transfixed the softening of those formerly stern features which now showed only childlike innocence; he saw appear the boyhood smile that had existed before the curse eclipsed it. He witnessed the flesh absolved of all its worldly weight of guilt; the thorn removed. His father begged forgiveness, pure love upon his countenance. Søren fell to his knees. So he was not lost to his father, after all! Plain now was the fact of Michael's always having understood the origin of his youngest son's waywardness. For his part, Søren discovered himself truly his father's son, heir as much to his godliness as to his sin. It was redemption and like Lazarus he returned to life half-blinded by tears. Numb-limbed, he rose and blundering into new reality embraced his father and took leave of him. Returned to the outside world he felt as naked as a newborn lamb, stripped of all ingenious intellectual armour to protect him from its storms, its cold and cruelty and its beauty on this bright May day of epiphany. Two weeks later on 19 May came a morning of cool, clear breeze, a day so limpid that it lit the whole of life in radiant bliss, life's now, then and tomorrow, so that the poet wrote ecstatically in his journal of indescribable joy... a gratuitous message of rejoicing 'in, at, with, over, by, and with my joy', a heavenly refrain which, as it were, displaces our other song, like the trade wind that blows 'from the Mamre to the everlasting habitations.'[7]

* * *

July brought *cri de coeur* from Kierkegaard to his confidant Emil Boesen, appeal for a *voice*, one as sharp as a lynx's eye, frightening as the groans of giants and lasting as nature's song. He needed an ability to call on range from deepest bass to the most tremulous treble, a symphony that moved from heavenly peace to frenzied volcanic eruption. That was what was required for him to catch breath, express what was on his mind, to make people tremble in sympathy and rage, and the more he contemplated the friends' motto "In the distance stands a church" the more Kierkegaard felt the truth of Boesen's remark that it had, indeed, come closer. But Kierkegaard felt unready for the challenge, fit only to be a listener. He felt his speech still too coarse, too unevangelical, uncircumcised. It died like a blessing on the lips of the mute. He begged his friend for the gift of words, for fitting eloquence.

August! Month of heat and madness, holidays and Copenhagen thronged with travellers. In the harbour the tall ships disgorged themselves of tourists, disembarking with their huge leather trunks and self-important stride. Lost in this strange place with its unknown tongue they covered their confusion with noise, boisterousness; imperiously they demanded of the humble townsman where to lodge, to eat, drink – for good as this place looked, nowhere is as fine as home of course, despite their having been so impatient to escape it. They strolled the lovely streets as though they owned them, casting about for someone who spoke their language to introduce them to new experience – which had better be good, for they were paying plenty for it. Kierkegaard, out on his daily constitutional, could not help finding something repulsive about these new world-wanderers, something repugnant, rapacious. He was particularly sensitive to the ingress of incomers, for his city was both his home and school. Copenhagen offered an endlessly changing pageant of people and place with which he engaged actively, imaginatively and intuitively.

---

7. Kierkegaard, *Journals*, p. 59.

He missed no opportunity for learning about the human condition in this great amphitheatre, and all fed into his work. His memory for incident and apparently 'casual' encounter was excellent, and every exchange he treated with respect. These simple daily outings offered an antidote to countless solitary hours at the writing desk; his city the arena in which he tested his ideas and his integrity among his fellow beings as an absolute equal. So the streets and citizens of Copenhagen kept him humbly grounded while making of him the genius translator of human nature he became. A solitary life bred in him love for the company of strangers, and he made of them his professors.

Barely had he found time to reconfigure his feelings for Michael Kierkegaard before a dated note appears in the journal:

> *Aug. 11.* My father died on Wednesday (the 9th) at 2 a.m. I had so very much wished that he might live another few years longer, and I look upon his death as the last sacrifice which he made to his love for me; for he did not die from me but *died for me* in order that if possible I might still turn into something. Of all that I have inherited from him, the recollection of him, his transfigured[8] portrait, not transfigured by the poetry of my imagination (for it did not require that) but explained by many an individual trait which I can now take account of – is dearest to me, and I will be careful to preserve it safely hidden from the world; for I feel clearly that at this moment there is only one (E. Boesen) to whom I can in truth talk about him. He was a 'faithful friend'.[9]

His father's death was a crossing of the Rubicon. Kierkegaard sensed a new spaciousness in his existence, as though the entire earth were bequeathed him. A world washed clean of his father's guilt, his suffering, his pain, the burden they had shared; all erased by having been spoken between them, thanks to God and to his father's courage, his ultimate beauty. The transfiguration which had poured over his son in streams of light had left the young Kierkegaard with a sense of having been baptised in the ebbing waters of his father's life; and after

---

8. The Danish *forklare* means both 'to explain' and 'to transfigure' or 'to glorify'.
9. Kierkegaard, *Journals*, p. 62.

forgiveness must follow reconciliation, penitence, repentance. Now the son swore to himself a solemn oath never to speak of these events, but to make his life henceforth bear testimony. Just a few weeks previously, on 6 July 1838, the young man had presented himself at Vor Frue Kirke and requested of the resident chaplain, Pastor Kalthoff, that he hear his confession. He then took Communion.

* * *

While Kierkegaard wrestled with the angel of his past, Hans Christian Andersen was trying feverishly to outmanoeuvre his own. Plagued by negative early experience, he found he could turn it back upon itself and, in sentimentalising childhood, neutralise and disarm the dangers it posed for adult life. The Odense street boys who had called him names and laughed at his patched coat, long legs and nose he transcended by a growing conviction of his superiority, his different destiny. Adopting an outer attitude matching this inner feeling would prove, like all such compensatory mechanisms, an over-corrective bound to backfire. Tragically for Andersen, once set on this course he could not reverse direction and it produced the caricature he became, a man whose personal relationships were marred by infantile fantasy and flight from reality. A man whose boundless hunger for love and approbation were matched only by the depth of his self-loathing and solipsism. His grandiosity knew no bounds; he saw himself as a wounded genius, the martyr whom no-one understood. He was sure, however, of one thing, that in the end his courage would carry him through, and he would attain the status of a saint. One day the whole world would hear of him. His name would be known to generations, his stories told to millions of children at their mothers' knees! He would win the hearts of the children, and they would weep and laugh at his command, for they were the only souls who truly understood him and appreciated his truth. The adult Andersen had managed to preserve the terrified child he had once been, embosom and romanticise it out of peril. Placing the child so powerfully at the centre of his work may in fact have saved him from himself, as transposing early trauma onto the page he consciously or unconsciously removed any potential danger of real-life acting out. Even considering the cruelly inhibitory sexual mores of his time, and the sensitivities of our own, one squirms a little at Andersen's writing to Jette Wulff in 1836 of grateful children offering him beautiful roses and kisses, 'but the girls are so very little, and I have asked several of them if I may be allowed to draw the interest on the capital in about six or seven years.'[10]

So the storyteller learnt to counter unbearable inner tension by insisting on the supremacy of innocence, stating that only the child is unafraid of reality; they may shriek in terror at the wicked witch, the genie and the sea monster, but they remain unmoved by verity. The storybook cruel stepmother, the evil queen, the bog-eyed hound towering above the town – they may make the child laugh or stare, but simple truth will be greeted with a smile. In Andersen's fictional world the child is misled, frightened, threatened and betrayed by adult figures, and almost always rescued by another child or supernatural creature, while his abuser often quietly escapes unscathed amidst the hubbub of a happy ending. Yet the child is altered by their adventure. A shard of ice remains in the once innocent heart. The memory of anguish taints a promise of immortality. The princess must pass through hell and face the gallows before she can marry her prince. Triumph, if it comes, comes only in the wake of terror. As Andersen's early experience is encoded in these stories it of course resonates with every child's deepest fears and the relief of release from them. From the safety of his parent's lap the child learns to face the horrors that await him in the grownup world. Sadly for Andersen, the more he honed his skills as society sauvage and literary chameleon through such transference, the less sugar-coating worked as camouflage for the real man. What strange irony that it was not the glittering poetic literary stardom so assiduously pursued in life that would immortalise his name, but precisely his disowned darkness. Not the shiny deceit by which he lived, but the eternal truth of Manichaean struggle between good and evil enshrined in the fairy tale that has won him universal recognition and acclaim.

The childhood naïvety of his earliest stories gradually makes way in the later tales and novels for older protagonists struggling with isolation and social estrangement. In April 1836 Andersen published his second novel. *O.T.* is a morality tale about a young man with the initials of Odense Tugthus ('prison'), during the creation of which he wrote, rewrote, and became increasingly committed to the vengeful narrative to be called *The Little Mermaid*. It was the point at which Andersen's focus sharpened on his fairy tales; a transition initially mediated by fresh familiarity with the transformative power of

---

10. Wullschläger, *Hans Christian Andersen*, p. 160.

German folklore, as evidenced in his new story, *The Wild Swans*. This is the piece that also marks the author's definitive departure from reliance on legend for the foundation of his stories; from now on he would depend more and more adventurously on his own imagination. There had been many versions of the 'wild swans' legend based on ancient European oral tradition, fables adapted by the Brothers Grimm as *The Six Swans* and *The Twelve Brothers*. A modern retelling had appeared in Matthias Winther's collection of Danish folk tales of 1823, which Andersen had read. His aim now was to appropriate the storyline, adopting its archetypal imagery while softening the more sinister and macabre Teutonic qualities endowed by Grimm. It is easy to identify elements which appealed to Andersen: the swans echo the image he used to signify humbly raised aristocracy, there is a wicked stepmother and a princess who must suffer to save her brothers. Other more pagan elements he discarded, replacing them with Christian characters acting out everyday events in land, sea and cityscapes familiar to a nineteenth-century Danish readership.

From the moment he set about the serious business of fairy-tale writing Andersen's style was all his own; it is impossible to mistake or misattribute his work. His use of the Danish language was idiosyncratic, charmingly chatty and parochial to the point of crudity; above all, it was radically new. The departure from traditional tone and syntax typical of his earlier stories generated shock among his first adult audience; it was so direct. Andersen now also discarded any show of approach via an adult protector and instead spoke straight to the child in their own vernacular, regularly relapsing into direct address and often ending a story by challenging his reader to accept an aphorism, narrative origin or denouement: 'Look you, this is a true story.'[11] It was not that Andersen had lost sight of his desire to convey his message to the mature reader. On the contrary, wishing as fervently as ever to reach an adult audience he had contrived a far more effective methodology for this than subterranean moralising; by adopting the diction of the street urchin he subverted adult bourgeois expectations and brought the parent forcibly down to earth while refusing to patronise the child. In shaping with such subtle candour his own transgressive style, he set himself apart from every

---

11. Hans Christian Andersen, 'The Princess and the Pea', in *The Complete Illustrated Stories of Hans Christian Andersen*, facsimile edn. (London: Chancellor Press, 1987), p. 34.

other children's writer of his time, gifting the genre truly innovative modern vigour and versatility as well as new dignity, and creating an exemplar for all who came after him.

His first efforts, *The Tinder-Box, Little Claus and Big Claus, The Princess and the Pea*, and *Little Ida's Flowers*, had been greeted by the critics with bewildered silence, but when at last a review appeared in *Dannora* it condemned the stories' lack of edification and deplored all the casual violence. More vicious and dismissive reviews followed, the *Dansk Litteratur-Tidende* ('Danish Literary Times') offering the author stern patriarchal correction: it was not by chance convention that words acceptably used in verbal intercourse should be employed differently or not at all in writing; words meant for children should always be above them, and this was how they preferred them. The reviewer hoped that this talented author would soon stop wasting his time writing fairy tales. That was not the plan. A little thrown by this sort of response to his new stories he might be, but Andersen was only just finding his feet. *The Wild Swans* followed on from *The Steadfast Tin Soldier* and *The Daisy*, and, as in *The Little Mermaid*, the new narrative equates female goodness with the adult archetypical motif of silent assent. With this story Andersen again found a reflective outlet for his anguish over loss of the past romantic attachment to Edvard Collin and the reader is struck by the tragic longevity, intensity and ambiguity of his feelings. In a cryptic addendum to *The Wild Swans*, completed that day, Andersen notes with emphasis: "Tenth of August… Edvard's second wedding anniversary." The brand-new piece was published for the first time in English in 1889,[12] and centres on a good king who has twelve children: eleven sons, and a girl called Elisa. The king marries a wicked queen who hates the children, banishes Elisa to grow up until she is fifteen far away with a peasant family and poisons the brothers' characters in the king's ears so that he no longer cares about them. His wicked wife then kisses each prince, turning him into a swan, and they fly away together to a distant land. Elisa must find her brothers and rescue them, in the process losing her tongue and almost her life.

On New Year's Day 1835 Andersen had written to his friend, Henriette Hanck, 'Now I have begun to write some fairy tales for children. I want to win the coming generations, you see.' By 16 March

---

12. In Hans Christian Andersen, *Stories for the Household* (London: George Routledge & Sons, 1889).

he was less self-assured, noting in a letter to his beloved 'sister', Jette Wulff: 'I have also written some fairy tales for children, of which Ørsted says that, if *The Improvisatore* will make me famous, my fairy tales will make me immortal, for they are the most perfect of all that I have written; but I myself do not think so.'[13]

Ørsted knew better.

* * *

Kierkegaard, increasingly infatuated with Regine Olsen, was also afraid for her, and his fear for her was of himself. He saw her as a child still, almost ten years his junior. Arriving to visit her at her home he would find her at the door. Quietly, composedly she would usher him through into her own little drawing-room, seat herself beside him on the sofa, a little way away but close enough for their conversation to become intimate. The Olsens lived on the third floor of a fine old town house near the harbour. Below, carriages clattered past, street vendors shouted their wares; broken fragments of conversation rose to reach the couple as passers-by greeted each other and exchanged news… the city speaking its own tongue, admiring its reflection in the water: high, stepped façades, clean symmetry of windows and doors, all serenity, grandeur. In the park nearby, watched over by nurse or mother, children played beneath the trees. Kierkegaard's glance took in Regine's simple sprigged frock, the same she had worn on that first day at Bolette's party. Often, he brought with him a sermon from Bishop Mynster for them to read and discuss. So long as he could keep their minds engaged, so long he felt safe. More and more he noted an element of subservience in her, a sort of humble desire to please. It troubled him, but he did not know how to counter it. He found it impossible to distract himself from the light touch of her hand on his arm, the fragrance of her skin. He attempted some explanation, began extrapolating from the text, but his heart was not in it. In her face he found utter compliance, trust. It was too much for him. Getting abruptly to his feet, he would pick up his hat, retrieve the book from the sofa, make his excuses and leave. She accompanied him downstairs to the front door.

It seemed to him long ages had passed since last he stood on the street. It was as though time had evaporated. He had existed for an hour or so in a shared present; the effortless timelessness she created

---

13. Andersen, *Diaries*, p. 94.

and inhabited. He could not get over how far this country lay from his own, where each frenetic hour fermented with thought, worry, dark foreboding. Where time was clogged with cerebration until he could no longer discern eternity. A reality wherein both consciously and unconsciously he sabotaged each living moment. It seemed extraordinary that, while with her, he simply rested in the now, in eternity. Time withdrew, ashamed of the absurdity of its finite state, while the room about her flowed with endless seasons. He was afraid for himself and for her. She made a poet of him, but he could hardly trust himself to let go of his melancholy, to join her in immediate reality. Yet perhaps he could change... Above all, he dreaded her falling in love with him, this was the great danger. That she might fall in love with him without knowing him. That he could become for her a sort of prince from a fairy tale; a being without a shadow, stripped of a past, of all the morbid movements of his soul. He shuddered at the thought of it, and of tainting her innocence. How could he begin to disclose to her his true nature, his real history? It was impossible. No, she must remain as she was, at the centre of her own world, pure and free. Somehow, he must foster some distance between them. He visualised their friendship as a clear running brook. He would be her friend, and they should not stray where angels fear to tread. Everyone had news to report today. He stopped and spoke and raised his hat. More than anything at such times he wished for silence and for solitude – and this was what he got: a gaggle of greetings every third step, words, grins, a long hello. Ah, here was the baker's shop. He would step inside and find something to go with his coffee. He should eat well tonight and drink some claret. That was the cure! All would be well.

Yet he knew his mind could not be stilled for long. The more he contemplated this girl's demeanour, the closer it seemed to the religious: her entire occupation, her complete habitation of the moment. It was the very flight of faith. Without relapse into the reflective state, she acted in exact accordance with the universe. Her behaviour and being was religious, and it was pantheistic. It followed no law but that of nature. It belonged to God. He saw it: the feminine as immediacy. She existed in eternity. For her now was always. She surrendered. She submitted to it without considering the consequences, not even for herself. It was sublime; and it terrified him. He felt a profound need not to dislodge her from this natural state. She must not love him. Yet they understood each other's very silence. There was not a nuance that passed between them unnoticed. They hardly needed words. He forced words between them, and she countered with her calm, her acceptance, her unselfconscious intellect: intelligence which had no need to declare itself, but which was always at large, at work upon the world. Since his father's death he had been struck by the consolation she afforded him – and all without a word of commiseration or condolence. His comfort lay in her warm fragrant presence and in the sense of eternity with which she surrounded him. He now knew he must not suffer as his father had suffered. Now he knew there was redemption, that he need not prostrate himself only to plunge back into pain. Most vital of all, he need not commit himself to the emasculating embrace of the Church.

The Church... it was always the same. It took a pristine truth and polluted it beyond recognition. He saw with absolute clarity how the adherents of the institution hung upon it all their own filth until truth was no longer perceptible, and then passed on the poisoned chalice. If his theological studies had taught him anything, then it was this: avoid the Church. And yet, and yet. There must be a surer footing for a sermon than this unforgiving Protestant doctrine. First they threw out the priests and icons and then they set themselves up as the iconostasis. No wonder they were lost and doing their best to lose everyone and everything else. What a miserable bunch! Love thy neighbour indeed! Do good! He scoured his brain for a preceding precept. Better look to the priest or to the poet? Or the philosopher? The concept was born in him of double destiny, attaching universal significance to individual event and experience by erasing discrimination between the two, merging motives in the search for solutions. He discerned in himself a marrying of the individual sense of responsibility with mass consciousness; his looking no longer towards another man for comfort but finding consolation only in becoming before God. A radical form of inwardness irrevocably committed to relationship. He recognised that what he tried to forget in order to engage with life his reflective intellect clung to as 'interesting', so that the moment his active side wished to act the reflective self intervened and he was rendered inert.

If only he could complete his studies and get the final exams behind him. Their presence was a blight on his life. He scribbled in his journal of his fear: everything frightened him, the whole of existence, from the smallest fly to the mystery of the Incarnation; everything was unintelligible to him, most of all himself. Prayer, nowadays, had become a kind of exercise in cleverness and wit, a kind of exhibitionism – repulsive! Where was the inner man? Every frantic search for God ended within himself; always it led Kierkegaard back to the individual. His analogy for the first step in the fear of God was that of a madman's sensing the mysterious spiritual superiority of a great doctor. The individual, that was it; here the battle was to be fought. He could not escape himself, and neither could he avoid his confrontation with the ideal. Did he confuse reality with the ideal? He thought not. Not yet. And yet, she reigned sovereign over his heart. Could he really believe the poet's tales, that when one first sees the object of one's love, one imagines one has seen her long ago; that all love, like all knowledge, is remembrance? That love too has its prophesies in the individual, its types, its myths, its Old Testament?

> Everywhere, in the face of every girl I see traces of your beauty, but it seems to me that I should have to possess the beauty of all girls in order to draw out a beauty equal to yours; that I should have to circumnavigate the world in order to find the place I lack and which the deepest mystery of my whole being points towards – and at the next moment you are so near to me, so present, filling my spirit so powerfully that I am transfigured to myself, and feel it is good to be here. ... Shall I find what I am seeking, here in this world, shall I fold you in my arms – or: are the orders 'FURTHER'?[14]

* * *

By 1839, given his growing fame across wider Europe in contrast to the mixed reception his three novels had met with at home, the growing success of the fairy stories alongside a collection of prose sketches and *The Mulatto*, and his one and only successful play, Andersen viewed his career with occasional mania, periodic disdain and his countrymen with almost constant contempt. In April 1843 he would write to Jette Wulff of this recurrent feeling: 'The Danes are evil, cold, satanic. ... I don't believe in love in the North, but in evil treachery. I can feel it in my own blood, and it's only in that way I know I am Danish!'[15] Yes, he knew this folk alright! He could snip them out of a blank sheet

---

14. Kierkegaard, *Journals*, p. 70.
15. Wullschläger, *Hans Christian Andersen*, p. 190.

Papercut by Andersen: - Pierrot, tree, angel, and a ballerina in the nest at the top of the tree.

of paper – and did so with consummate skill. Scissored whole rows of identical citizens, long prancing lines of them cut out from life: self-satisfied, over-pious, over-educated, over-everything. He could see them now, very pleased with themselves, strutting along their straight streets with the air of a nation quite on the right footing. What was more, given an appreciative audience, he would cut out another procession too, this time of Copenhagen's circus clowns, dancers and theatre people. Here was the audience on their way to the latest performance, not to absorb culture, of course not, but to swap a few little titbits of gossip and stare at one another's new outfit, take a few minor characters down a peg or two, stick the knife in where it hurt. The close-knit world of Copenhagen's literati was oppressive and insular and, although the Collins were mainly kind and encouraging, they did not hide from him the fact that they considered him a lesser writer than Heiberg and Oehlenschläger. The critics had done their best to destroy his faith in his own fairy tales, but in February 1837 he rallied, writing bravely to the writer and critic, Bernhard Severin Ingemann, whom he could not forgive for a previous wounding review, to commend *The Little Mermaid*. It was better than *Thumbelina*, he wrote, and apart from 'The Little Abesses's Story' in *The Imprisovatore*, the one which had most affected him in the writing. The emotional backdrop of his unrequited love for Edvard Collin explains the depth of feeling behind Andersen's defensiveness regarding this tale, and now he described how he felt during the writing: 'You smile perhaps? Well, I don't know how other writers feel!'[16] but he suffered with his characters, Andersen went on, he shared their moods, whether good or bad, and he could be pleasant or the reverse according to the scene on which he might be working.

Thus Andersen oscillated between overweening self-confidence, vanity even, and a crushing sense of failure during which his mood reflected a world entirely populated by evil and loveless compatriots, provincial, small-minded, sniping and jealous. It was a mortal sin to rise above your station here; they did not tolerate talent, couldn't bear anyone to put their head above the parapet; no room at the inn for the genius! He had tried so hard to write for the theatre but failed to find favour with the most culturally celebrated literary couple in Copenhagen, Johan Ludvig Heiberg and his wife Johanne Luise Heiberg, and a year later when he submitted his next play, *The Moorish Maid*, the couple were to undermine him even further with their withdrawal of support. Andersen felt the city's suffocating grip around his throat. Foreign trips were his only salvation; he never wrote much underway but found he could settle back down to work well when he got home. Andersen's discovery of the benefits of travel may have arrived at just that moment in the nineteenth century when the world was opening up, but oh the misery of it! Seasickness; the dreaded jolting of the carriage over broken, pot-holed thoroughfares, tipping over into puddles of icy mud and water; foreign languages and food, fear of fire and dogs, bandits and pandemic and ailments of every kind! Caught between the desire to be gone from here and the dread of going, he vacillated before deciding to miss the latest of his productions, including the opening night. He would rather risk foreign miasma against which he had no immunity than the usual home-grown ennui. After all, he was a good tourist; like all the best venturers to a land larger than their own, he was humble, curious and thankful. He needed sunshine, wine, company that loved him, people capable of love. New faces, fresh ideas and places. On his itinerary was another extended tour of his beloved Italy, perhaps he would even include the Orient. Into his capacious leather portmanteau he packed his sketch- and notebooks and, respecting old superstition, added to his luggage a lengthy coil of rope in case of fire.

---

16. Ibid., p. 165.

* * *

Kierkegaard was hard-pressed at home to fulfil the least but most onerous of his ambitions. He began working for his final theological exam at the end of 1839, at which point the journal empties of entries. He took the exam and passed on 3 July 1840, 'Magna cum laude!' Having successfully petitioned the king for permission to submit his dissertation, *The Concept of Irony*, in Danish rather than in Latin to allow for what he knew to be its idiosyncratic style, he had to face the colloquium conducted in Latin. As predicted, Kierkegaard's departure from academic conventions in style and structure caused consternation, despite the judges recognising the work's intelligence and noteworthiness. On publication in 1841 *The Concept of Irony* received scant reviews, although one critic praised it highly only to be coolly rebuffed by Meïr Aron Goldschmidt, renowned editor of the periodical *Corsair* (*Corsaren*), to the effect that it was a mistake to scrutinise style rather than content. For Kierkegaard, who later disowned its Hegelian tropes,[17] it was simply the end of a long and dusty road: 'I am always accused of using long parentheses. Reading for my examination is the longest parenthesis I have known.'[18] Journal entries resume the following day, but all but six of these pages have been lost. A couple of notes remain concerning his ensuing visit to Jutland; all else has been destroyed.

---

17. Kierkegaard understood the 'negativity' of irony to indicate its relation to divine infinity. He accused Hegel of fleeing from this into the 'positivity' of knowingness and systematisation: his thesis, antithesis, synthesis. In Kierkegaard's view Hegel is antithetic to irony; he believes Socrates when he says he is ignorant, feels this is a defect and therefore beneath his dignity (Plato). See D. Anthony Storm's *Commentary on Kierkegaard*, 'First Period, Works of Youth 1835-1842', commentary on *The Concept of Irony*; available online at sorenkierkegaard.org.
18. Kierkegaard, *Journals*, p. 83.

Chapter 5

Lily of the Valley

If there is one area of striking personal similarity between Søren Kierkegaard and Hans Christian Andersen, it must be their ability to hide their true feelings. In their emotional lives both men were masters of dissimulation. Kierkegaard perfected the art of literary disguise, adopting one persona and *nom de plume* after another, as ever taking his cue from Socrates in promoting and nurturing the cause of dialectics. In this way too he decisively erected a barrier between his own persona and personal experience, and the point he wished to make. Such mercurialism was an effective device, enlivening, clarifying, illustrating and making accessible otherwise obscure and difficult material in Kierkegaard's writings – and providing a vehicle for his brilliant, often excoriating wit. Again, guided by Socrates' 'Know thyself', Kierkegaard's most profound expositions are leavened with hilariously acerbic metaphor, epithets and bywords, most self-pillorying. His style may only very loosely, however, be described as 'humorous'; these interjections and extrapolations are not meant as comic relief, and neither is he trying to convey scepticism. His intention is to employ the 'negative' as Socrates used it to imply the infinite by gesturing towards its opposite and beyond towards an unknown (divine) end. It is a deployment of irony that was, according to Kierkegaard, misunderstood, misinterpreted or missed by Plato himself, and has been by many scholars since. Kierkegaard uses irony as Socrates does to deny and disarm 'knowing'. Irony is the means by which both Socrates and Kierkegaard provide forward propulsion for dialectic by illuminating their interlocutor's false premise and irritating them into self-defeating defence of it, so to reclaim, refocus and right their wandered attention from (eternal) truth. A note from 1847 outlines this purpose:

> What the age needs is *pathos* (in the same way that scurvy needs greens); but not even the art of drilling an artesian well is more subtle than the calculated dialectics of humour, emotion and passion, with which I have tried to produce a beneficial gust of feeling. The misfortune of the age is understanding and reflection. No one, however immediately enthusiastic, can any longer help us, because they are consumed by the reflection of the age. ... In order to defend marriage nowadays one must be able to enchant its licentious inclinations with *The Seducer's Diary*, and the same applies everywhere.[1]

Andersen's own need for emotional camouflage was a survival strategy that permeated every aspect of his life. Most expertly, explicitly and economically in his literary works it is exploited in his fairy tales: desperate sentimentalisations of love, loss and retribution. The novels and plays carry the same leitmotif, with the rejected outsider as major protagonist – all projections of himself. The undercurrent of self-pitying aggression is always palpable, as so often in his diary and personal correspondence. It can sometimes feel to his reader that the writer's negativity must surely subsume his narrative, but it never does. Instead, the apparently self-sabotaging compulsion to forge on against the flow serves only to animate and invigorate the work, just as it has fed Andersen's fame. The same contrariness may be detected in his conduct of personal relationships. In 1839 we find him basking in international acclaim for his stories, but intent upon pursuing his career in the domestic theatre. His play *The Mulatto*, about a doomed cross-cultural love affair, had been due to open in December, but King Frederik VI's death on the night of the premiere led to two months of mourning, so that the play only opened at the Royal Theatre on 3 February the following year. Johanne Luise, wife of Johan Ludvig Heiberg, played leading lady. The new King Christian VIII was at the performance, bowed to Andersen and invited him to court next day. However, the play's initial success was soon eclipsed

---

1. Kierkegaard, *Journals*, p. 201.

when its author was accused of plagiarism because the printer had unfortunately omitted his acknowledgement to the originator of the storyline. Andersen reacted swiftly with a new drama, *The Moorish Maid*, similarly themed but far less well written. Andersen had meant it for Johanne Luise, by now prima donna of Danish Golden Age theatre, but her husband hated the play, and she refused the lead role. The actress and Andersen were not always in accord. He needed her professional status to enhance his stage plays but resented the ease with which marriage to Heiberg had propelled her from humble origins effortlessly up through the ranks to the heights of Copenhagen's cultural elite. The storyteller's outrage at this new slight found expression in a pettish preface to the second play, a display of grandiosity which made him a lifelong enemy of the Heibergs; doubly self-defeating given his patrons' admiration for Copenhagen's literary giant.

Seething with suppressed rage and humiliation, Andersen reacted in his usual way, leaving at once for the new extended foreign tour. *En route*, he wrote a faux love letter to a Lady Matilde Barck he had met a year or so before in Sweden and with whom he was conducting a public flirtation, pleading for her support and affection. She responded warmly and at once, but her letter never reached Andersen, having been mislaid by the courier just as the resultant emotional impact upon her is lost to history. Andersen seems completely oblivious to the effect he has upon the women he habitually used as camouflage and discarded at will. Again, even taking into account the crippling sexual prohibitions of his time, it is hard to credit or excuse the degree of duplicity and disrespect with which he treated the women in his life. Embarking for Rome in wild weather with big seas driving in off the Baltic, he recorded in his diary another rapturous farewell to Edvard Collin: 'I said goodbye; he pressed a kiss on to my mouth! Oh, it was as if my heart would burst!'[2] The chameleon in his diary, unclothed.

*   *   *

Meanwhile, the nearly two years of intensive preparation for his examination that Kierkegaard called 'the great parenthesis' proceeded to the bemusement of numerous friends and acquaintances. Most had assumed that when upon his father's death Søren came into a fortune

---

2. Wullschläger, *Hans Christian Andersen*, p. 189.

and inherited the great house on Nytorv he would lapse into a life of comfort and leisure. Not so, the opposite seemed true. Any refined observation along these lines he countered with the explanation that so long as his father lived it had been possible to produce arguments against sitting the theological exams, but now things had changed he found himself taking his father's part in the debate and being unable to win it. With any less than circumspect commentator he was more succinct: 'It's because I can no longer put the old man off with stuff and nonsense.'[3] The months of reclusive study allowed Kierkegaard time and space to attend to himself in a deeper sense. In truth, he found the present enforced scholarship deadly dull. Of far more interest to him was the need he felt for integration of his personality. The recognition of schism between his capability to act in the world and the 'reflection' which constantly impeded him was causing him increasing anguish. Understanding his very real capacity for active participation, he felt this must be where his true integrity lay, and yet he longed to be free of it, to explore a landscape of reflection which seemed so much more absorbing, abstracted from personal consciousness and thus potentiated by its 'assuming to be a universal consciousness'.[4]

The connection is apparent with Kierkegaard's adoption of authorial pseudonyms and his vehement disavowal that they represented aspects of himself. He did not want the reader diverted by simplistic assumptions and he offered many and various reasons for the pseudonymity. They were probably indeed numerous. The simplest might lie in character: his extreme introversion, personal diffidence and shyness; an inability to communicate directly leading to the need for 'indirect communication'. Or it may simply have felt to him, especially as a very young man, intellectually unedifying to share his most private experience with the world without some veil, however flimsy. He was, after all, never intent on writing fiction. Given his determination and acuteness in observing and assimilating aspects of human response, and his peerless pursuit of self-knowledge, there is no denying the works' obvious devolution from personal experience. Yet such truth is superficial. The curious simultaneous proximity and distance he perceived between the personal and the universal led Kierkegaard to feel increasingly free

---

3. Lowrie, *A Short Life of Kierkegaard*, p. 129.
4. Ibid., p. 128.

to extrapolate characterisation to its farthest logical limit, and this produced a distinctive estrangement far outflanking that described by many fiction writers in relation to their creations. In following a trait (including his own) through to its utmost extremity, isolating and stripping it bare of moderating features, he arrived at pure similitude. He was thus capable, as Kierkegaard scholar David Ferdinand Swenson (1876-1940) described it, of 'making a map of the emotional cosmos' by delineating the characteristic capabilities of the human soul. The result was a completely new form of psychology, 'a comparative philosophy of values.'[5]

In evolving his unique genre, Kierkegaard strove for and achieved an ability to depict persona and event without identifying with them, however close they lay to his own life experience. It was an extraordinary measure of objectivity that allowed him to escape the dry 'systematisation' he had rejected in philosophy (particularly in Hegel) and instead animate his dialectic with an almost endless procession of permutations in human character and behaviour, pure and unalloyed, from the pious to the profligate. So that although, unlike the polymorphous characters of general fiction, there rarely if ever exists a human nature so quintessential as one of Kierkegaard's pseudonymic stereotypes, we cannot help but find ourselves in them – his expressed religious intention. His brilliance in the art of inventing *dramatis personae* may also be attributed both to inborn mischievousness and to his passion for the theatre. In all, he continues with typical courage and integrity to address 'Everyman' in even his most exacting writings, and manages still to elude the more enervating effects upon his work of academic enquiry, however energetic. The depth and degree to which Kierkegaard perfected generalisation outwards from the self is quite stupendous and directly related to the search by the artist's *'autonomous complex'* for symbols described by Jung.[6]

Nonetheless, and tragically for this nineteenth-century Hamlet, Kierkegaard's genius could not protect or help him find an integrated inner state. Insight, however acute, famously fails to work in liberating synchrony with the need to act, and he remained locked in reflection until in 1839 his life took a direction which would lead to the decisive moment. The only diversion he allowed himself from his studies was

---

5. Ibid., p. 155.
6. See Chapter One, footnote 13.

Letter to Regine: Kierkegaard sketches himself standing on the Knippelbro, peering through a spyglass over to her house on the other side of the water. He explains the principle of refraction, then its 'secret *genie*' whereby to he who understands how to use the instrument is revealed what he most longs to see – for everyone else it is a 'useless contrivance…'.

the thought of Regine Olsen. He would later summarise how he had decided upon her before his father died, after which event Kierkegaard read for the examination, during which time he allowed her existence to entwine itself with his own. This period of falling deeply in love for the first and last time in his life, offered the 26-year-old Kierkegaard the only sort of education he truly valued. Now he discovered and began to perfect his genius for the delicacy and discretion he considered best honoured the mysteries of love and human relationship. His feeling for Regine grew so deep within him that he was incapable of expressing it directly. He could not speak its name, but during their meetings elaborated on his reading of Plato and finding one's lost other half. His virtuosity in tender expression spans a thousand octaves, from loftiest to most lowly note. He tells her how he places her knitting close to him on the sofa as he writes, and his undated letters are a masterclass in evasion, evoking the verbal void and emotional incoherence of their encounters as vividly as their passion:

> My Regine!
> The other day when you came to see me you told me that when you were confirmed your father had presented you with a bottle of lily of the valley (*Extrait double de Muguet*). Perhaps you thought that I did not hear this, or perhaps you thought that it had slipped by my ear like so much else that finds no response within. But not at all! But as that flower conceals itself so prettily within its big leaf, so I first

allowed the plan of sending you the enclosed to conceal itself in the half-transparent veil of oblivion so that, freed from every external consideration, even the most illusive [sic.], rejuvenated to a new life in comparison with which its first existence was but an earthly life, it might now exude that fragrance for which longing and memory ('from the spring of my youth') are rivals.[7]

He would write most powerfully about such experience, the anxiety and the defensive response it provoked in *Quidam's Diary*, the final part of *Stages on Life's Way*, the book he published in 1845 and which is effectively a 'repetition' of *Either/Or*. Here he expands on the capacity to hide the melancholic nature by subtle means, with help of the sagacity which belongs to it. So deep is the deception that melancholy may be deferred, or rather disguised, kept at bay until he is in solitude, where the dreaded state of mind simply awaits him. Since he fell in love, the writer has trained himself to an even more refined degree in this art. Whereas displays of exuberant mirth would raise suspicion in even the least astute observer, the best deception is an attitude of common sense, passionate reflection and an open face and heart. Here is the show of confidence and security in life which masks the insomniac anguish of 'sleepless and melancholy reflection'.[8] Did he know that lily of the valley (also called 'Mary bells', 'Our Lady's tears', 'Mary's tears') symbolises marital happiness? Perhaps. In any case, among the many little gifts he sent her this was special, to be reprised at crucial moments in their relationship. More ardent words accompanied a picture he sent Regine on another occasion, a young woman with a flower in her hand. It is not clear to him, he writes, from whom she has received or to whom she is giving this flower. In the picture a young man seems to turn his back upon the world, the letter muses:

---

7. Søren Kierkegaard, *Kierkegaard Letters and Documents*, with Introduction and Notes, transl. Henrik Rosenmeier, Letter 18, p. 64. Available online at: https://zlib.pub/download/letters-and-documents-1afjrcm67mg0?hash=95b39cf248098014f3ff9c3dc707b794. Accessed 5 November 2024.

8. Søren Kierkegaard, *Stages on Life's Way*, trans. Walter Lowrie (New York, NY: Schocken Books, 1967), pp. 188-89.

Perhaps he has sat like this for centuries; perhaps the happy moment was only a brief one and yet sufficient for an eternity. With the picture my thought also returns to its beginning, and I tear myself away, flee from everything that would imprison me in chains of sorrow, and I cry out louder than sorrows ... yet, yet, yet in all of this I am happy, indescribably happy, for I know what I possess. ... I am enclosing a scarf. I ask you to accept it and desire that you alone know that you own this trifle. ...
Your S.K.

On the reverse side of the image is transcribed a German love poem, *Des Knaben Wunderhorn*:

Es vergeht keine Stund in der Nacht,
Da mein Herz nicht erwacht,
Und an dich gedenkt,
Dass du mir viel tausandmal
Dein Herze geschenkt.

Regine has added: 'And if my arm doth give such pleasure, Such comfort and such ease; Then, handsome merman, hasten; Come take them both – oh, please.'[9] So few of her words survive (she swore she had burned almost all her letters to Kierkegaard) the more eloquent and piercing these. As for the tiny phial of perfume in its velvet pouch, she wore it around her neck and throughout her long life held it in her hand at times of greatest grief and stress.

* * *

Andersen's ship weighed anchor in Copenhagen at two o'clock on 31 October 1840 and immediately began listing and heaving. His seasickness worsened as time went on; they got hit so hard by a wave he thought they had run aground. Once back on dry land he travelled by rented carriage down through Schleswig-Holstein: miles of rough highway over heathland, chimneyless houses from whose wide-open doors the smoke billowed. Everything was mire and muck, he recorded in his diary. On through Neumünster to Itzehoe, where

---

9. Søren Kierkegaard, *Kierkegaard Letters and Documents*, Letter 27, p. 73.

Lily of the Valley

Andersen was fascinated by the oldest church in the country, dating from the time of Charlemagne and half swallowed by the earth; he saw a church interred, bizarre figment of his Romantic imagination. Throughout the region, ambassadors and important figures in the arts emerged to greet him. He loved it when people read his name on his luggage and asked whether he was the famous Danish author. In Altona he was fed oysters and champagne, and everywhere hosted in fine style by local aristocrats and feted for *Only a Fiddler* and *The Improvisatore*, an eventuality for which Andersen had come prepared with copies to give away. There are regular ingratiating poems penned *en route* for ladies of the grand houses, but as ever while travelling it is his diary that displays the fluency and lyricism of his prose when not written for public consumption. Gone is the whimsy of his fairy tales. His almost daily entries are as expressive and uninhibited as the line drawings that fill his sketchbooks, and these meticulous and detailed observations on people and place reveal the writer's own vulnerability and a rare and refined sensitivity to foreign realities.

Such openness to unfamiliar cultural values is moving enough in itself, but Andersen also brings to his vignettes a sharp eye for human idiosyncrasy. Like Kierkegaard, he is alert to individual traits but, rather than dissecting them, Andersen's reportage demonstrates the diarist's own unworldliness. Gifted a ticket for a concert by Liszt, he scribbles for posterity an unforgettable pen-portrait of the composer. Perhaps a little awestruck at the sight of him in the flesh, Andersen begins by comparing great men to mountains, best seen from a distance to fully appreciate their grandeur. Poor Liszt looked to the storyteller as though he'd just been discharged from orthopaedic hospital after straightening-out surgery, there was something so spidery and demonic about him. The way he sat at the piano, his pale face contorted with violent passion, he looked to Andersen like a devil trying to play his soul free. Every note flowed from heart and soul – the composer seemed tortured. As his music filled the air, Andersen watched garlands of flowers being hurled up onto the stage. He would later note how in fact the bathing attendant at the hotel had brought most of the tributes and asked people to throw them… and he can't resist a parting shot at his compatriots; had this happened in honour of Miss Grahn,[10] what a fuss would have been made about the

---

10. The famous ballerina, ballet mistress and choreographer, Lucile Grahn, born in 1819 and trained at the Royal Danish Theatre.

prearrangement – 'for we Copenhageners are good at seeing everything in the worst light.'[11]

In the fortified city of Magdeburg, he rushes off to the railway station to book the first train journey of his life, feeling as though he is surrendering himself to his God. Only the day before he had seen a steam engine for the first time, hurtling along the ground like a rocket, and here he was trying it for himself. Train travel proved completely disorientating, the earth spinning while the near landscape fled past and only the distant vista stayed put. Maybe this was how migratory birds felt as one after another town disappeared in their wake. His fairy-tale imagination got to work at once on the new experience. He felt like a magician in a carriage hitched to a dragon, swooping past mortals on side roads moving along like snails. As for the steam whistle, it was hideous, like the screaming of a stuck pig.

Andersen's sojourn in Germany was to end less than happily, but before leaving Leipzig on 11 November he called on Felix Mendelssohn and attended a rehearsal of a Beethoven symphony. Leaving for Munich via Augsburg later in the afternoon, he was shown an example of the newly invented daguerreotype; in Munich he renewed his acquaintance with the philosopher Friedrich Schelling. Here too, however, he quarrelled with the poet Hans Peter Holst, with whom he was to have journeyed on to Rome, and so set off alone and disgruntled. His arrival in the Italian capital on 19 December was miserable; the weather was unusually bad and Andersen had flu as well as one of his regular painful toothaches. Of the people he had once known in the city, the painter Küchler remained, but nothing of the romantic sentiment Andersen had once felt for him. Alone in the city, chilled and uncomfortable, he impatiently awaited Holst's late arrival and letters from Copenhagen, and on 8 January 1841 to add to his misery received word from Jonas Collin that the premier of *The Moorish Maid* had been a fiasco. That night Andersen slept badly, dreaming his head was made of stone and refused to break despite someone hitting him over it with an axe.

The treasures of Rome had lost their appeal, he was desperately lonely. Depression settled over him, with its accompanying pall of self-pity. Instead of being out socialising as usual, he was back in his lodgings by 5.30 p.m. each evening, unable even to enjoy reading, watching the clock to see if it was after nine yet so that he could go to

---

11. Andersen, *Diaries*, p. 100.

bed. Such solitude at least dispelled lesser fears, even that of assault, his abiding worry whenever a fellow traveller appeared slightly odd to him. He contemplated with some serenity the artistic drama and beneficence of a violent death. He had nothing more to live for, after all, even his art was difficult for him these days. His need for attention was so overwhelming, he admitted to himself, that the idea of sudden demise rather intrigued him. He knew his own weakness, he could see his own faults! He prayed for the dawning of a great idea, for God to send him either joy or death.

All through January he continued to be plagued by low spirits and petty ailments, dizziness, a sore throat and headaches. In mid-February he heard from Copenhagen that Heiberg had satirised him (in fact, he'd been subject of a single scornful sentence), prompting Andersen to draft a viciously cathartic response which, although never posted, served to improve his mood. Arriving in Naples, his spirits were further lifted by news from Denmark that the king had granted him a stipend to enable him to continue his travels. By 20 March he was sailing along the coast of Greece, ecstatic at his first glimpse of the snow-covered mountain of Morea, ancient name of the Mani district at the southern tip of the Peloponnese peninsula. Behind the idyll, however, pandemic raged. No cases of cholera are recorded before the beginning of the nineteenth century, but there followed seven successive global outbreaks, six in the nineteenth century; the seventh beginning in 1961.[12] In this context it is interesting to note that Andersen's travelling companions included Germans, Dutch, Americans and Russians, while increased commerce and sea trade were all cited as causes of the pandemic. Despite his worries, Andersen was again revelling in exotic company, conversing, watching, listening and later recording everything, including his

---

12. Seven distinct pandemics of cholera have been recorded during the past two centuries. The seventh pandemic, which is still ongoing today, is considered to have occurred principally between 1961 to 1974. During this period, following (re)introduction, many countries transitioned to becoming cholera-endemic. While global incidence greatly decreased in the late 1990s, cholera remained prevalent in parts of Africa and Asia. World Health Organisation, Disease Outbreak News, Cholera – Global Situation, 16 December 2022. https://www.who.int/emergencies/disease-outbreak-news/item/2022-DON426. Accessed 5 November 2024.

disapproval of incidents of disrespect and racism which offended his sense of propriety; he had met a man from St Petersburg, he noted disapprovingly, who was ultracritical of the Greeks and the Orient in general, having been robbed by Albanians.

It must have taken quite some courage for anyone to risk voyages and foreign hotels on such a prolonged trip, especially Andersen, given his morbid imagination and extreme hypochondria. Perhaps an almost constant sense of cultural estrangement and misery at home outweighed many fears, but he was certainly more than aware of the dangers. Every personal health concern is meticulously noted, from a suppurating nodule on his gum which he fears might be infected to his perennial preoccupation: 'My penis is giving me trouble, and, heaven knows, it isn't my fault.'[13] 'Penis still bad; if only I haven't caught something in the ship's loo!'[14] Other serious diseases abounded alongside cholera, and deaths due to poor hygiene were endemic; one travelling acquaintance went down with smallpox and Andersen anxiously feared contamination, noting how after being with him the evening before the man had got home and looked at his body to find the pocks had broken out. The mid-nineteenth century, still floundering in antiquated notions of pathology and epidemiology, nevertheless found the world on the cusp of groundbreaking medical advance. Louis Pasteur (1822-95), known as the 'father of microbiology' was to describe airborne disease transmission and originate the 'germ theory of disease', soon followed by cholera vaccine and identification of the causative organism by Robert Koch and Filippo Pacini. Nevertheless, while treatments for cholera improved, global understanding of hygiene and sanitation lagged far behind, prolonging each outbreak. The traveller had constantly to comply with quarantine regulations and cope with ships delayed in port, stringent passport checks, enforced pauses and sudden alterations in planned trajectories.

At Piraeus, Andersen and fellow passengers were summoned onto boats at nine o'clock in the morning and sailed ashore without visiting the quarantine station or showing their passports. He drove into Athens with four Americans and one Russian to find the road which several years before had been a bog was now a fine highway, rousing respectful wit: 'It was very dusty, but it was, to be sure, classical dust.'[15]

---

13. Andersen, *Diaries*, p. 112.
14. Ibid., p. 113.
15. Ibid., p. 111.

Lily of the Valley

So through a small forest of olive trees into Athens. The new city also took him by surprise after so long an absence, antiquity transformed into a town seemingly built in a hurry for a big market, now in full swing. He soon relaxed and spent a month in Greece before travelling on to Constantinople, where he managed to view the burial casket of the Sultan's grandfather, Abdul-Hamid, before being chased away as an infidel by an attendant: "Christians must not see such things!"

Sailing onwards to Pera, Andersen visited the dervish's monastery to be mesmerised by the spirituality of their dance in homage to the planets, while a priest walked quietly and majestically among the white-skirted whirling mystics. It was all entrancing and the monastery beautiful, unlike the one he had seen in Scutari, where he had been rather shocked and repelled by the dervish's antics. Back at his hotel, Andersen was drawn outside by the sound of regimental music. As ever, the erotic charge returned at the sight of dark-skinned soldiers dressed in indigo blue trousers, jackets with scarlet-bordered collar, and fezzes, some in boots and some slippers... After dinner he received a visit from a young blond Russian fellow from the Caucasus, also staying at the hotel on his way to Egypt and then home via Copenhagen. The closing diary entry on Saturday 1 May graphically records the writer's physical arousal, followed by a collage of spontaneous impressions that illustrate the sheer delight and openness with which Andersen greeted new surroundings; a

Whirling dervishes at Pera, from Andersen's
letter to Jette Wulff, 29 May 1841.

typically chimerical response to the wide world of his experience, at times jaded but just as often one of unalloyed wonder:

> Wandered around Pera; its mosques full of praying and prostrated men in rows. ... The sea of Marmara like glass, the mountains in Asia seem ethereal; in the clear air beyond lay a chain of snow-covered mountains. ... Happened in the street on all the foreign ambassadors who are meeting to confer about the disturbances in Bulgaria, some had servants both fore and aft and secretaries on either side. At dinner a young German who was only eating here to catch a glimpse of me; he had read my novels and my biography. Walked down to the quay in Galata. What a throng of boats! ... Encountered another corpse today, a Greek woman. An Asiatic sensuality is torturing me here. Oh, How I am burning with longing![16]

On the morning of Tuesday, 4 May, Andersen started out early and watched something of the procession for the Prophet Mohammed's birthday: music and horses, their magnificent caparisons studded with precious gems, and, following them, pages wearing peacock feathers and the young nineteen-year-old sultan in a jacket and fez with bird-of-paradise feather; he looked very pale. Amid all the festivities Andersen began to fret about the journey ahead, anxious that something might be wrong with his passport; he chided himself for worrying and said his goodbyes, due to set off homewards at 6.30 a.m. next day. Rumours were rife of uprisings in the Balkans, with the massacre of thousands of Christians. He had been warned against taking his planned route via the Danube but, as usual, Andersen's complete self-absorption eclipsed the perils of geopolitical upheaval. Far greater than his fear of worldly catastrophe was that of infection from other passengers, and letters from Cairo and Constantinople reported two hundred people daily dying of the plague.

*   *   *

On 7 September 1838, before he entered the 'great parenthesis' and less than a month after his father's death, Kierkegaard had published his first literary work, the small critical monograph on Andersen's

---

16. Ibid., p. 120.

novel *Only a Fiddler*. Kierkegaard's cryptically entitled pamphlet, *From the Papers of a Person Still Living, Published Against His Will*, comprised a merciless critique of Andersen's third attempt at full-length fiction. It was vicious, but Kierkegaard's invective stemmed not from complete contempt for the storyteller novelist *per se*, but rather indignation at Andersen's defeatist attitude towards the gift of genius. This was a matter greatly occupying Kierkegaard's mind, as in the aftermath of great bereavement he tried to discern his path and define a task that might give meaning to his life. How to justify his own gift? How make amends for time wasted so far? As he read Andersen's work, Kierkegaard was struggling with his own lack of courage and commitment and writing the critique may even have helped him arrive at some resolution. Repelled by the self-indulgence and pathos of the new novel, Kierkegaard pours scorn on Andersen's belief that genius may be crushed and succumb to adverse circumstance. No! genius was not daunted, did not flinch from life – and lame excuse indeed to plead suffering as reason to refute its challenges.

Poor Andersen! He had unwittingly presented his friend with a few thousand words of exactly the sort of moral cowardice calculated to unleash a murderous riposte, Kierkegaard's blood was up, and the rapier thrust: genius did not shrink from adversity, countered the critic, it was like thunder as it comes up against the wind, a conflagration which the wind only rouses to fiercer flame. It might have been a warning salvo fired against himself. Kierkegaard's first published work, generally dismissed as stylistically ponderous and over-academic, nonetheless offers a foretaste of the passionate commitment he was to bring to all his future writings. He never put pen to paper without the emotional impetus and integrity that animates this first work. To these qualities would be added innate intellectual and lyrical genius: 'No other philosopher except Plato has known how to adorn and vivify the strictest thinking with imagination and poetry.[17] He was arriving at the hitherto untrodden way he would take from now on and follow to its ultimate conclusion.

Having passed the theology examination, and suffering mental and emotional torture over Regine, the new graduate set off for his father's birthplace and on 19 July 1840 records, amidst a flurry of somewhat obscure and overwrought reports, a long and comical conversation overheard onboard the ferry from Kalundborg to

---

17. Lowrie, *A Short Life of Kierkegaard*, p. 134.

Aarhus in which four fellow passengers, all parsons, discuss the fair weather expediting the crossing. Back and forth between them they pitch the old superstition about no skipper wanting a parson onboard as it bodes contrary winds... which, they triumphantly chorus, cannot be true, for see how well the sailing goes today! Hearing which Kierkegaard, who had in vain strained his ears for a whisper of wind, remarks on the dubious blessing of the freedom of the parish, for here onboard there was complete freedom of the parishes, and he could have listened to whichever parson he liked and been none the wiser! Not one of the four could bear to let go of his privileged version of the story, so none would. All in all, it left the young theologian praying for a bout of seasickness, or that the other passengers might be so stricken... Irony was always a safe first and last resort for Kierkegaard, but he was in a fragile state. To his journal he confided the dullness which pervaded his being. His soul was so empty he could not imagine what might fill the void, not even the blessedness of heaven itself. Not lack, he ruminated, awakened the truly idealistic longing, for lack embodied some worldly scepticism ... but superabundance... so long as he had been full of ideas he was afraid of the ideal and so gave birth to deformities, thus reality failed to meet his burning desires. If only this should not be the case also with love. He dreaded confusing an ideal with a reality, and while that was not yet the case, some mysterious terror made him long to know the future whilst quaking at the prospect.

For a long time he had lived in horror of his potential to seduce, now he feared Regine's propensity to fall prey to it. Already he was shielding himself and their future from the shadow of his past while abandoning himself 'secretly and clandestinely' to this love. The first thing he had done after passing the exam was to visit the Rørdams. He was then plunged into more immediate anticipatory dread with the approach of departure for Jutland. How ambiguous a feeling for this young man at such a moment to be on his way to his father's birthplace! The scene that featured so sorrowfully, so poignantly and terribly in his father's life story that it had bred in his youngest son a sort of mortal terror. Yet Søren's recently reborn love and reverence for his late father made of this pilgrimage also a precious opportunity to be reunited with him in spirit. No longer an impressionable child, the son must have hoped now to be able to set the stories of his childhood within some subjectively conceived context. Perhaps he would at last be able to make mature sense of his father's suffering and thus come closer both to him and to his own independent adult self.

Approaching Sædding, he considered the possibility of preaching his first sermon at the little church but was shocked to see the Gospel for that Sunday was Mark 8:1-10, the feeding of the four thousand: 'From whence can a man satisfy these men with bread *here in the wilderness*.'[18] Again he felt his soul subsumed beneath bleak imagery of that barren, destitute and godforsaken heathland. Surely the whole meaning of his life could not lie in that little cemetery, that he might fall ill and be buried in the garden of graves around the church where he had contemplated preaching? What an extraordinary thought! His father's last wish fulfilled... and yet the son rejected any such imagined fate, feeling it incommensurate with the recompense he felt he owed his father. From Michael Pedersen he had learned the meaning of fatherly love, and thus gained some idea of divine fatherly love 'the one unshakable thing in life; the true Archimedean point'[19]. As such reflection gave way to actual sight of the settlement, he found arrival calming.

Time at last to ruminate on the effect of this landscape as it lay before him in reality; how open everything was to the vast skies, naked and unclothed before God. How such surroundings affect the human spirit; how humbling was such a landscape, how one might be brought to one's knees. He saw how powerfully the spirit would be permanently shaped by such a place, where there was no room for distractions, 'the many little crevices where consciousness can hide, and where seriousness has such difficulty in running down one's scattered thoughts.' He saw how this landscape might prove formative of a fine mind. Here, he felt, human consciousness must firmly and scrupulously shut itself off from the world, close about itself. He wept: 'Just as people say: *nulla dies sine linea*, so I can say of this journey "*nulla dies sine lacryma*".[20] Things became clearer to him: he had revelled in reflection; it had become his

---

18. Holy Bible, St James version, Matthew 15:33 'And his disciples say unto him Whence should we have so much bread in the wilderness, as to fill so great a multitude?'.
19. Kierkegaard, *Journals*, p. 86.
20. Ibid.

favourite diversion to consider defection from the Church in elevated terms – those of intellectual critique, informed refusal, the act of a superior intelligence. Now he had to face facts. His father was dead and, in the light of his confession, the son saw the unedifying truth of his own adolescent rebellion. Not merely humbled but mortified, he wrote how moral courage was required to grieve; religious courage to rejoice. A world of difference lay between the proud courage, which dared to fear the worst, and the humble, which dared to hope for the best. His Jutland pilgrimage was coming to an end, but the confrontation with himself continued, reinvigorated. By mid-November he would be lambasting himself and, in naming his weakness, vowing to dispel it:

> I have the courage to doubt, I believe everything; I have the courage to fight – I believe against everything; but I have not the courage to know something, not the courage to possess, to own something. ... I have only the pale, bloodless, hard-lived midnight shapes to fight against, to which I myself give life and existence.[21]

So he set the scene for what would become the altarpiece of his life and work. From the very beginning he had been afraid for her and for himself, as the religious is afraid before his God, and indeed theirs would become the greatest of love stories, built not on consummation but silent sufferance, not worldly happiness, but faith that oversteps the temporal to realise divine fulfilment. His return to Copenhagen in August meant renewed proximity to Regine. Obsessed as he was with worldly thoughts of her, he was far more preoccupied with the mystery of her soul. Any demeaning attempt at getting to 'know' her was anathema to him; he shrank from the idea of so desecrating an attempt to investigate Regine's nature. In order to preserve her inviolability, he must exercise the utmost caution and restraint. Of paramount concern to him was the seriousness of his love; he must be vigilant, guard against himself, neither flirt with nor mislead her. He knew his own nature, feared both its sprite and solemnity of soul, that bringer of betrayal satisfied with nothing less than full disclosure. He trembled. He had never loved another woman and knew he never

---

21. Ibid., pp. 87-88.

would. There was no room for error. Only after the most profound reflection could the leap be made.

The lengths to which he would go to glimpse Regine during this period were extraordinary. They met at her home and in society, and he followed her unobserved. This last he found the least obtrusive way of simultaneously refreshing and marshalling his thoughts and feelings. It also protected her from the possible pain and embarrassment of public scrutiny; if he was careful no one would suspect secret liaison, and she would not be angered or he thus distracted from his studies. Kierkegaard discovered a little café on her route to and from her weekly singing lesson from which, if he chose his seat, he could watch her pass unobserved. Like everyone else, his friends and acquaintances knew he was a creature of habit and they wanted to know why the departure from routine. He told them the café served the best coffee in town; he simply could not resist a second cup. In fact, the place was awful in every way, from dingy decor to the stale croissants and filthy brew, but soon his friends were frequenting it. When they told Kierkegaard they found the coffee vile, he insisted it was delicious, a most superior blend, he said he drank it every day. When at last they abandoned the ghastly venue he continued drinking its coffee and eating the desiccated pastries, overjoyed at reclaiming his privacy. His friends were equally happy to leave him to it; they knew he was eccentric and stubborn as a mule.

He had met his match. In quarrels Regine stood her ground, refusing to capitulate. They would part in acrimony only to meet again another day with fresh joy to discuss the same matter calmly. Their two souls felt to her so securely moored fast against each other that neither could set sail alone. The sense of eternity was shared, and the reason they never dated their letters. It was how he would explain his hesitation in sending her his first gift, the phial of lily of the valley: so that delay might cause it to be concealed like the bloom within its sheath of green, for so long that it lost all former associations for her and would thus exist at the interception of now and soon; here and there; home and away; present, past and future: 'because I know that you, too, know the infinity of the moment'.[22] The moment of truth was upon them, and he knew it. Especially upon him, for Regine was much more than an infatuation, she represented nothing less than his hope of joining the world, as he saw it, in 'realising the universal';

---

22. Kierkegaard, *Letters*, no. 18.

and, as the position he had reached in regard to his true being and the ethical problems it posed involved excluding the woman he loved, he now faced the ultimate dilemma. He chose, determined to remain meticulous.

* * *

The difficulties and dangers of travel that may have helped to keep Kierkegaard at home and focused on his life task but for a few outings to Berlin, were for Andersen by now an established mode of escape from himself and a vital defence. He was perhaps the most well-travelled Dane of his time, as well as the most fearful. So susceptible was he that dread of fire, the stranger and disease became almost incapacitating. After it was rumoured that on burial his old benefactor, the composer Weyse, 'was not quite cold about the heart', Andersen kept a note on his bedside table reading: 'I am not really dead' and begging anyone who found his 'corpse' to bleed him thoroughly. Everyone who knew him well was familiar with his whimsy, so in response to Andersen announcing his forthcoming Balkan trip, Jonas Collin had written back saying the planned jaunt to Greece would probably come to nothing, which he would welcome, for only God knew why his ward wanted to go there. Not even discouragement from this source could put Andersen off his new venture and, fuelled by foreign fame and desperation, the unknown perils of the region only added allure to his plans. Again he discovered the trusted remedy worked; the farther south he ventured, the more remote despair. Adventurousness repaid him well. The impressions left by this trip were to feed into his travel writing, especially the travelogue, *A Poet's Bazaar*. Most of all, though, they would add sun-drenched splendour, exoticism and a thrill of restrained sensuality to one after another fairy tale, introducing his stolid northern European readership to hitherto unimagined worlds of beauty, colour, excitement, spirituality and mysticism.

He was proud, in retrospect, to have chosen the most hazardous return route, by steamer via the Danube northwards through the war zone of Wallachia, Bulgaria and Serbia to Orsova on the Hungarian frontier, where all passengers had been quarantined for ten days. At the beginning of the journey, three weeks previously, he had disembarked in Constanta and been upset at the sight of a dead stork, his most loved bird, and near it a dead dog, stoking his superstitious mind to conjure up calamity. Andersen's lifelong adulation of the stork speaks eloquently of his childhood privations; emblem of birth and happy family, the bird must have signified all he had felt he missed. The bad omen remained with him as they emerged into a blustery Black Sea shrouded in chill fog but later, as the steamer plied its stately way up the great river, he was glad to have chosen it over the land, where all he saw beyond the conflict-ridden riverbanks were ruined towns and settlements and blackened fields and forest. As the voyage progressed, Andersen thought his hard-won courage increasingly vindicated, and in Budapest on 30 May had been further gratified to discover himself already well-known here thanks to translation of the French biography; he even found copies of *The Improvisatore* in a bookshop. At Vienna, though, came the dawn of new and unwelcome reality. Only one letter awaited him, from his dear friend Jette, and nothing from the benefactor he called The Father or his son Edvard. Flooding back to Andersen came all the unpleasantness of home; 'this German-northern atmosphere' – and by 4 June he was looking back with nostalgia and forward with dread: 'I wish I had died in the Orient!'[23]

In Dresden he sat for the court painter, Carl Christian Vogel von Vogelstein, who produced a sensitive portrait which Andersen would come to regard as the truest ever made of him. It emphasises an intelligent, high forehead beneath receding hairline and enhances the hooded eyes with dreaminess. The storyteller is uncharacteristically poised in this likeness, a smile playing about his mouth and his bearing dignified despite the foppish dress and pose. For once he seems at ease beneath the other's gaze, sure of his own place in their shared world. In Dresden, too, he found awaiting him letters from the Collins that completely disarmed him, dispelling former mistrust and making his evening 'the happiest of my trip'. Leipzig greeted him with accolades and invitations from all the city's most noted artists, as though contrived to provide the grand finale needed for his trip. Back on Danish soil he crossed to Funen on 13 July, visiting friends in Odense and there meeting with common parochial delight at his having come home specially for the town fair! Consoling himself with memories of cosmopolitanism and foreign fame, he travelled on to stay on Count Moltke-Hvitfeldt's country estate at Glorup.

Once home, things turned out better than expected. Cultured Copenhagen showed itself capricious enough to allow the sun to set on failure one day and rise on glory the next, so that the dismal flop

---

23. Andersen, *Diaries*, p. 126.

of Andersen's play *The Moorish Maid* was eclipsed by the drawing-room appearance of a swashbuckling Balkan explorer. Invited to every salon, he was thrilled to discover himself centre of attention; the Collins warmly welcomed him home, and all in all he felt far better disposed towards his home country than he had previously thought possible. Diary entries are paused while Andersen works on stories and completes *A Poet's Bazaar*. Although poorly received when it appeared in April 1842, this book became very popular with the reading public both at home and abroad and is generally considered the finest of his travelogues. He simultaneously produced a new instalment of *Tales Told for Children* to come out just in time for Christmas. Every celebrity visiting the city sought him out, among them Franz Liszt and Clara Schumann, who found the renowned storyteller still quite young and very ugly… 'a ghostly appearance.' although she noted 'a poetical mind'.[24] Arresting that Andersen should be thus described, as Kierkegaard was to pin the same epithet on himself, once remarking that 'There is something spectral about me – and this is both the good and the bad in me – something that makes it impossible for anyone to endure having to see me every day and thus have a real relationship with me.'[25]

* * *

On 8 September 1840, a scant month after his return from Jutland, Søren Kierkegaard left home 'with the firm purpose of deciding the matter'. It so happened that Regine was just leaving her house, and they met on the street outside. She told him there was nobody in and he took this as an invitation, 'just the opportunity I wanted' (by the time he got to his journal, he knew this had been 'foolhardy' of him). They went upstairs together. Regine, he reports, seemed a little uneasy as they stood alone in the living room. Kierkegaard asked her to play a piece on the piano as she usually did for him, but this time it did not help his nerves. Suddenly he snatched the score away, threw it down on the piano and burst out: 'Oh, what do I care about music now! It is you I am searching for, it is you I have sought after for two years.'[26] She remained a few moments silent while Kierkegaard said and did

---

24. Wullschläger, *Hans Christian Andersen*, pp. 201-202.
25. Kierkegaard's Journals and Notebooks, Volume 6: Journals NB11 - NB14 https://bibleportal.com/bible-quote/ Accessed 19 November 2024.
26. Kierkegaard, *Journals*, p. 92.

nothing more to impress her, other than warn her of his melancholy. At her mention of Fritz Schlegel, her tutor and betrothed, Kierkegaard records having told her to leave the former relationship as parenthesis. In fact, it was two days later, on 10 September, that Regine referred to Schlegel by name and Kierkegaard voiced his own impassioned prior claim upon her. Two days earlier she had been so struck dumb by his outburst that Søren was shocked at the strength of the effect he may have had, fearing it might lead to misunderstanding and even hurt her reputation. She had fled the room, and he immediately left the house and made his way straight to her father, Etatsråd Olsen. The councillor said neither yes, nor no, but Kierkegaard saw that he was willing enough to give his blessing to a betrothal. Søren asked her father for a meeting with Regine, which was granted for the afternoon of the tenth: 'On this occasion I did not say a single word to persuade her. She said Yes.'[27] Kierkegaard immediately began conducting himself as one of the family, particularly in relation to her father, whom he had always loved. By next day Kierkegaard realised inwardly that he had 'made a false step':

> A penitent such as I was with my *vita ante acta*, my melancholy, that was enough. I suffered unspeakably at that time.
> She seemed to notice nothing. On the contrary, her spirits were so high that once she said she had accepted me out of pity.[28]

It was the beginning of the end. The more Regine succumbed to her feelings, openly worshipping him, the more he suffered. In her joyous exuberance she tested and teased him, declaring that if she thought he only visited her out of habit she would at once break off the engagement. He recoiled; if she did not take it more seriously, he was saved, he glimpsed escape. However, the more loving she became the more he realised his own responsibility for this. On one occasion, when determined to break through his melancholy, he had begged her, 'Surrender to me; your pride makes everything easier for me'.[29] It was, he grieved in his journal, perfectly true, honest to her, but

---

27. Ibid.
28. Ibid.
29. Ibid., p. 93.

treachery towards himself. A note is added to the effect that Regine certainly suspected his state of mind, accusing him of never being happy whether she remained with him or not. She had also once promised never to ask him anything, if only she might stay with him. At this point Kierkegaard knew he could extricate himself with a modicum of grace, leaving Regine with the sense that she herself had made the decisive move, and on good grounds. However, he could not betray his own integrity to this degree, knowing he still clung to the fragile hope of marriage. So, even as his misgiving deepened, he threw himself wholeheartedly into their affair. It was a situation he interpreted directly as God's punishment on him. A period followed of tragic dissonance while the engagement limped on month after month, both partners so profoundly and poignantly involved with the other that each lost sight entirely of their differing states of mind.

On 17 November Kierkegaard entered the seminary. It was bound to be a rocky ride. Bishop Mynster, revered by Kierkegaard as his father's pastor, was a great source of sorrow and annoyance to the young seminarian due to what he saw as Mynster's obstructive attitude towards him. What would become an endless irascible discourse began between Kierkegaard and the cleric over what seemed the latter's implacable opposition to Kierkegaard's every plan for his future. While Kierkegaard cherished the hope of a position on the staff of the seminary, where his particular skills in extrapolation, exploration and expression might find their natural place, the lord bishop ignored his wish. The younger man reacted furiously, interpreting the bishop's attitude as indicative of his finding Kierkegaard too dangerous and wanting him out of town, safely ensconced in country parish where nobody would hear his heretical ideas or come under his influence. Nothing was achieved by attrition and the malevolent undercurrent kept on tugging them in differing directions.

Bishop Mynster, painting by C. A. Jensen (1792-1870).

The day after he entered the seminary, he and Regine had quarrelled about who owed whom a letter.

Regine offered to bring hers to him by hand, which Kierkegaard vehemently forbade her to do. As they made up, he evoked for her the tremendous impression she had made upon him at their second meeting, when, on leaving he had seen her at the window, dressed in his favourite summer frock. She had suggested walking 'with bowed head' on her letter-bringing errand to the seminary, and now he went on fatuously or fawningly to portray her as a humble emissary of love. She was in no mood for patronising sentimentality and told him to desist. So, two days later, and a year since he had first sent her lily of the valley, she received a second tiny phial, this time 'enveloped in an abundance of leafy wrappings', and accompanied by an ominous little note referring to 'leaves' that might either be floral or pages of a letter:

> But these leaves are not the kind one tears off hastily or throws aside with annoyance in order to get to the contents. On the contrary, they are precisely of that kind which gives pleasure, and I see with how much care and solicitude you will unfold every leaf and thereby recollect that I recollect you, my Regine, and you will yourself recollect.[30]

The words sent a shiver through her. In her mind's eye she saw the tiny flowers, entombed, glacially pale. The cold leaves seemed for some reason to ward off her hands. On 11 August she received her ring, returned with another note from him:

> In order not to put more often to the test a thing which after all must be done, and which being done will supply the needed strength – let it be done. Above all forgive a man who writes this, forgive a man who, though he may be capable of something, is not capable of making a girl happy.[31]

---

30. Kierkegaard, *Letters and Documents*, Letter 42, p. 86.
31. Lowrie, *A Short Life of Kierkegaard*, pp. 38-39. The letter appears in the subsection attributed to Frater Taciturnitus in *Quidam's Diary, Stages on Life's Way*. It is repeatedly referred to, usually cryptically, throughout Kierkegaard's writings in which he repeats the narrative of his engagement.

In response, Regine 'overstepped her limit', according to her lover, and tried to force him to overstep his own. Rushing to his chambers and finding him away from home, she left a note begging him to reverse his decision and in the name of Christ not to leave her. She also invoked the memory of his dead father. Kierkegaard was deeply moved, even more so when Regine's father, interpreting his behaviour as eccentricity, begged him not to forsake her: she was willing to submit unconditionally to everything. The moment of truth provided painful clarity. Under such stress Kierkegaard defended himself in the only way he knew how, by hardening his resolve and playing devil's advocate in the pages of his journal. Well then, what if he had let himself marry her, he could have played a despicable game of tyrant and martyr, keeping a monopoly on power by doing her the favour. Charity! He could have attended to a young girl's imprecations and taken full advantage of her. She trusted him, and he might easily have abused her trust. There was one objection: the only person he could never fool was himself. He might tell himself that he was too heavy for her, and she too light for him, and that both burdens caused strain, but ultimately, as he confessed in writing, reason could never have been strong enough to keep him from yielding to her. He could never have defied her tears, her father's suffering and his own wish had he not 'had to fight the case before a much higher tribunal, and hence my firmness.'[32] 'She fought like a tigress. ... If I had not believed that God had lodged a veto, she would have been victorious.'[33]

He was appalled, mortified on her behalf when Regine fell on her knees before him. The more she opposed him, the more Kierkegaard felt the depths of his love for her; her pleas that she be allowed to love him almost broke him, for precisely then he perceived that his response was something more than passion. At this moment he realised, in contravention of his main contention (that she loved without knowing or understanding him), just how perfectly she perceived his inner state and intended anxiety to drive him to extremes. It did, and all his strength was needed to constrain himself and repel her. He begged her to set him free, for her own sake. She swore she would bear anything rather than let him go. He suggested that he make it seem that it was she who broke off the engagement and so spare her any offence or public embarrassment, to which she

---

32. Ibid., pp. 139-140.
33. Kierkegaard, *Journals*, p. 94.

replied 'not unsocratically'[34] that in her presence no one would let anything be noticed and what people said in her absence remained a matter of indifference.

After two months of this she grew desperate and, for the first time in his life, Kierkegaard scolded, walked out and made for the theatre, hoping to find the comforting presence of Emil Boesen there; instead, his appearance gave rise to a rumour that glancing at his watch he had issued the Olsens with an ultimatum: if they had anything more to say they'd better hurry up and say it, because he was going to see a show. When he got there the act was over, Councillor Olsen approached and asked to speak to him. They went back together to the Olsen house, where Regine's father told Kierkegaard that she was in absolute despair, the end of the affair would be the death of her. She had ceased eating and sleeping. Kierkegaard promised to calm her down but reiterated that the die was cast. Her father replied he was a proud man and found it hard to ask such a thing, but he begged Kierkegaard not to break with her. The following morning a letter came from the councillor saying Regine had not slept all night and asking Kierkegaard to go and see her. He went, and tried again to persuade her of his decision. She asked whether he would ever marry. He replied with what he described as necessary cruelty, that, yes, he would perhaps do so in ten years' time when he had sown his wild oats 'then I shall need some young blood to rejuvenate me.'[35] She asked forgiveness for the pain she had caused him; and he responded that it was he who should beg forgiveness. She made him promise to think of her, and he did so: '"Kiss me", she said. I did so but without passion. Merciful God!'[36]

---

34. Ibid.
35. Ibid., p. 95.
36. Ibid.

Chapter 6

A Palace of Pretend

In his Translator's Introduction to Schocken's 1967 edition of *Stages on Life's Way* (1845), Walter Lowrie lambasts Kierkegaard's endless exposition of his engagement: 'I heartily wish S.K. had never written this 'Diary' – nor written the hundreds of pages on the same theme which he confided in his Journal. I am tired of reading it all and find it still more tiresome to translate it. …'[1] In writing this, Lowrie continues, Kierkegaard made a bad impression and did himself a disfavour. A caricature that appeared the *Corsair* at the time, of a young girl on all fours with S.K. sitting astride her with a whip is judged to be cruel but 'not undeserved'. Such outspoken condemnation by so great a scholar and 'lover' of Kierkegaard is remarkable, although as commentator, translator and biographer Lowrie is never inhibited by gratuitous etiquette. Accused by his most generous critic, historian Professor Wilhelm Pauck, of over-sympathising with his subject and so failing to write so historical a biography as he might have done, Lowrie defends his position, freely admitting that warmth of feeling imbues his biography with sympathy, admiration and occasional pity for Kierkegaard. Lowrie goes on to point out that when, however, he lost patience with his object of pity and ventured to abuse Kierkegaard for what he later realised was a misreading of a particularly sentimental exposition of his engagement in the Journal, the biographer came in for reasonable rebuke by no less a figure than

---

1. Walter Lowrie, Introduction, in Søren Kierkegaard, *Stages on Life's Way*, p. 14.

Kierkegaard scholar Professor Swenson ('who is only a philosopher') for being 'unhistorical'.[2] Nonetheless, and despite his indignation at what he saw as Kierkegaard's misjudgement on this point, Lowrie declares his undiminished pity and reverence, 'I bow before him in admiration'... signing off with some aplomb: 'If this be unhistorical, make the most of it!'[3]

More regrettable than any lapse on the part of his translator, and far more moving, is the ineradicable impression left by Kierkegaard's writings of his own unresolved bewilderment. Despite the immense and lasting significance of the works devolved from his inability to marry the woman he loved, there remains at their core some curiously weighty and elusive mystery: an elemental but earthly 'thou shalt not'. His comprehensive attempts at hiding from posterity the reality of his life's agony do not veil this void. Lowrie felt it, but refrained, perhaps through discretion and loyalty, perhaps due to the ageless taboo associated with any critique of motherhood, to elaborate beyond the merest mention.[4] Yet it seems obvious that fundamental to the genesis of Kierkegaard's tragedy were the grave emotional effects of an essentially unmothered life, the one aspect of his private experience he neglected publicly to examine. So glaring is the omission that it illuminates the sheer traumatic force required to expunge such experience from a brilliantly reflective mind. Whether due to conscious psychological recoil from the facts or simple unconscious banishing of them, it is hard to believe that such an intellect could have tolerated even the most remotely perceived denial; such would surely have been tracked, pinned down and duly annihilated as teller of untruths. Yet what remains unspoken at the centre of Kierkegaard's life is his silent and comprehensive disavowal of the woman who bore him, evidenced in the absence of her name or any reference to her in the many thousands of words he wrote. The effect on his life of this lacuna, counterbalanced with excessively dominant paternal

---

2. Ibid, p. 15.
3. Ibid.
4. See Chapter Two: 'The fact that there was something which impeded S.K. from honouring his mother, and from loving her as a son ought, was certainly a principal cause of his tragedy, and perhaps it accounts in part for the particular misfortune that he was not able to "realize the universal" by marrying the woman he loved.' Lowrie, *A Short Life of Kierkegaard*, p. 25.

influence, was catastrophic, and juvenile reconstruction of relations between his father and mother must fatally have shaped Kierkegaard's view of marriage. The precocious powers of observation and imagination he demonstrated as a child may, in Jungian terms, have entirely eradicated faith in a 'good' stereotype, but prohibition may also arise from some far more esoteric source. More is 'known' about such things now. Adverse childhood experience was not named in Kierkegaard's day, let alone the lasting holistic effects on body, mind and spirit of suppressed emotional response to trauma.[5] In any case, it is clear that as an adult Kierkegaard dared not risk the potential moral degradation inherent in human love, marriage and parenthood.

* * *

Having resolved to stay at home and ride out the storm for eighteen months after breaking with Regine (so that she might witness his nonchalance as the city explored the depths of his depravity), he found himself so vilified and humiliated by the uproar that life became unbearable. After a fortnight he left on a study trip to Berlin, the excuse for which was what turned out to be a short-lived enthusiasm for the great philosopher of Romanticism, Friedrich Wilhelm Joseph Schelling (1775-1854), who was giving a series of lectures there debunking Hegelian theory. Just before leaving, after a night spent weeping on his bed, Søren found his elder brother on his doorstep. The younger was used to 'sound advice' from Peter concerning his clerical career, but not in such intimate affairs, and opening the door to his brother one can imagine Søren contemplating evisceration. Peter had apparently come to discuss his little brother's reputation – my reputation, *note bene*! exclaimed Søren in his journal – and was minded to sally forth and work for his salvation, spreading the word that, contrary to public opinion and superficial appearances, his younger sibling was in fact a saint. Indeed, Peter was keen to visit Regine's family and persuade them there was no finer fellow in terms of integrity, goodness and grace. Kierkegaard was brief but to the point, 'If you do so, I will put a bullet through your head',[6] which was, he wrote, the best proof of how concerned he was. Shortly after Peter and Boesen had watched him board ship for Germany on

---

5. See Gabor Maté, *When the Body Says No, The Cost of Hidden Stress*, Wiley (2011).
6. Kierkegaard, *Journals*, p. 95.

25 October 1841, an anguished Kierkegaard consigned to his journal the outpouring too painful for public consumption, charging anyone who had anything to say about his loss of Regine of being incapable of understanding it and recommending that they hold their tongue:

> – and how should anyone know it better than I who have made the whole of my tremendously reflective soul into as agreeable a frame as possible for her pure depths – my dark thoughts – my melancholy dreams, my brilliant expectations – and above all my inconstancy, in short all that brilliance by the side of her depths.[7]

The moment the bonds were broken he had known that there were only two paths open to him now: either he threw himself into the wildest life or he must become absolutely religious, but not in the manner of the parsons.

A little later, installed in his Berlin lodgings he expands on the anxiety of being unsure whether or not it was possible to turn back to her and begs his God for courage. How hard, how cruel to have set his whole heart on her, his whole hope for life, having never really thought about marriage before meeting her, having never imagined how deep a wound relinquishment of this hope would leave behind. How often he had almost encouraged her, he had only to tell her that he loved her, and the die would have been cast and, as he saw it, his young life ended. His mind retraced its steps, again and again arriving at the same conclusion, each time with more urgency. The decision had been the right one; he had always kept his relations with her in so vague a form that he could interpret it in any way he wished. In giving it to mean he was a deceiver he believed that humanly speaking he was saving her, providing her soul with necessary resilience. He did not doubt his reasoning on this score, but now came face to face with the fact of his own lack of faith: faith that to God all things are possible, but where lay the boundary between this and tempting God? His sin had never been that he did not love her. He could certainly seek intellectual refuge from the crisis, displace the problem by laying the blame on Regine for loving too wholeheartedly and too well; if only she had not stopped living for herself in order to live for him the disaster might have been averted. His conscience immediately

---

7. Kierkegaard, *Journals*, p. 96.

bounced the blame back onto his own shoulders; to fool the whole world, he wrote, did not weigh heavily upon him, but to deceive a young girl... after all, as he had already wryly observed, it was not his well-shaped nose she loved, nor his beautiful eyes, nor his small feet, nor his fine head; she had simply loved him, 'and yet she did not understand me.'[8]

The impossibility of 'understanding' presented Kierkegaard's rationality with an impassable barrier; the same that lay at the core of his exploration of religiosity. Here the objection took earthly form, the earthliest, for human love pivots on the paradox of incarnation. He longed for Regine to know him fully and love him for what he truly was, while his introverted intelligence precluded him from enlightening her. To validate this reality involved betraying hers by denying her autonomy; he could not allow her capacity for understanding, let alone understanding of him, even at its most artless. From this position of intolerable disequilibrium, he saw the only ground for their union lay in the absurd, that which he would later designate 'divine folly'. This involved acceptance of the paradox, and rejection of the mediating mind. Back in Berlin on 17 May 1843, he would write retrospectively of this realisation and thank God for it. He knew now that he had perhaps better not have got engaged, but after that point he had behaved with complete integrity towards Regine. Feeling as though he had lived through aeons of poetry in the intervening eighteen months, he did not wish to convert this experience into literature and so 'volatilise' his relationship to her; it had a quite different quality. She had not become a fairy princess and, if possible, she would become his wife.

One thing she almost certainly could not have understood in her teens was his real dread of her abandoning her own life and subjugating it to his, although this is what every young girl does when she first falls in love. He had seen the signs, and felt if it was allowed to happen the danger was real that loving her as he did he would lose his own life's meaning and direction. So, embarked on a frenzy of 'monologue' writing examining the moral rectitude of leaving her, he diverted himself with visits to the theatre to see a popular farce playing in Berlin and for the rest exhausted himself body and soul with work. In writing *Either/Or* he employs five pseudonyms; further evidence of his need for 'indirect communication', particularly

---

8. Ibid., p. 97.

in relation to the '*one* reader' whom he is addressing in this huge two-volume book. His true and deeply hidden hope was that in reading it she would be persuaded to review any impression she had formed of his villainy. Time and time again, in revisiting recent circumstances from which he had fled, his purpose in life would seem to him revealed as that of one who presents the truth as he discovers it in such a way as simultaneously to destroy all possible claim of authority. By disowning authority, by being in the greatest possible degree unreliable in the eyes of man, he would offer them the truth and put them in a contradictory position from which they could only escape by themselves unequivocally adopting it. The commission was weighty, and left him wondering whether in finding his own truth a man (himself) became a speaking Balaam's ass or a laughing jack-ass, an apostle or an angel. One thing was certain, to be an author had become the most miserable of occupations. He thought of the grovelling involved, the pleading and offering of references, humiliating beyond belief! Either you knew your subject better than your reader, or you shouldn't write. The alternative was a sort of taking the reader for a ride, and he refused to do this. If he was to write, he had to do so in his own way, whether or not his work was ever to be read or reviewed.

After Schelling's second lecture Kierkegaard's attendance dropped off. He was quickly disenchanted with the thinker whose 'positive philosophy' and concept of human freedom he had hoped would shed fresh light on 'reality' for him and clarify his situation. The truth was that nothing helped clarify it. If he thought he could still make Regine happy he would have left Berlin the same evening. It was hard to have made someone unhappy, especially to do so as almost the only hope of ensuring her happiness. By now he was involved in a double game reflective of the dilemma. He detailed Boesen to spy on Regine and report back to him her every movement. The extent of his obsession is revealed in a letter asking his friend to provide him with news and including minute instructions based on Regine's precise movements around the city. He emphasises the secrecy of the mission. Boesen advises against any such espionage. Kierkegaard goes further, fabricating fascination with a young actress currently playing in Berlin of whom he writes to Boesen that she reminds him of 'someone'. Knowing how gossip spread in Copenhagen he could be pretty sure the wildfire would reach Regine. The dastardlier the picture he painted of himself, the further he hoped to help her out of her love for him. On 2 February 1842 he sent another long missive to his confidant, this time concerning himself, concluding with an itinerary of each of his days in Berlin to illustrate its fullness and the lasting significance of this winter. He had been attending three or four lectures daily and making handwritten fair copies of each, he said, as well as attending a language lesson, and had still managed to get a lot written, i.e. a considerable portion of *Either/Or*. In addition, he'd read a good deal. All this fuelled by a dread sense of mortality; the briefer the term, the more intensely lived. Such meticulous itemisation, and no mention of the dreadful suffering which came out in torrents of incoherent poetic prose, whole pages of which he tore out of his journal and destroyed.

However, he could not keep his distance, and on 27 February told Boesen of his immediate plans: Schelling having proved himself a terrible driveller, he was returning to Copenhagen at once, not to commit himself afresh in any way except to finishing *Either/Or*. The same day he again dismisses the German philosopher in a note to his supercilious elder brother just insubordinate enough to soothe a younger sibling's self-esteem and sufficiently dissembling to cover his tracks concerning recent history. Repeating his contempt of Schelling, he added that he was coming home but would be leaving Copenhagen again as soon as he'd completed a little job he had on hand. Otherwise, he was well; like a schoolboy on holiday, in fact, able to fool about as he pleased. He was sure he'd have been reduced to complete idiocy had he gone on listening to Schelling. He got back on 6 March after a scant four and a half months away, in his luggage a substantial part of *Either/Or*, including *The Diary of a Seducer*. All his works from now on would be dedicated to his 'one reader', but this manuscript was by its timing particularly destined for Regine to convince her of his villainy. In his letter from Berlin asking Boesen to spy on her Kierkegaard had said that he did not consider this the final break. Nevertheless, he had always underestimated the furore his broken engagement would cause in Copenhagen. While he still hoped for a rapprochement, his home city was in ferment, the scandal on everybody's lips and almost all the sympathy with Regine. He too feared most for her; he knew her temperament well enough. Recalling her threat, one that her father had repeated in his own words, he recoiled from the thought that he might in actuality become responsible for murder. He felt that if he could go back to her he would do so, but that would literally end his own life. He was far from unfamiliar with the thought of suicide, which made separation from Regine doubly hard for him, 'for who loves like a dying man' and that was how he had always thought of it each time he devoted himself to her, yet to live with her 'in the peaceful and trusting sense of the word'[9] never occurred to him.

To understand the extremity of Kierkegaard's struggle with intimacy requires of his reader an ability to return to the moment of his young manhood when he was faced with his father's fallibility. To relive with him the crisis with the same passionate intensity, plunge with him into its fathomless depths of grief and shame. What Kierkegaard lost at that moment was more than his innocence; it was a lifetime's existential equilibrium. His soul so shuddered to its foundations that love could never again be for him a thing of comfort and stability, but only moment-to-moment dread of extinction. That he was able to turn such extreme terror of abandonment into a religious task presents a completely new and challenging paradigm for the love relationship.[10] Henceforth his being would remain too restive for the *status quo*. He would never be able to offer himself, let alone a woman, the conventional notional secure haven of marriage. He knew he did not have it in his power to protect her from contingency, from change, from sacred reality. It was, he felt, impossible for him to bind himself irretrievably to another person – and he doubted whether this were possible or even *permissible* between human beings. What then of sacred separation, space for the divine? Whenever he had glimpsed the possibility of marital contentment he had soon been returned to himself, to his cleverness, intrigue, his need to reflect, and then the crucial moment was past. Yet now, precisely when he had thrown them both into the void and she thought he deprived her of her happiness, when all accused him of faithlessness, he was more faithful than any. The paradox was exquisite – and intolerable. One day science would, he believed, discover his true sickness, the nature of this perversity, and name it. However, it would never be cured, this much-travelled

---

9. Kierkegaard, *Journals*, p. 98.
10. Kierkegaard prefigures by a century the premise of Martin Buber's *I and Thou* (Germany 1929, English translation, Dover Publications, 1937, 1970, Walter Kaufman).

path from the crossroads to the monastery of silent vows, of the dilemma, of contradiction, of the dialectic of love, of dread.

* * *

Christmas 1841 brought *Tales for Children*, a batch of new dark and moralising tales from Andersen, all related to death and punishment. The central story, *The Sandman*, was certainly aimed at entertaining Danish parents rather than their children, for the characters are Copenhageners transformed into animals, all perfectly recognisable and accompanied by some touchingly comical self-portraits of the author. In *The Buckwheat* Andersen takes his compatriots down another peg or two. It is the day after a violent thunderstorm over fields of wheat, barley, oats and buckwheat. Among the crops stands a venerable willow tree, so old that it has been split almost in half; in the cleft grow grass and brambles. All the crops know how wise the willow is, for it has stood here since time immemorial. All night as thunder raged across the fields the old willow tree watched the crops cower, all but the buckwheat, which stood up proud and tall. When the old willow asked the buckwheat why it seemed so impervious to the storm, it replied, "I bend to nothing and nobody," and stretched its lovely leaves and tossed its beautiful flowers. Just then, a terrible flash of lightening streaked across the sky and all the crops but the buckwheat knelt low and covered their ears. When the fiery night had passed all the crops lifted their heads into the cool air to enjoy the scent of refreshed earth and sky and feel gentle droplets of rain. Only the buckwheat lay seared and razed to the ground and the old willow wept for it: "See what pride and vainglory have done?"

A Poet's Bazaar came out in April 1842 and did very well in Denmark, outselling its author's previously popular travel books, *A Walking Tour* and *Picture Book Without Pictures*, and going into German, Swedish and English translation. This book memorialises the 1840s coming-of-age of the Grand Tour, by which time large-scale rail transport had expedited exploration of the wider world by privileged young men from Western Europe and the Americas; soon joined by their female counterparts. They went via Italy and sometimes, like Andersen, ventured as far as Greece, Turkey and south into the Balkans, discovering along the way the sites and treasures of antiquity. First encounters with the Orient led visual artists of the era to record early impressions of a sun-drenched other world, canvases featuring dusky peoples in previously unimaginable settings. Here were bustling Arab souks and coffeeshops, narrow shady streets where the water-seller offered refreshment to robed drinkers from a leather saddlebag; desert camels, and serene alabaster cupolas silhouetted against a flawless sapphire sky. They discovered the pale pillars of a mosque spiralled with coloured marble mosaiced morning glory; fragrant jasmine and cypress groves, towering date palms, and the calm symmetry of an Islamic garden – all bathed in sultry golden light. The culture-shock, colour, heat and vibrancy of this new reality Andersen captured perfectly with his painterly eye for landscape and character, and his sketchbooks evidence the same untamed immediacy of place and face that energises the writing. In what he saw as a typically parochial response, the Danish critics were less enthusiastic about this new travelogue than his public, homing in on frivolous detail to attack him for the name-dropping that peppered his book. Andersen was in truth an obsequious and over-thankful guest who brought to his work the naïve, indulgent attitude of the outsider overjoyed at last to feel accepted somewhere. He tended to overlook his host's serious shortcomings while quavering at the smallest slight or criticism. If anything tarnishes *A Poet's Bazaar* it is this tone of servility, and the book's most scathing critic was the brilliant editor of literary/satirical magazine *Corsair*, Meïr Aron Goldschmidt – the same whose mordant pen would later cause Søren Kierkegaard so much anguish and suffering.

While Goldschmidt admired Andersen's landscapes in *A Poet's Bazaar*, he found the writer too much ignored the poverty and suppression of the people among whom he travelled. Predominately a political commentator, Goldschmidt ignored Andersen's sensitivity to people and place, instead slamming into his uninformed naïvety. Given the ferment across Europe at the time, Goldschmidt might be excused for wondering why there was no mention of it in the storyteller's new book. The Carlsbad Decrees of 1835 had effectively killed off free speech in Germany, poets were languishing in prison or, like Heinrich Heine, in exile, while it was rumoured that the news periodical, the *Rheinische Zeitung*, edited by a young man called Karl Marx was about to be closed down. Wullschläger offers local context for Goldschmidt's review; in her opinion just five years previously nobody in Copenhagen would have written it. Now, against the backdrop of the dissent and unrest that had led to the 1848 uprisings and war in Germany and Denmark, the article was indicative of newly emergent interest in politics which Christian VIII was unable to check. The cosy atmosphere of Biedermeier Copenhagen was succumbing to German and French societal influences which pushed aside previous emphasis on the arts nurtured by the king and marked the waning of Golden Age culture.[11]

If this was indeed a watershed moment, it was one that entirely passed Andersen by. A paragraph in his autobiography records his riposte to Goldschmidt's accusations of political naïvety, as the storyteller asserts his complete disinterest in such things and what is more declares politics a danger for the poet. The subjectivity of the forest-floor view was one thing, wrote Andersen, but it was easy to forget how different things may look from the top of the tree. He would bow to the man of noble conviction whatever his social standing, but politics were not his business. God had given him another task; he'd known that in 1848, and he knew it still. It was a task always facilitated by beautiful, cultivated and convivial surroundings, and these he tirelessly sought out. Unwelcome memories and misery were kept at bay in the company of the high-born of Europe, for whose flattery and praise Andersen remained insatiably hungry. There was nothing he loved more than to find himself invited to a country estate, the seat of one or other aristocrat, in the company of finely dressed ladies and gentlemen whose servants jumped to meet his every need. He loved the ambiance of the nineteenth-century Danish stately home, modest by British standards but quietly assertive, an unostentatious mansion house set in peaceful parkland dotted with solitary oaks and ancient beech trees. So long as Andersen was strolling the manor grounds, admiring an ornamental lake, he could forget his past, the faces of his mother and dear lost father; even his own young self, the changeling child whose ugly features and overgrown limbs had suffered the bruises, kicks and cuts of his peers, and whose huge feet touched an earth that seemed to repel his presence on it.

He had first experienced such bucolic freedom in 1838 on Funen. From 1842 onwards, he regularly stayed at a couple of the most exclusive rural retreats, both deep in the Zealand countryside. Gisselfeld was a former monastery, a towering, red-brick gabled edifice, austere but for the surrounding parkland, and owned by the elderly Countess Danneskjold-Samsøe, mother of the Duke of Augustenborg. From here he regularly went on to Bregentved, a moated, French-style, seventeenth-century manor house on the

---

11. Wullschläger, *Hans Christian Andersen*, pp. 203-4.

country estate of Count Moltke. Here Andersen enjoyed the extensive woodlands, lawns and lime-tree avenues, and lakes that offered the sight of white swans and shimmering water lilies. Relaxed by these surroundings and luxuriating in his host's generous hospitality and an air of refinement, ease and privilege, Andersen felt free of city stress and social obligations. Here he found space and leisure enough for dreaming, the essential nourishment for his imagination. It was wandering the grounds at Gisselfeld on 5 July 1842 that had given him the idea for 'The Story of a Duck' and, returning three days later, he noted that the swans had young and were 'very irritable'. Three weeks later, at Bregentved, he started to write 'The Cygnet'. It would take Andersen eighteen months to hone this story, in which his own experience is so perfectly sublimated. The circumstances of its writing are charmingly described in the opening lines:

> It was so pretty out in the country in the glorious summertime. The corn stood yellow, the oats green, the hay was stacked in the meadows, and the stork strode about on his long red legs, and chattered Egyptian, for he had learnt that language from his mother. Round about the fields and meadows were great forests, and in the midst of the woods deep lakes; yes, it was truly delightful out in the country.
>
> In the sunlight stood an old country house encircled by deep ditches. From the walls right down to the water grew large dock-leaves that had shot up so high that little children could stand on tiptoe beneath the tallest. It was as lonesome there as in the thickest wood, and here lay a duck upon her nest; she was engaged in hatching her young, but by this time she was nearly tired of the task, it had lasted so long and she seldom received visitors; the other ducks preferred to swim about in the ditches to waddling up the bank and sitting under a dock-leaf to gossip with her. At last one egg cracked, and then another and another.[12]

The story ends with the swan, now fully grown from the ugly little grey cygnet it once was, accepting the world's praise and adulation

---

12. *Hans Andersen's Fairy Tales:* 16 plates in colour by Margaret W. Tarrant (London and Melbourne: Ward, Lock & Co. Ltd, London and Melbourne (*c.* 1930s), *The Ugly Duckling*, p. 7.

while his admirers feed him bread and cakes. Andersen ends his tale on a note of candid self-identification – among his society friends, *he* is the swan:

> It felt so bashful that it stuck its head beneath its wings, it did not know what to do. It was almost too happy but not a bit proud, for a good heart is never proud. It thought of how it had been persecuted and despised, and now all said that it was the loveliest of lovely birds. And the lilacs bowed their branches down into the water towards it, and the sun shone so nice and warm, and then the swan swelled out its plumage, raised its slim neck, and cried from the bottom of its heart: 'I never dreamed of such bliss when I was an ugly duckling!'[13]

The story marked a highly significant moment for Andersen, both personally and professionally. His first attempts at the apparently simple but richly allegorical tale coincided with an abrupt abandonment of risqué allusion in Andersen's writing, especially in reference to the royal court and upper echelons. There would be no more fairy tales such as *The Emperor's New Clothes* and *The Princess and the Swineherd*, in which, respectively, he satirises the throne and mocks an aristocratic lady. The reason for the *volte face* was that Andersen had been brought to heel by the king himself with his sudden gift to the storyteller on 12 July 1842 of a ruby ring set with thirty small diamonds. Why such a gesture was made at this moment is a mystery, for the date marked neither birthday, anniversary, nor any significant occasion – at least, none publicly acknowledged. Christian VIII was by now in a weakened position, his absolutist reign attenuated and facing the loss of the prime southern territories of Schleswig and Holstein as they passed from the Danish to the German crown. His reign so far had been marked by the most benign potential possible of an absolute monarch, bearing as it did the hallmark of a perceptive, creative and pragmatic personality. Christian VIII had also enjoyed huge popularity among his subjects for pursuing a liberal agenda. But no creative artist can resist poking fun at the higher-ups in society, and the king must have been at the very least discomfited by Andersen's ridicule. The storyteller's

---

13. Ibid., p. 18.

worldview mattered in Denmark; he now figured among the most widely read and acclaimed of the nation's writers. Any appearance of royal discouragement aimed at him would have caused the throne even more embarrassment. The king put on discretion with his kid gloves and presented Andersen with the ring.

Aficionados of the 'royal lineage' theory insist that this gift accompanied some important private disclosure to Andersen concerning his birth: namely, that he was the king's illegitimate son. Christian VIII is known to have had at least ten extramarital offspring, for each of whom he carefully provided. Andersen certainly grew up listening to his mother's claim that her son's blood ran blue, but whatever actually occurred in July 1842, it quashed insurrection in the storyteller and brought him firmly back into the king's fold. Even were it established that the ring was a father's gift to his son, this fact would not materially have affected Andersen, who would have been sworn to secrecy. However, two consecutive, single-sentence, stand-alone paragraphs towards the end of *The Ugly Duckling* may plausibly be interpreted as pointing to such a seminal change in his fortunes:

> It doesn't matter a bit about being born in a duck-yard when one has lain in a swan's egg.
> The large swans now swam round and round about it and stroked it with their beaks and were quite friendly.[14]

Andersen completed 'the tale of the young swan' on 7 October 1843, and a month later, on 10 November, it was published by Reitzel to an ecstatic response from the writer's rags-to-riches muse Jenny Lind. Wullschläger claims Andersen to be 'the only writer' whose invented tales match the archetypal quality and double articulation of traditional folk stories described by child psychologist Bruno Bettelheim (1904-1990) as having over millennia confronted the child with unconscious dilemmas and helped resolve them through fantasy by reaching 'the uneducated mind of the child as well as that of the sophisticated adult.'[15] This interpretation hints at intrinsic jeopardy for an age of infantilisation intent on evading dark realities. Precisely their qualities of supreme eloquence and naïvety lend to Andersen's most unconsciously conceived and universally loved archetypal fairy

---

14. Ibid., pp. 17-18.
15. Wullschläger, *Hans Christian Andersen*, p. 224.

tales an irresistible sentimentality that tempts the adult mind away from deeper processing. If fantasy acts identically on both child and adult, only the latter may wilfully take refuge in its superficial shape to prevent more profound truth reaching the unconscious.

In 1854 Kierkegaard would relate a corresponding farmyard autobiography, searing in its self-exposure, and later designated by Lowrie one of the pieces representing Kierkegaard's last words. This was the sketch entitled *The Wild Goose: A Symbol*, in which the wild bird of the title becomes enchanted by its domesticated counterparts and tries to get them to fly away with him, to liberate them from a pathetically mediocre life of captivity waddling around as respectable tame geese. At first the farmyard geese, who live a life of ease and comfort, find the wild goose likeable and quite entertaining, but soon they grow tired of him, deride and scold and treat him as an immature fantasist who doesn't know what he's talking about. Unfortunately, the wild goose has by now so committed himself to them that he cannot disengage from the tame flock, they have gained power over him, the wild goose becomes a tame goose and so the tale ends – or almost. Kierkegaard then supplies his parable with a closing moral flourish: while what the wild goose tries to do may be viewed as a fine altruistic act, it is completely mistaken; for the golden rule is that a tame goose never becomes a wild goose, but a wild goose can very easily become a tame one. So Kierkegaard impresses on the genius the need for self-preservation. As soon as the wild goose notices the tame geese are acquiring power over him he must be gone, away with the wild flock! Though the same rule does not apply to Christianity, which teaches what a man can *become* in life. 'Here there is hope that a tame goose may become a wild goose… Therefore, stay with them, occupied only with one, to win the individual to a transformation – but for the love of God in heaven…'[16] and he repeats his warning. Here is an exact and potent antidote to Andersen's sugar-coated pill for the spiritual sickness of their time.

External change was accompanied for Andersen by inner turmoil. During the writing of his story, from its inception as he walked round the lake at Bregentved through its many iterations in content and title ('The Story of a Duck', 'The Cygnet'), Andersen was plunged into past pain. At Gisselfeld, despite the warm embrace of the ducal family of Augustenborg, he was deeply depressed, remarking that work on

---

16. Lowrie, *A Short Life of Kierkegaard*, p. 257.

the story helped his sunken spirits. His past was never far to seek. In February 1842 he had returned from the theatre in Copenhagen to the startling discovery of a letter from his mother's daughter. His half-sister, Karen-Marie, a washerwoman in the Copenhagen slums, had found him, awakening memories of family shame and scandal; lascivious stories overheard as a boy in the spinning room, and with them the inchoate feelings they'd engendered. After a feverish night of sensuality and despair, Andersen rushed off to see his protector Jonas Collin, who immediately put a lawyer on the track of Karen-Marie's whereabouts and situation; her common-law husband was sent for and Andersen gave him four *Rigsdalers*. Karen-Marie would appear again later in the year, when he gave her a single *Rigsdaler* to leave him alone, but she looked him up once more at his hotel a year later for the last time. She would die, unbeknown to him, in 1846.

The Ugly Duckling is a fairy tale so freighted with hidden meaning that it survives the worst literary fate, from bad translation to inane filmic fantasy, hitting the heart each time with the same shudder of pity and recognition. Andersen's contemporaneous reader was unencumbered with Freudian psychology: a ball was a ball, a pine tree a pine tree. Today his story leads down many more possible avenues. *The Ugly Duckling* is no simple rags-to-riches narrative, and Andersen may be drawing attention to the absolute alienation and disenfranchisement of both the pauper and homosexual of his day; his duckling may obviously be read as metaphor for the repressed individual at last 'coming out', and at least one commentator has carefully dissected a relevant paragraph:

> When the cygnet, driven out of the poultry-yard by the other birds because he is 'different', meets up with two wild ganders, specifically stated by Andersen to be male, with whom he strikes up a friendship, the association is brought to a swift end by a couple of hunters' bullets. Although the author had covered his tracks by making the ganders a laddish pair with an eye to the maiden geese who swam on a distant swamp, he still made the point that association with one's own kind is not allowed.[17]

---

17. Alison Prince, *Hans Christian Andersen, The Fan Dancer* (London: Allison & Busby Limited, 1998), p. 211.

Speculation concerning Andersen's complex orientation and attitude to sex is far from new, and sexual agitation, alienation and agony scream from the pages of his diaries, whispers between the lines of every story. Andersen repeatedly evokes a sense of incarceration within a closed inner space, fortified by false persona and self-prohibition. It is often as difficult for the more perceptive reader to persevere through these many unconsciously revelatory pages as it is to suffer with Kierkegaard through his own. For every fan of fairy tale, there is a reader for whom it is too much: a dissenter, one whom the author alienates. Yet something powerfully irresistible in the crafted innocence, directness and disingenuous depths of Andersen's writing beckons back each new generation. In forswearing the adult world, in remaining a child celibate, he is become the arch seducer of storytelling.

Chapter 7

Into the Silence

A photograph of Regine Olsen Schlegel taken when she was 33 shows a woman of considerable character. The image dates from 1855, the year she left Copenhagen with her husband to take up his new post as governor of the Danish West Indies, a move that would fatally alter the constellation and course of Søren Kierkegaard's life. Regine appears quietly but singularly robed in dark lustrous silk with matching wide velvet trim and a cream, crocheted lace collar and front ruff. Securing the collar at her throat is a brooch of heavy knotted silver. Her glossy dark hair is parted in the middle and gathered in bunches of ringlets over her ears. She gazes gravely and unselfconsciously at the camera, front-lit, her whole demeanour composed. Yet these features convey unmistakeable spirit. She declares that she is herself; she belongs to no one else, to no social class or category. One is struck by the steady expression in her eyes, in discord with the shy half-smile. The oval face retains the soft curves of youth, but symmetry lends it classical beauty. These are not the features of a flirt, a fairy-tale princess or fickle wife, but of a thinking woman, one

Regine Olsen Schlegel, 1855.

Regine Olsen Schlegel and Søren Kierkegaard.

who has considered life and come to her own conclusions: a woman who grew up in a large family under the protection of a kind and loving father, and especially close to her sister, Cornelia. Grief, dignity and self-determination lie in the depths of these eyes. Her smile is dutiful, but she holds back, refusing surrender to the camera; rather, she in turn interrogates and repudiates its image-making. As though it is she who regards us calmly through the lens, reserving judgement – an attitude we seem to recognise from another familiar portrait. However, the astonishing extent of this likeness to that of Søren Kierkegaard becomes apparent only when the two images are juxtaposed. Evident now is the lovely unearthly transparency in both their faces; the unmistakable intensity that seems to echo back and forth between them. The intelligence of each brow, the self-containment; the humour in each expressive mouth: it seems the most obvious thing in this world and the next that they belong together.

During the period of religious crisis which culminated in Regine's engagement to another man, Kierkegaard was working prodigiously hard. He still cherished the thought of a future with her and wrote with this at the forefront of his mind. As was his wont, he hoped, he vanquished hope. He recapitulated:

> At the wedding I will have to take an oath – consequently I dare not conceal anything; and on the other hand there are things which I cannot tell her. The fact that the divine enters into marriage is my ruin. If I do not let myself be married to her I hurt her. Can an unethical relationship be defensible – in that case I begin tomorrow. It was she who asked me and that is enough. She can certainly trust me, but that is an unholy existence. Dancing on a volcano

as I do she would have to do the same as long as it lasted. And so it is humbler of me to remain quiet.[1]

No sooner were his first two *Edifying Discourses* ready for the printer on 6 May than he was off again to Berlin two days later. It is in these short lyrical pieces written to accompany *Either/Or* that Kierkegaard makes plain the vital correlation between the ethical stage and faith, and here too is his declaration of intent regarding readership. A collected edition of all *Eighteen Edifying Discourses* would appear in early August 1844, each contributory volume dedicated to his father and all carrying much the same preface. However, the first, dated 5 May 1843, includes a disclaimer regarding the author's calling 'this little book' 'discourses, not sermons' as he has no 'authority to **preach**'(*sic*) for he does not consider himself a '**teacher**'(*sic*). There follows a short trail of whimsy starting out from the 'almost romantic hope' that the book might embark upon its journey along solitary paths and, after encountering one after another mistaken reader, finally find the one individual to whom it has stretched out its arms. Then, despite weary from its search, the book waits patiently as the humblest wildflower of the forest floor… until a bird 'which I call **my** reader' suddenly swoops down, plucks and carries it off… So Kierkegaard introduces with his bold '**my**' what would henceforth be adopted as his special category, 'the individual', but of course he is here referring specifically to Regine Olsen. Closing the preface (dated November 1842) to the 'found papers of A' (the aesthete) and 'B' (the ethicist)', which form the basis of *Either/Or* and of which he purports to be 'The Editor', Kierkegaard pretends uncertainty as to what B would make of it all, suggesting he might wish to reproach K for publishing A's papers, or even to disown the content before sending the book on its way. At the end of all this 'the editor' adds his own plea: avoid the attention of the critics, he suggests, address a single reader in a quiet moment, and if encountering a lady reader advise her that she might find in these pages something worth knowing; '"so read the first something in such a way that you who have read it can be as though one who has not read it, the other in such a way that you who have read it can be as one who has not forgotten what has been

---

1. Kierkegaard, *Journals*, p. 124.

read.'"[2] As editor he would only add the wish that the book meets the reader at an auspicious moment, and that she is scrupulous in adhering to B's well-meant advice.

Thus the author begs his beloved simultaneously to read the entirety of this new work as though both aspects were of equal weight, validity and truth, while at the same time counselling her to cultivate innocent forgetfulness of having read the first part and insisting her memory not fail her regarding the second. *The Seducer's Diary* in the first volume aims precisely at disabusing Regine of any illusions regarding certain aspects of masculinity (his own), so safeguarding herself in or against her love for him. In the second part his aim is the same: he puts the case for marriage in such ideal terms as to imply its serene heights while simultaneously presenting the impossibility (for himself) of attaining them. This latter, the first part of the second volume of *Either/Or*, was written before the rest, while Kierkegaard was still engaged to Regine but despairing of his ability to realise 'the universal'. Into the mouth of Judge Williams Kierkegaard places his entire predicament – and in such a way as to break his reader's heart. The loftier this exaltation of the married state, the more palpable the writer's self-denying desolation; the more convincing his exhortation to self-realising faith, the farther it slips from reach. Here Kierkegaard states most unequivocally his concept of the paradox of faith: it is the absurd that allows a man to aspire beyond reason, to make him 'lighter than the whole world'; the same sort of faith that makes it possible to swim.

This then was the magnificent petition by which Kierkegaard hoped to persuade Regine Olsen to learn and accept his whole truth. It was tactically tenacious, yet he knew what he was doing in advocating 'neither/nor'; throughout his writing his premise is essentially a protest against the Hegelian philosophy of 'mediation'. Offered in its place is a non-directive dialectic of faith as the *only* choice. On 20 February 1843 *Either/Or* burst upon an unsuspecting world as an entirely new and innovative form of literature; in Copenhagen it caused a sensation – nothing like it, either stylistically or in content, had ever before appeared in print. It was confounding; eccentric and extreme as his narrative is, this dialectician has no apparent designs

---

2. Søren Kierkegaard, *Either/Or: A Fragment of Life*, ed. Victor Eremita, abridged, trans. and with Notes by Alastair Hannay (London: Penguin, 1992), p. 37.

upon his reader, no interest in instructing as to what is good and what evil, no ambition even to substantiate the existence of such binaries. He simply wants to bring the individual to the point at which choice acquires true and immediate meaning for him, to indicate possible passage from the 'aesthetic' into the 'ethical' stage, thus securing access to the farther shore. Here he leaves his reader exactly where he wants them: rudderless, with the prospect of swimming 'over seventy thousand fathoms without a lifebelt'. The thing, then, was to choose, but not primarily between good and evil. The thing was to choose to *will*. For with this choice good and evil are posited anew. To choose the ethical is to choose the good, but this is a purely abstract concept proposed by the ethical; it does not preclude the chooser choosing evil again, despite having once chosen good. Only in retrospect may the choice be judged, but the choice is the ethical option; only indifference is unethical. He elaborates, underlining the importance of choosing, that the crucial thing is not deliberation but 'the baptism of choice'[3] by which it passes into the ethical. Yet still the act of choosing becomes increasingly difficult as time goes on and the soul finds itself constantly arrested on one side or the other of the dilemma and must *will* to fall definitively on one side or the other for choice to be made and, most significantly, for choice to mean anything. Later in 1843, Kierkegaard underlined in a since much (mis)quoted aphorism this perpetual shuddering on the brink:

> It is perfectly true, as philosophers say, that life must be understood backwards. But they forget the other proposition, that it must be lived forwards... life can never really be understood in time simply because at no particular moment can I find the necessary resting-place from which to understand it – backwards.[4]

A small preceding journal section under the same heading, *Esquisse*, describes in the process of choice 'one little obdurate point of madness' haunting the mind of the genius which embitters and threatens him with suicide, for it turns him into 'a servile spirit, a man'.[5] He is excited by this, because it poses the possibility of liberation, if

---

3. Ibid., p. 487.
4. Kierkegaard, *Journals*, p. 127.
5. Ibid., pp. 126-127.

only he can resolve the matter of freedom. This would be simple if the truth were simple that the proper effect of ethics was to turn a talent into one's vocation. The real problem arises when considering the role of religion in the choice. For example, Kierkegaard says that had he employed his own talents optimally without this consideration, he would have turned his acuteness outwards and lived a happy life as a police spy. Religion would have remained important to him, but not paramount. By going through religion, he turned his acuteness back on himself. If so-called reality is the highest of all things he ought to have chosen differently.

The author of the mystifying new publication was gratified to hear that neither Goldschmidt of *Corsair* nor the critic Heiberg had understood a word of it; apparently the latter had said in his 'effusion'[6] about *Either/Or* that it was hard to judge the profundity of certain remarks. To which Kierkegaard drily replied that the great advantage of Heiberg *et al* was that one knew beforehand, even before one had heard what they had to say, that it would be profound because one seldom or never discovered an original thought among them. What they knew they took from Hegel – and as Hegel was always profound, so must be Prof. Heiberg. Kierkegaard was not too much concerned with the critical faculties of Copenhagen's intelligentsia. His impassioned wish was for the woman he loved to know and accept him as he truly was. In this, his most read and renowned work, he reveals himself in the only way possible for him and begs her to find a favourable moment in which to absorb the full extent of his (potential for) perdition. He knew there would be no point in his humanising elucidation of the ethical and no power in his plea for marriage without its preceding shadow, a portrayal of the extremities of an aesthetic life. The strength of his argument lay in its dichotomy, the second part of his book being the exact antithesis of the first, so that the author's paradoxical intent becomes obvious: Part Two of *Either/Or*, establishing that it is the duty of the individual to become manifest, represents the opposite of the whole implication of the first part. To emphasise this Kierkegaard carefully notes the hidden nature of the aesthetic, expressing itself, when it does so, in a 'coquettish'[7] manner: his reason for never allowing "A" to speak out

---

6. Ibid., entry 464 footnoted: In the *Intelligensblade* for March 1, 1843.
7. Ibid., p. 130. The second part of *Either/Or*, in which there is a long characterisation of 'A' by 'B' is also a description of Kierkegaard as a

openly of what lay in his heart. In becoming manifest, the individual humbles himself into the hands of God.

Writing from Berlin to his friend Boesen on 25 May, he described finishing one new work which he regarded as important, *Repetition*, written in less than a fortnight, and his pressing on immediately with the next, *Fear and Trembling*. He had been ill when he first started on this work, he wrote, that was to say his mind was expanding and presumably killing his body. Never before had he worked so hard, going out for a little while in the morning and then working straight through until mid-afternoon, by which time he could hardly see. He would then get to the restaurant somehow, leaning on his cane, but all the time dreading anyone calling out his name in case hearing it he simply fell down dead. He would then recommence working. Both new books, which Lowrie considers 'the most perfect he ever wrote',[8] were published on the same date and both dealt with his love affair – but in such a way that much of their content would be understood only by Regine. Kierkegaard was apparently satisfied with his coining of 'repetition' to supplant Platonic 'remembrance', but it was not a rubric to which he would return. The category was vividly relevant to him at the time of writing because of his hope for repetition with Regine. Lowrie in his lyrical translation of *Repetition* reveals Kierkegaard the poet, despite his disclaiming the status. In fact, he vacillated on this point, knowing the scope of imaginative play of which he was capable and occasionally allowing its free expression. Kierkegaard always used the word 'poetic' to denote writing by 'maker' or 'creator', as derived from the Greek, and placed this in the category of the religious, signifying it's not belonging in the category of the aesthetic. On arrival in Berlin, Kierkegaard had rushed to his old lodgings to test this possibility of repetition:

> Gendarmes Square is surely the most beautiful in Berlin. The theatre and the two churches make a fine appearance, especially as viewed from a window by moonlight. The recollection of it contributed much to hasten my steps. One ascends a flight of stairs in a house illuminated by gas, one opens a small door... Beyond this are two rooms exactly alike, the effect of seeing one room doubled in a mirror.

---

young man seen from the outside.
8. Lowrie, *A Short Life of Kierkegaard*, p. 157.

> The inner room is tastefully lighted. A branch candlestick stands on the writing table, beside which stands a handsome armchair covered in red velvet. The first room is not illuminated. Here the pale light of the room is blended with the stronger illumination from the inner room. One sits down upon a chair by the window, one looks out upon the great square, one sees the shadows of pedestrians hasten along the walls. Everything is transformed into a theatrical decoration. A dreamy reality looms up in the background of the soul. One feels a desire to throw on a cloak and slink along the walls with a searching glance, attentive to every sound. One does not do it, one merely sees oneself doing so in a renewed youth... One retires to the inner room and begins to work. ... Midnight is past. One extinguishes the candles, one lights a small night lamp. The moonlight triumphs unalloyed. A single shadow appears still darker, a single footstep takes a long time to disappear. The cloudless vault of heaven seems sad and meditative, as though the end of the world were past and heaven undisturbed were concerned only with itself.[9]

But, alas, repetition proves illusionary:

> My host, materialist that he was, *hatte sich verändret*, in the pregnant sense in which the Germans use this word, and as it is used in some quarters in Copenhagen, if I am correctly informed, in the sense of getting married. I wanted to wish him good fortune; but as I have not sufficient command of the German language to be able to turn a sharp corner, nor had promptly at my disposal the phrases appropriate to such an occasion, I confined myself to pantomimic motions. I laid my hand upon my heart and looked at him, while tender sympathy was legibly depicted upon my countenance. He pressed my hand. After we had thus come to an understanding with one another he proceeded to prove the aesthetic validity of marriage. In this he was

---

9. Søren Kierkegaard, *Repetition: An Essay in Experimental Psychology*, trans. with Introduction and Notes by Walter Lowrie, (Princeton, NJ: Princeton University Press, 1941), p. 55.

extraordinarily successful – just as he was formerly in proving the perfection of the bachelor life. When I am talking German I am the most compliant person in the world.[10]

The irony is cruel, inflected, unmistakable.

In *The Seducer's Diary* Kierkegaard had presented the naked truth, imagined or real, of that of which he was most deeply ashamed, and he was appalled to find it leapt upon and devoured by a general public heedless of his repeated request that they proceed to the second part of his book. He knew of course that many readers would see through the pseudonyms and identify him with the character of the seducer; he was by now used to public censure, but this did not lessen his shock when *The Seducer's Diary* quickly appeared in a self-standing English-language edition. It may safely be assumed that 'his' reader, Regine Olsen, read *Either/Or* at once and in full. That year Easter Monday fell on 16 April and at Evensong in Vor Frue Kirke during Bishop Mynster's sermon Kierkegaard thought he saw her nod at him. He was bemused, unsure whether the gesture was imploring or forgiving. In any case, he asserted in his journal, it was full of affection. He had chosen a secluded place to sit, but she discovered him anyway. He wished she had not. He was thrown by the thought that despite all his efforts she still believed in him. At this rate it would not be long before her trust in him led her to think him a hypocrite. All his efforts had been self-defeating, he despaired that a man of his inwardness and religiosity should behave as he did. Yet he felt unable to abandon his position, go on living for her alone and expose himself to more contempt? He had already lost his honour – where to now? Might he in a fit of madness do something utterly despicable to force her to believe in his badness – but what would be the good? She would only believe he was not like that before. Then a quiet but ominously attenuated observation: 'Every Monday between nine and ten she meets me. I took no steps to bring it about. She knows the road I habitually take, which way she… [page torn out of the journal][11]

Thrice more before the end of the year journal pages are removed, but after mid-summer entries are markedly changed in tone, becoming short, fragmentary, and distracted. Sometime in July

---

10. Ibid., pp. 55-56.
11. Kierkegaard *Journals*, p. 119.

Kierkegaard returned to Copenhagen to get his books printed and discovered that while he was in Berlin Regine had become engaged to her former tutor and betrothed, Johan Frederik 'Fritz' Schlegel. Completely disorientated by this turn of events in which he was so subtly and certainly implicated, Kierkegaard reacted with stunned indignation. Now he recalled how she had once greeted him in the street after her engagement but before he had heard of it; how friendly she had been, how 'ingratiating'. At the time he had not understood her attitude, given her a questioning look and a shake of his head, but now he saw that she must have been looking for his approval. Until this moment, definitive separation from Regine must have seemed to Kierkegaard almost an abstraction. As long as he had deliberately hovered over his decision, there was a chance of reversing it and retrieving her. Now suddenly that possibility was gone, and with it all illusions. The horror of this unexpected certainty was complete, disabling and diminishing. The most terrible thing that could befall a man, he wrote, was to become ridiculous in his own eyes, to discover, for example, that the content of his feelings was twaddle. It was easy enough to run that risk in human relations. You just had to believe enough in loud shouts and alarms etc. ... 'The thing is,' he told himself, 'to be strongly built'.[12]

He knew very well the limits of his strength; he was grief-stricken, and grief can quickly become petrified as rage. Resisting this, he summoned all his resources to channel renewed shock and despair, discovering in himself unsuspected reserves won since his broken engagement. Soon he was revising *Repetition* in accordance with the new status quo; not a radical rewrite, as with his usual comprehensive redrafting, but rather amending a few pertinent words and rewriting just the last ten pages. The final text is so focused and definitive as to make palpable the transmutation of emotional energy into the writing. Work had a revivifying effect on Kierkegaard and these two books accompanied by *Three Edifying Discourses*, all directed at Regine, appeared on the same day, 16 October 1843. They supplement the aesthetic works with religious commentary and for the first time in the pseudonymous writings frankly confront the Christian concept of faith. On 6 December he published a further *Four Edifying Discourses*.

---

12. Ibid., p. 128.

During his lifetime Kierkegaard referred indignantly to people paraphrasing him, insisting that what he offered was not 'results', but an approach which every subjective thinker must follow for themself. By 1843 Regine Olsen had grown into a woman who thought for herself. It seems plausible that she arrived swiftly and certainly at a radical understanding of her predicament: the one course left open to her if she wished to continue clandestinely to 'live with' the man she loved was to marry another. Only in this way could she render herself effectively invisible to an intrusive outside world and so protect and preserve her emotional and spiritual integrity. Having faced the fact that her lover was locked into his agony, she now accepted that it was beyond her capacity and his will for her to release him from it. Her love for him left her no choice but the religious. For herself she chose the cloister: a quietly pedestrian marriage to Fritz Schlegel. He was a man she liked and had known since childhood, the man whom she had betrayed and yet who would almost certainly have offered comfort in the wake of her broken engagement to his rival. Regine's decision may be seen as commensurate with Kierkegaard's choice of the religious path of penitence. She chose the silence. It must have taken enormous strength and all her courage to walk her way as she did, with grace, discretion and dignity for the many remaining years of her husband's life, for so long as she was married she would never speak of Kierkegaard. In case this construction seems conjecture, it is based on the character not only of Regine Olsen, but of Kierkegaard himself. A man of his discernment, emotional intelligence and intellect could not have fallen so passionately, comprehensively and lastingly in love with anyone he could not consider his equal.

He would recall time and again how at the moment of separation she had thrown herself on her knees before him, imploring him to allow her to live with him, be it only in a small cupboard in his house. The horror of it! How could she so demean herself? She chooses the cry, he thought; I choose the pain. As so often in extreme moments, he had resorted to levity, "'You shall become a governess!" Teasing, he had hoped for a smile; he got only her tears, a brief flash of anger, and more tears. Now he realised how monstrous had been his remark, and how hideously mistimed. How he had turned their Rubicon into farce. His beloved, his most beloved, a governess! With what strange prophetic irony have those words echoed down the century and more since they were uttered. The crisis was now reached. He had always known he should either marry her, or never marry. As usual in his agony and misjudgement of her, he felt the pain belonged only to himself. He would have a copy of each of his twin books bound exquisitely in silks and keep them for her. Finally, she would understand. He ordered a little cabinet to be made of Brazilian rosewood to his own design. It would have no shelves, as she wished to live in it. Here he would place all his souvenirs of her: the diamond cross, the scarf, the letters, some stems of lily of the valley pressed between leaves of tissue paper and her little gold ring. Here too he would deposit the twin volumes written in Berlin, revised on homecoming, and any other papers touching on the matter. At the last all would pass into her hands and she would understand.

Surely she had long understood. It was not essential in mid-nineteenth-century Denmark for a woman of Regine's social standing, or even lower, to marry for reasons of prestige or financial security. Denmark was ahead of many European countries in terms of women's rights, and already at the time of her renewed engagement Regine would have known contemporaries embarked on a career outside the home as a *købekone*, a businesswoman. City laws gave the right to a widow to inherit her late spouse's trade, although women were not granted membership of the guilds which monopolised most professions. In practice, however, it was very common for women to be given a dispensation to run a small business for their own support and very soon, in 1857, women would gain equal rights with men in commerce. That same year unmarried women attained legal majority. Regine Olsen could simply have chosen to live alone, exposed as every solitary woman is to the world's scrutiny. Here is evidence, should any more be needed, of her perspicacity not only in recognising the distinctive anonymity of the married state, but clearly perceiving its benefits despite the strictures. So the young Regine set out quietly to perfect the art attributed by the American poet James Merrill to Elizabeth Bishop: a lifelong impersonation of an ordinary woman. Meanwhile, the silent, erotically charged and secretly contrived encounters between herself and Kierkegaard continued on their daily walks. They took great care not to be noticed, each signalling and diverting their course when another pedestrian came into sight. They never missed their meeting. If a day passed without it, they managed two on the following.

* * *

Andersen spent autumn 1842 in Copenhagen working on his epic drama about the wandering Jew, Ahasverus, and Christmas holidays in a whirl of balls, amateur dramatics and readings of his work to aristocratic friends at Gisselfeld and Bregentved. The early new year found him stopping briefly at Breitenburg Castle in Holstein as guest of Count Rantzau on his way to Paris. He could hardly afford the trip, but plundered his savings, desperate to escape the Danish winter. He planned two months away. Diary entries resume on the evening of his departure, 30 January 1843, after a farewell dinner given by Jonas Collin. Vignettes from this holiday offer a quintessential glimpse of the by now so multifaceted storyteller. Underpinning his daily life is always the need for God to reassure him of eternity, and his regular prayers are as simple and direct as might be expected of a man of his background. Overlaid on insecurity and the fundamental sweetness and transparency of his personality are all the affectations, petty vanities, despair, and self-absorption accumulated in his struggle to establish his place in the world. Equally eclectic and volatile is the melange of trivia, exoticism, ornamentation, irony, terror, rage and hypochondria detailed in his diary, which he knew would one day be made public.

That he never learned the basic rules of syntax and grammar, despite having been forced to attend school into his twenties, is commented upon in the introduction to his American translators' selection from the diaries. Patricia L. Conroy admits the language posed 'problems'[13] for them. At best Andersen could be spontaneous and witty, but she also encountered carelessness, awkwardness, and ambiguity. Always intimidated by the risk of disappointing benefactors, Andersen did his best to read, learn and benefit culturally from his foreign travels, but he lacked discipline enough to apply himself to mastering the finer details of anything. In his lifetime he must have visited literally hundreds of churches and mosques, tombs, museums and galleries, as well as attending innumerable theatrical productions all over Europe. It is very possible that he accumulated a degree of expertise in areas of cultural life which he never acquired the confidence to show, even in his writings. He never numbered the pages in his diaries, which at his death were found scattered about in notebooks and on loose leaves of

---

13. Patricia L. Conroy, Translators' Preface, in Hans Christian Andersen, *Diaries*, pp. xi-xii.

paper. Material archived for the most part at the Royal Danish Library in Copenhagen remains incomplete. For Andersen these randomised jottings and drawings constituted the invaluable raw material for much of his work, most significantly, his travel writing. The fresh and engaging nature of the travelogues may be directly and ironically attributable as well to their author's comparatively unschooled mind as to his dismal view of Denmark. The instant he is away from home Andersen sheds his inhibitions and shares feelings and reactions with refreshing candour.

En route to Paris on 3 March and passing through Brussels, he remarks of the masterpieces at the museum: 'I'm not fond of Rubens – these fat, blond women with simple faces and faded clothes bore me.'[14] On 8 March, ten years after his first visit, he arrives in the French capital and makes straight for the Café du Danemark to meet up with fellow countrymen, among them Theodor Collin, the youngest son of Jonas, who will later become his *de facto* brother's travel companion and personal physician. At the café a delighted Andersen learnt that his name was well known in Paris, thanks to a French edition of his novel, *The Improvisitore*, although apparently in terrible translation, and to Xavier Marmier's biography of him in *History of Literature in Denmark and Sweden* (1839). This discovery and the rapturous welcome awaiting him from the Parisian artistic community failed, however, to set his mood fair and steady for the remainder of the trip. Awaking irascible on the morning of 20 March, he marches off to Café du Danemark to write letters, including one to Jette Wulff and another a prima-donna-ish cancellation of a *soirée* to which he had been invited that evening. An encounter with a Danish engineer over morning coffee did nothing to lift his spirits, but his next appointment was at the Hôtel de Paris to meet Alexandre Dumas, who welcomed him with open arms, 'dressed in blue-striped shirt and baggy trousers!'[15]

The great novelist and playwright soon had Andersen in transports of delight at his bohemianism, the bed being unmade and the table overflowing with papers. Dumas delighted him by relating a pleasing little name-dropping anecdote about being invited to Stockholm and St Petersburg by the king of Sweden, which satisfied Andersen's eternal preoccupation with his host's social status. Dumas then offered to

---

14. Andersen, *Diaries*, p. 127.
15. Ibid.

take him up to the Théâtre-Français that evening and introduce him to Rachel Felix. This young actress, daughter of a Jewish gypsy, was a tragedienne crowned with early fame for the emotional power of her onstage presence. On discovering that she was in fact playing a day later, Andersen took his rancour with him in search of company for the evening and found Theodor Collin. Dinner at a restaurant fell far short of the storyteller's culinary expectations, and at the theatre he was disgusted to find himself sitting behind a whole row of his countrymen who treated the performing Danish singer with contempt. It was all Andersen expected from his compatriots: the singer was one of them, so well qualified for a put-down. That was how Grahn had been treated; the more obvious her talent, the more disdain heaped upon her, especially by the culture cliques... the Danes were a cold, clammy people. He was feeling no better by next day, when he rounded off his letter to Jette Wulff, demanding to know whether or not his long-cherished and reworked play, *Agnete and the Merman*, was going to be put on in Copenhagen: this must of course, he simmered, be classed as a favour!

That evening he met Dumas in the street with his son of eighteen ('he is himself thirty-six', noted Andersen primly of Dumas) and they set off for the Théâtre-Français. Andersen had dressed in his best with his hair parted on the left, what was called at home "the king's side". Backstage, behind a screen, he found Rachel costumed in character as Phaedra, who 'received us graciously'. He found her beautiful, her face interesting, her reality far surpassing any of the portraits he'd seen of her. The tenor of her voice was lovely to him too, seductively low, and he told her how revered she was in Denmark. She refused to believe her portrait hung in every home, but promised that when she found herself in Copenhagen, she would look him up as a friend, to which he simperingly replied that she would find herself so surrounded by friendship that she would not need his. Andersen was soon pluming himself in his diary on a mildly titillating exchange with Dumas following his remarking how his heart had pounded in anticipation of speaking to Rachel. Dumas had apparently passed this on to her, and she'd replied that artists did understand each other! Captivated by Rachel's dark, androgynous looks and flouting of conventional feminine dress and behaviour, Andersen wanted to hang around in the hope of speaking more with her, but Dumas dragged him off instead to watch a street pageant at which he knew they would be in short skirts. The Frenchman, never one to deprive himself of a bawdy moment, took Andersen's arm as they walked and told him Rachel was the lover of one of Napoleon's sons. On arrival at the *tableaux vivants* the novelist went off to speak to the director, leaving Andersen stranded amidst a noisy crowd and taken aback at the sight of a stagehand flirting with one of the *figurantes* on his knee. Andersen could never quite cope with overt heterosexual display, which simultaneously repelled and fascinated him.

In Italy he had once been mortified at an inability to tear himself away from the sight of a naked young woman. Now his imagination fastened on Rachel and he could not control the effects. His passion is fully delineated in the diary, where he calls her a personification of the tragic muse who gives him cold shivers down the back, like watching a sleepwalker acting out his most secret feelings. It was typical of the immature, sexually repressed Andersen that such ethereal effusion evaporated at the slightest diversion, as revealed by the following sentence in which he casually records his neighbour in the theatre, an Englishman, remarking on the recent death of the poet Southey. The infatuation with Rachel would last until she cooled sufficiently in her response for Andersen to repeat his usual pattern of retreat into self-pity followed by plunge into a new *faux* love affair. The rest of his time in Paris he spends complaining of stomach troubles whilst gadding about having a pretty good time, frequenting museums, theatre and the opera and taking every advantage of invitations to dine and shine. On 1 April Theodor left for Rome, so Andersen spent the following day – his birthday – alone, and without any post. He decided on a visit to the handsome Heinrich Heine, who complimented him on his narrative skills and invited him to come round again, but Andersen mistrusted the poet, recalling something derogatory he had written about him ten years previously. Heine remembered it too, noting how Andersen had called on him looking like a tailor. His visitor's servility was what had made the most vivid impression on Heine, illustrated in an exchange about a big tie pin Andersen was wearing. When Heine asked him about it, Andersen had unctuously announced it was a gift which the Electress of Hessen had been gracious enough to bestow upon him. Otherwise, Andersen had struck Heine as quite spirited.

On 8 April, labile as ever, Andersen grouses about every theatre performance attended that day, and the next gushes joyously, "Was in Notre-Dame!" The following day he visited Victor Hugo, and was kept waiting for quite some time before being received by the writer in his dressing-gown and asked to lunch. His excitement at foreign environs and habits unabated, Andersen continues to hurtle from one such encounter to the next, recording every conversation, along with weather and modes of transport. After climbing the Arc de Triomphe in a violent winter storm, he wrote that it left Paris lying in a cloud of snow, the outskirts of the city lit by the sun, all in all a lovely panorama for the delectation of the tourist. Ten days after his birthday he is furious at having received only a note from Jonas Collin and accuses the family of having no care or consideration for him. The day limps on: he is not served half quickly enough in a shop, and suffers similar neglect in a restaurant, but does manage sulkily to record sending a letter home to the Privy Councillor. All this while, Jonas' son Edvard and his wife Jette are mourning the loss in early 1843 of their fifteen-year-old eldest daughter, about which Andersen mentions nothing in the way of condolence or empathy for his friend. Instead, he adopts a whining, wounded tone for a letter to Jonas complaining of Edvard's oversight, to which The Father patiently replies that Andersen is always recalled lovingly by them all, even if this is not expressed in words.

On 27 April Andersen received an invitation from Rachel to a *soirée* at her home where he was disenchanted by the absence of a single Danish author on her bookshelves, and at the theatre the following evening he heard of Copenhagen daily *Berlingske Tidende* reports that his play *Agnete and the Merman* had been hissed off the stage. Andersen vented his own venom in a continuation of his letter to Jette Wulff, declaring his hope never again to set eyes on home. They had not a jot of appreciation for the great gifts God had bestowed upon him, he fulminated, all he ever felt from Denmark were its cold draughts that chilled him to the bone. Overwhelmed with righteous indignation and self-pity, he begged his long-suffering faithful friend to pray for his death. He longed to be put out of his misery, he wrote, and knowing she fostered sisterly feeling for him in her heart he was sure that in her he would find understanding. Jette did indeed care and feel for him, but he tried her patience sorely. She was the only friend who spoke truth to him, fearlessly pointing out his failings, self-glorification and ingratitude. He was chastened by her words and they always did him good, bringing him back down to earth and into his better nature. His remorse was genuine, but chronic insecurity constantly undermined his capability for self-examination and amendment. Within a few hours of the melodramatic outburst to Jette it was forgotten and he was rejoicing in an invitation from the poet and statesman, Alphonse de Lamartine. A new round of visits, salons and farewell calls continued up until his departure from Paris on 8 May.

* * *

Andersen spent most of the summer of 1843 visiting friends on Funen and Zealand and working on the four new tales which would appear in November in *New Fairy Tales for Children*. He also fell out of love with an old flame, and in love with a new. While staying on Funen he had met a family called Bøving and discovered the wife to be none other than the former Riborg Voigt, his first romantic interest. It was thirteen years since he had seen her, he noted in his calendar, and his feeling for her lay far in the past. His new muse was the 22-year-old opera singer known as the 'Swedish Nightingale', Jenny Lind, whose childlike beauty and ethereal voice beguiled and thrilled everyone who saw her perform. She had recently arrived in Copenhagen, where she and Andersen had been fellow dinner guests of ballet master August Bournonville: 'They drank to her health and mine – in love!'[16] Jenny appealed to Andersen on all levels, including sexually. She was young and fresh, and he was beginning to feel rather middle-aged. Artistically talented and passionately interested in theatre, she was also his equal in social status, so that for once he need not feel disconcerted by a disparity. She too came from an underprivileged background and exhibited the same artless plebian prudery and insecurity as he; she too mined her experience to reinterpret, elevate and give contemporary voice to the traditional folk tales and legends of her land and people. Jenny also carried with her from her past a sort of fragile simplicity and naïvety which Andersen recognised, and her unforced naturalness allowed

Jenny Lind, (1820-1887).

---

16. Andersen, *Diaries*, p. 140.

him to relax rather than having to guess at and combat the wiles of the more sophisticated women he was used to.

Born in 1820, Jenny Lind was fifteen before her mother married her father Niclas Jonas Lind. Like Andersen she had a half-sister born illegitimately to another father. The whole family had lived in a small Stockholm apartment, along with girl boarders from the school run by her mother from home to provide the only family income while her husband was either in the debtors' prison, or drinking. The majority of Jenny's childhood had been spent with foster parents or, by another strange coincidence, in the care of a couple who ran the home where her gentle grandmother lived, and just like Andersen she had found shelter there, dancing and singing for the old ladies until at the age of nine she was discovered by Mademoiselle Lundberg, a dancer at the Royal Opera House. Such parallel histories made almost inevitable the immediate feelings of kinship that sprang up between herself and Andersen.

Jenny had not come to Copenhagen to work, but was soon introduced to Bournonville who persuaded her to stay in his household where his Swedish wife made her feel very much at home. She loved hymn singing with the many Bournonville children, and their father was soon doing all he could to persuade her onstage at the Royal Theatre. The current production was Meyerbeer's sensational *Robert le Diable*, in which Jenny had excelled when it was produced in Stockholm. Here in Denmark she could even sing the opera in Swedish, but the prospect terrified her. Bournonville found himself inviting Andersen to the house one Sunday to divert his guest with conversations about fairy tales and international theatre, subjects upon which the storyteller was an acknowledged expert. Jenny was familiar with some of Andersen's stories, and he was enchanted by her unselfconscious observation that she would never be invited to sing in Paris thanks to her potato nose. At last Andersen had found his perfect muse, and Jenny Lind an older protector; the kind, humorous, gentle man whose love of the dramatic arts matched her own. Two stories from his pen mark the storyteller's transition from old love to new: *The Sweethearts* (also translated as *The Top and the Ball*) refers wryly to Riborg's proud dismissal of Andersen's former feelings for her; and *The Nightingale* pays homage to the character and artistry of Jenny Lind as she stood on the cusp of international celebrity.

On15 August 1843 Copenhagen's new and innovative recreational facility, the Tivoli Gardens, swung open its twin-turreted wooden gates for the first time to great fanfare and the citizens of Copenhagen poured through to express their awe and amazement at the attractions. A notable exception, Søren Kierkegaard dismissed the project as a frivolous vulgarity typical of the social levelling he associated with the modern city. One of the first amusement parks in the world, the Tivoli Gardens was designed and built with the permission of Christian VIII by an army officer, Georg Carstensen, who had persuaded the king of the efficacy of a fun park in distracting people from politics. The location granted by royal consent was a roughly fifteen-acre slope of military fortifications beyond the city ramparts, and the new park included the first wooden roller-coaster, a scandalously unceremonious seven-second thrill. Carstensen's inspiration had been to imbue his Gardens with oriental exoticism; among the many attractions there remains today a four-tier, gable-and-hip-roofed Chinese pagoda, its gold and crimson splendour reflected in the waters of an ornamental lake. Soon added to his amusement park were the smartly uniformed Tivoli Boys Guard, whose musical instruction and inspiration has lasted until today among both girls and boys. The amusement park would inspire Walt Disney to design Disneyland in California, opened by the entrepreneur himself in July 1955. In its early heyday the Tivoli Gardens were hung with myriad-coloured lanterns, peacocks strutted among its flowerbeds and all was lit up at night by fireworks and gas lamps. Among the great and the good who attended the grand opening was Hans Christian Andersen, who discovered here the setting for a new story.

Inspired by Jenny and written in a 24-hour frenzy, *The Nightingale* comes complete with jaunty oriental introduction. In his own inimitable style, Andersen instructs his reader that the emperor is a Chinaman, those surrounding him are also Chinamen, and that it all happened a long time ago, which is why it's worth listening to the story before it is forgotten: the Emperor's palace is made entirely of precious porcelain, and the gardens surrounding it are most marvellous and so extensive that even the gardener does not know where they end. If you walk on forever, you come to a glorious forest that goes right down to the seashore, and in the branches of its high trees lives a Nightingale… The emperor loves the nightingale's song, and has a little mechanical bird made to look like the wild one but studded all over with precious gems. It can even sing a duet with the real bird, but this shows up the shortcomings of the mechanical toy and the real bird flies away. When the emperor falls sick he sees Death sitting on his chest wearing his golden crown and calls for the nightingale to come out of the forest to sing to him. The little grey bird flies in at the window, sings, and Death retreats, returns the emperor's insignia and floats away out of the window like a cold white mist. The emperor tells the nightingale it must stay forever, but the bird replies that it loves not the emperor's crown, but his heart, and will only return to sing to him of its own free will. At daybreak the servants enter the emperor's bedroom expecting to find his corpse, but instead are greeted by his joyous, "Good morning!"

Ever since arriving at his extraordinary denouement to *The Little Mermaid*, Andersen had been struggling with the idea of redemption. Meeting the unspoilt Jenny, with her faith in the transformative power of art, restored his trust in transcendence over untruth and death. His finding her led to four of his finest tales: *The Ugly Duckling* (completed on 7 October 1843, three weeks after Jenny's departure from Copenhagen), *The Snow Queen*, *The Fir Tree* and *The Nightingale* and among these the last stands out as a masterpiece of morality-tale telling, a parable for the newborn modern age. On 10 November Reitzel published *New Fairy Tales* in time for Christmas, omitting from the title the 'for Children' of previous editions. The collection was ecstatically received, marking Andersen's late breakthrough in his home country. The book also contains a typically mawkish story of child death and transformation, *The Angel*, which may have arisen from Edvard's recent loss and exactly chimed with Biedermeier public taste of the time. Andersen's obsession with premature death, especially his own and that of children, would follow him throughout his writing life and into old age, though without in any way translating into real-life sympathy for bereaved friends. By 18 November the first edition of 850 copies of the new book was sold out and scheduled for reprinting and Andersen was writing to Jette Wulff of its enormous success. He felt he had at last learnt how to write fairy tales. In a flood of new self-confidence, he told her that he had given up on the old stories he had himself heard as a child and instead begun relating tales that arose completely from his own imagination. The new production came from a desire to reach the adults whom he knew were reading to their young. He wanted to provide something for the adult mind, offered in the shape of a story for children. This was the birth of the ingenious and revolutionary idea the realisation of which at first caused such perturbation among the reading public.

His mood of optimistic renewal fed into the rest of Andersen's life. While he celebrated success and enjoyed the flirtation with Jenny, he received a letter from her which he interpreted for Jette as foreshadowing the singer's coming betrothal. Yet Andersen responds simply by distancing himself, telling Jette that he is really in no position to have an opinion on the matter – which was all too true. He was preparing to leave again for the Nysø estate, where Thorvaldsen had his sculpture studio and the young Baron Henrik Stampe his home. Smitten he might be with Jenny Lind, but Andersen was covering his tracks once more, meanwhile courting the 22-year-old Stampe, law student son of wealthy artistic patrons and heir to a fine house at Nysø. Andersen had first met him in 1839 and their attachment would deepen, ending only in 1844 with the latter's engagement in which the unknowing Andersen would be indelicately involved. A bas relief of the handsome young aristocrat by Thorvaldsen[17] reveals an idealised masculine torso crowned with a somewhat disgruntled looking Grecian head. Stampe and his younger brother often modelled for the sculptor as classical youths, nude or loincloth clad, sometimes on horseback. Visits to Thorvaldsen were convivial, the sculptor loved evenings entertaining and during these Andersen played centre stage, telling his stories to the assembled company. During the fortnight of this November visit Andersen and Henrik fell in love. It was intoxicating in a way romance with a woman could never be for Andersen, and there was added frisson in that he was feeling in need of erotic rejuvenation. The relationship ripened rapidly and passionate letters were soon passing between the two men. Sadly for Andersen, though, Stampe too was dissembling, using him to meet seventeen-year-old Jonna Drewsen, the eldest granddaughter of Jonas Collin and Andersen's favourite of the younger generation of Collins. Andersen had been close to Jonna ever since she was a baby, and very fond of her mother; Jonna's trust made him the perfect go-between for Stampe, and Andersen had soon outlived his usefulness.

The spring of 1844 was to bring the storyteller little joy. On 23 March a letter came from Jenny addressing Andersen as 'My Good Brother'. Bournonville had told her of Andersen's grief at her silence.

---

17. https://www.thorvaldsensmuseum.dk/soeg?q=+Hendrik+Stampe. Accessed 20 November 2024.

Gently the singer now set their relationship on a new footing, begging forgiveness and offering thanks for his gift of new fairy tales, telling him how proud she was of their friendship. She confided in him that her struggles were abating, that she was able now to accept her fate with gratitude for the grace shown her by God. She sent blessings to her 'brother' and wished him protection and farewell, signing herself his 'affectionate sister, Jenny'. Andersen habitually referred to the women in his life as 'sister' and Jenny continued to occupy his mind for years to come, despite her rejection. However, next day a new sorrow filled his heart: the sudden death of Thorvaldsen, with whom Andersen had dined as guest of Baroness Stampe at her Copenhagen home the very evening of his passing. As Andersen describes it, the company had been in high spirits. 'The powerful old man' had frolicked into the room in his dressing gown, slippers and drawers, 'swinging his Raphaelian night-cap, dancing, and joined in a chorus'.[18] Andersen sat by his side at dinner on what would be the last day of the sculptor's life. Thorvaldsen had been unusually lively, repeating some of his favourite jokes from editions of *Corsair*. He talked of returning to Italy the following summer.

It was a Sunday, and Oehlenschläger offered to stay and read something, but the sculptor wanted to go to the theatre instead to see a tragedy. He invited Andersen to accompany him, but the storyteller said he preferred to go the next night as he had no free seat for that evening. The two men shook hands and said goodbye and Andersen left the sculptor dozing in his armchair. Thorvaldsen opened his eyes, smiled and nodded at him. The next morning a waiter at the Hôtel du Nord remarked to Andersen how strange it was, Thorvaldsen dying so suddenly like that yesterday. Horrified, Andersen shrieked out his friend's name, exclaiming that he could not be dead, he had sat at dinner with him only the previous evening! The waiter reiterated that Thorvaldsen had died at the theatre that same night. Still insisting that there was some mistake and his friend must merely have been taken ill, Andersen snatched up his hat and, fighting a rising tide of anxiety, hurried to the sculptor's home. He found Thorvaldsen's body lying stretched out on the bed in a room full of strangers who on hearing the news had somehow forced their way in. The room was stuffy, the floor pooled with slush from snowy boots. Seated on the edge of the

---

18. Andersen, *My Fairy-tale Life*, p. 245.

bed was a weeping Baroness Stampe. It was beyond comprehension. Andersen stood by, paralysed with shock.

This loss, on top of Jenny's letter and cooling relations with Stampe, was too much for Andersen. He always found relational realignment disorientating, almost impossible to process and accept, and would for years continue his erotic fantasy involving Jenny and Stampe. Only decades later would he at last confide in Edvard's wife, Jette, how painful had been his being used as 'a stepladder' to be passed over by Stampe for one of the Collin family. Now he beat his customary retreat from darkness, departing on 23 May 1844 for a ten-week trip to Germany. One more blow awaited him *en route*. Calling in at Breitenburg in anticipation of comfort, he found his old friend and patron, Count Rantzau, dying. He stayed two weeks then set off via Hamburg, Hanover and Braunschweig for Weimar, a destination he had long looked forward to visiting. Mid-nineteenth century Weimar stood at the epicentre of European culture, lauded as one of its most treasured architectural gems: the German Athens. An enlightened aristocracy had patronised the arts here, establishing a Court of the Muses which attracted, nurtured and cherished the most accomplished artists of the era. Bach had been choirmaster at the court chapel; both Goethe and Schiller had lived and worked here. Andersen had always yearned to see the city. He arrived on the twenty-sixth birthday of Hereditary Grand Duke Carl Alexander, son of Grand Duke Carl Friedrich of Saxe-Weimar-Eisenbach, and the warmth generated between Andersen and the young hereditary grand duke was instantly apparent. This mutual attraction would quickly mature in all aspects, despite the young hereditary duke having recently married the Dutch Princess Sophie.

From Weimar Andersen travelled south to see old friends in Dresden, where on 4 July news reached him of an engagement between Henrik Stampe and Jonna Drewsen: 'It is a lie!' spluttered Andersen in his diary. Leipzig was his next stop, where Clara Schumann played him three of his songs set to music by her husband, Robert. In Berlin he called on Jacob Grimm without a letter of introduction and was humiliated to find the great editor of German folk tales had never heard of him. Back home in Copenhagen he received a late summer invitation from King Christian VIII and his queen to visit them on the North Frisian island of Föhr. He could not afford to go but there was obviously no refusing the royal couple, and so he set out against his will on bad roads, staying at miserable inns in impoverished marshlands where he was outraged to discover people speaking Frisian instead of German or Danish. An hour's crossing by ferry brought him to the island, which he was delighted to find looked inviting and the town well-kept. The royal couple were 'gracious' and he read them *The Top and the Ball* and *The Ugly Duckling*, the latter tale he reports as having greatly amused the king. Andersen was relieved to hear that he would be reimbursed for his trip, and called in again on the failing Count Rantzau on his way home.

Chapter 8

Shadow Boxing

Towards the end of 1843 Kierkegaard enters on a strange period of transition from the state of longing for 'repetition' with Regine to attaining new equilibrium and composure without this hope. In Berlin he makes no mention whatsoever of his current ferment of book writing; instead, journal entries indicate quietly impassioned resistance to expectations, along with contemplation of Regine's definitive absence from a henceforth unshared life. Many of the journal fragments refer to themes he will develop later in *Stages on Life's Way*. He is concerned with self-examination in these short, subdued reflections following on realisation of his lack of faith, and another recap on his relationship with his fallen father is followed by remarks on recovery from it:

> And therefore faith hopes also in this life, but be it noted, by virtue of the absurd, not by virtue of the human understanding, otherwise it is merely human wisdom, not faith.[1]
>
> Faith is therefore what the Greeks call divine folly. That is, not merely an intellectual observation but something which can be directly carried out.[2]

---

1. Kierkegaard, *Journals,* p. 122.
2. Ibid.

He continues, describing the origins of the second of six autobiographical passages in the last section of *Stages on Life's Way*. 'The Two Lepers' was written to rid himself of all this mental and spiritual darkness by reflecting on the contrast between two lepers, one of whom is gentle and does not wish to show himself to people for fear of frightening them, the other who avenges himself on others by doing so. The first leper discovers that his brothers have suffered exactly as he has; the whole family had contracted leprosy. The first autobiographical passage, 'Silent Despair', also appears in his journal. The third idea (pertaining to 'the great earthquake') concerns psychological foreboding of guilt and follows the story of David and his son, Solomon. Kierkegaard makes the mature Solomon's intelligence and sensuality consequential upon David's greatness in framing repentance ethically, while the youthful Solomon descries only his father's great agitation, awakening the son's suspicions. These in turn 'kill all energy (except in the form of imagination) and rouse the intelligence, and this combination of imagination and intelligence, where the factor of will is lacking, is really sensuality'.[3] Kierkegaard goes on with the most exquisite understanding of female susceptibility to give an example of the dialectic of guilt and innocence derived from Nebuchadnezzar; this would be included as the last autobiographical insertion in *Stages* and concerns an old voluptuary who takes some young people into a museum of Greek sculpture. One of the girls, the most innocent, senses something in the old man's expression which embarrasses and makes her blush. The old fellow notices this, she reads disapproval in his face, and at the same moment one of the young men glances her way. Her modesty is violated, she is unable to confide in anyone and becomes depressed.

These frankly autobiographical sketches, unguarded by pseudonym, leave Kierkegaard castigating himself for his self-indulgence. Literature, he writes in his journal, should not be 'a hospital for cripples' or 'the abortions of impotent thoughts, or the dregs of painful consequences'.[4] Journal entries are few while he is working on *The Concept of Dread*, which he termed 'simply a deliberation on psychological lines in the direction of the dogmatic problem of sin'[5] and attributed to Vigilius Haufniensis (the 'Watchman' of Copenhagen). This important work,

---

3. Ibid., p. 123.
4. Ibid., p. 124.
5. Lowrie, A Short Life of Kierkegaard, p. 163.

published on 17 June 1844, describes Kierkegaard's journey to faith along lines previously sketched, as he gradually and meticulously charted and recharted his relationship to his father; essentially, it treats premonition of fall occasioned by the son's suspicion of paternal fallibility. He dedicated the new book to the late Poul Møller, as though humbly to convey how his student had taken the beloved mentor's advice in abandoning an original grandiose plan to instead concentrate on identifying a core concept.

After the previous year's closing journal notes relating to *Either/Or*, 1844 opens with a remark casting light on Kierkegaard's adoption of 'repetition' as leitmotif in his uniquely unapologetic literary experiment. No other writer has so determinedly covered the same ground in subsequent works. The subject of this note is the characterisation of 'A' by 'B' in the second part of *Either/Or*, which describes Kierkegaard as a young man. Because Repetition is classed as a religious category, the youthful reprobate is stuck, one might say hoist on his own petard. He is ironical, clever, challenges the 'interesting' but does not see that he is himself immured. In Kierkegaard's terminology the first form of the interesting is to love change; the other is to wish for change, but without concomitant pain. The young man is unable to see a way out of the trap. This is shortly followed by 'A Story' called *Silent Despair* which appears in the journal in 1844 and will be included in *'Guilty?'/'Not Guilty?' Quidam's Diary*. Relating once more what happened between himself and his father, it is pithily introduced with an apocryphal story of the Anglo-Irish writer Jonathan Swift (1667-1745) who, having founded a lunatic asylum, ended up himself detained there, gazing at his own reflection in a mirror and commiserating with it as a 'poor old man'. In order to extricate himself from his own dilemma Kierkegaard had to 'venture far out' and find himself defenceless over seventy thousand fathoms. This was the radical religious project behind *Stages on Life's Way*, which reiterates *Either/Or*, employing many previously used pseudonymous characters using similar arguments, but now greatly refined and focused. Kierkegaard regarded *Either/Or* as unfinished, arrested at the 'ethical' stage. Now he was rewriting the work, consolidating it with the section he called *Quidam's Diary*, an open interrogation of his own role in his doomed love affair, and culminating in an exposition of faith. The new project would be uncompromisingly rigorous: 'Let no one understand all my talk of pathos and passion to mean that I am proclaiming any and every uncircumcised immediacy, all manner of unshaven passion.'[6] Four years later came the definition: 'Faith is a second immediacy ... immediacy after reflection'.[7]

Kierkegaard's work process is always the same; during gestation book motifs are rehearsed in the journal, while, as soon as serious work is under way it falls practically silent regarding the present project but for the odd note and laconic progress reports in letters to Boesen. An exception is his 'Report' on 'In Vino Veritas' in the first part of *Stages*, which on 27 August he describes as going badly. He continues, outlining his aim with the five speeches in 'In Vino Veritas' to offer caricatures of woman as she is commonly seen, i.e. in a false light. The Young Man only apprehends sex; Constantin Constantius discusses the spiritual aspect in the guise of faithlessness, i.e. talkativeness; Victor Eremita considers woman spiritually as sex in terms of its significance to man, i.e. that it has none. The Fashion Designer focuses on the sensual, beyond the erotic, as vanity, which Kierkegaard describes as woman's relation to woman on the basis that she does not dress to please men, but only herself. Johannes the seducer is interested only in the sensual in relation to eros. Kierkegaard had planned to write *'Guilty?'/'Not Guilty?'* immediately on reaching Berlin, as he noted on 17 May, but changed his mind with awareness that he might still marry Regine and did not wish to turn her into a fictive character evaporated into poetry. So the story was kept for *Stages*, written after she was definitively lost to him and published on 30 May 1845. Meanwhile, Kierkegaard takes regularly to his journal with cryptic commentary on himself and the world around him:

> Where feelings are concerned the same thing happens to me that happened to the Englishman who got into financial difficulties because no one could change his £100 note.[8]

> Goethe is nothing but a talented defender of solecisms. At no single point has he realised the idea; but (whether the subject is girls, love or Christianity) there is one thing he can do, talk himself out of everything.[9]

---

6. Kierkegaard, *Journals*, p. 133.
7. Kierkegaard, *Stages on Life's Way*, p. 364, fn. 1.
8. Kierkegaard, *Journals*, p. 134.
9. Ibid.

Just as no writer since Kierkegaard has used irony to more riveting effect, none has had comparable courage, stamina and distinction in reinvention. The result is stunningly cumulative. Kierkegaard himself boasted of having produced a literature within a literature (something akin to his likening his puzzling pseudonyms to Chinese boxes, one fitting inside another). In *Stages on Life's Way*, the Judge's speech at the banquet and *Quidam's Diary*, respectively, elaborate on subjects covered in *Either/Or* and other works but far outclass earlier attempts at exemplifying marriage and describing Kierkegaard's love. For example, the latter is documented in *Stages* with absolute candour rather than symbolically, offering a devastating critique of the emotional state we call 'falling in love' and an exposé of the mortal risks implied, most notably the jeopardy it poses for the beloved; here the dialectic closely mirrors that of Socrates and Phaedrus. Unflinching in self-scrutiny, Kierkegaard proves by dissecting his own ineptitude the full extent of our inability to know another person, pursuing his premise until we are fully convinced of the futility of any such attempt; no one in their right mind should try – and Kierkegaard was always in his right mind.

Revealed in the service of truth through *Quidam's Diary* is progressive terrorisation of heart by head until two creatures emerge from the text unrecognisable as their real-life counterparts. Kierkegaard's portrayal of Regine is fictive, one of an eternally naïve girl; a betrayal of reality which corresponds with one of Socrates' list of threats facing the beloved as the lover tries to turn him/her into his ideal. In thus annihilating her existential potential, the lover kills and at the same time preserves her; by pinning her down in immanence he, predatory as the lepidopterist, protects himself from the ineffable he both longs for and dreads. To further underline his thesis, Kierkegaard lays blame at Regine's door for having had the temerity to turn the erotic into the religious by calling upon him in the name of God and his father to turn back to her, and by threatening to end her life. Appended to all this literary reinvention must be recognition of the agonising self-betrayal employed, for its author had long ago recognised and loved the most sacred in Regine; her feminine being epitomised for him the pure 'immediacy' he recognised as truly 'religious' and with which his reflective nature endlessly warred. Thus the crucial turning point gave rise to this great book in which Kierkegaard unlocks, universalises and sanctifies the predicament with which she left him. *Stages on Life's Way* is accompanied by three

Discourses on Imagined Occasions, published within a day of *Stages* and each differently illuminating the moment of transition from the 'ethical' to the 'religious'.

A year earlier, on 13 June 1844, he had published the slim volume of *Philosophical Fragments*, having abandoned another tract, *De omnibus dubitandum est*, in which he attacked the followers of Descartes, a reversal occasioned by Regine's nodding to him in church which turned him against Hegelians instead. Both small books are ascribed to the pseudonym Johannes Climacus, as would be a weighty 'postscript' to the former, published in February the following year as the *Concluding Unscientific Postscript to Philosophical Fragments*. Lowrie devotes a whole page in his *Short Life of Kierkegaard* to a surmise that, in choosing this pseudonym, Kierkegaard may have been referring to the Greek monk, John Climacus, (d. c. 600) abbot of the monastery on Mount Sinai, who was famous for a treatise on ascetic mysticism, entitled *Scala Paradisi*, and so given the surname *klimax*, Greek for 'ladder'. In *De omnibus* Kierkegaard refers to a youth's ardent intellectual activity as 'a ladder of paradise'; Kierkegaard's religious works 'authored' by Anti-climacus are of course apologia for an opposite striving. The *Fragments* pretends to be 'a thought-project', discussing the themes of Christianity without using the word or referring to supposed historical events in which the religion is founded. The *Concluding Unscientific* (from the German *unwissenschaftlich*) *Postscript to Philosophical Fragments* was promised as a sequel and 'historical costume' but is in fact an overt attack on pedantic philosophers and revolt against their stripping the subject of all humour and poetry. Because it refutes the style and mannerisms of the profession, this 'simple' (Kierkegaard's working wording for the title) treatise offers the lay reader much food for thought. It is also strong medicine; Kierkegaard, master of both transparency and arcane detail, never defaults on analytical rigour. The book was complex and never became popular. Several years after publication he noted that only 60 copies had been sold and it had never been reviewed.

In mid-October 1844 Kierkegaard moved from Nørregade 230 back to the house of his birth at Nytorv 2, where he would live until its sale in 1847. His literary output between March and August had been extraordinary: nine *Edifying Discourses*, the term he used to denote a 'lay sermon' or address founded not in authority but rebellion against the 'insubordination' of disliking Christian obedience, along with *The Concept of Dread* and *Philosophical Fragments*. There were also numerous papers and journal entries, one of which records pertinently enough two remarks made to him after his father's death:

> When father died Sibbern said to me: 'Now you will never take your theological examination' and it was precisely then that I took it; if father had lived I should never have taken it. – when I broke off my engagement Peter said to me: 'Now you are lost.' And yet it is clear that if I have become something it was by that step.[10]

From 13 to 24 May, back in Berlin, Kierkegaard ruminated on recent writings and the paucity of readers for *Stages*, far fewer than for *Either/Or*. Bemoaning the fact that he was faulted for duplicity, he hit back at his detractors – they should try it for themselves – 'The bawling protestations of the direct method are infinitely easier.'[11] He had earlier sketched a mettlesome little intro to the pseudonymous writing in a journal entry under the by-line 'Nicolaus Notabene' where he relates how he came to be a writer of 'difficult' works as antidote to the anodynes offered by contemporary literature. It happened like this: one day he'd been sitting on a park bench watching the girls go by when the thought occurred that one genius after another appeared and made life, existence and eternal happiness more and more easily accessible to the populous – and what was he doing? Surely, he could make himself useful to the age by making things difficult? After all, when things get *too* easy, well, it's just no fun anymore... so henceforth, armed with this new resolve, he had applied himself bravely and happily to the task... well, not entirely happily, because it had cost him money... you obviously can't ask people to *pay* to have things made difficult... that would make life far *too* difficult... A sober addendum notes how the skipper of any ordinary vessel knows his course beforehand; but it is different with a man-of-war. So it goes with genius: most of us have a notion of what we have to do in life, but the genius, like the skipper of the warship, is far out on the deep before he gets his orders.

Kierkegaard had once likened his manifestation in the age to that of the small bird known as the storm petrel which appears when a

---

10. Ibid., p. 137.
11. Ibid., p. 143.

squall is brewing. A new tempest was now approaching which would permanently divert him from philosophy. If in *Either/Or* and *Stages on Life's Way* Kierkegaard had distilled from his own struggles two distinct types of religiousness – the ethical and the religious, on one hand, and the aesthetic speculative on the other, his new work, which he thought would be his last but in fact provided the impetus for freshly inspired output, defines these Christian categories far more sharply. The *Concluding Unscientific Postscript to Philosophical Fragments* speaks of 'religiousness A', the religion of immanence or immediacy, and 'religiousness B', that of transcendence or 'paradoxical religion'. The former passivity towards the divine births guilt and suffering but retains sight of the Godhead; the latter is characterised by so great a qualitative distance imposed between God and man that guilt is converted into 'sin', leading to so intolerable a degree of qualitative alienation from the ideal that the temporal self, unable to realise it, is cast off from the divine and feels irretrievably loosed from the law of God. Now Kierkegaard places these two religious categories in contrast to the aesthetic speculative emphasis on objectivity. In the *Fragments* 'Climacus' had questioned and dismissed a historical perspective as point of departure for an eternal consciousness; interesting as historical data might be, it could never form a basis for eternal blessedness. With his emphatic insistence on the supremacy of subjectivity in the *Postscript*, Kierkegaard now laid to rest any doubts regarding the personal appropriation of 'truth' in his definition of it as 'objective uncertainty held fast by the personal appropriation of the most passionate inwardness',[12] declaring this to be the highest truth there is for an existing individual.

He is pointing indubitably to the individual as standard of truth in the sense in which Socrates understood the Delphic maxim 'Know thyself'. The 'infinitely interested subjective thinker' stands in sharp contrast to the speculative, whose speciality is a claim to disinterested objective truth – from a safe experiential distance. In contrast to the dissociation of speculative philosophy, Kierkegaard's subjectivism rests on the intimate relationship between the individual and the world in which he *exists*. To exist does not mean simply *to be*, but to become manifest, to step forth from shared objective reality as discrete but involved individual: to stand out from (*ex-stare*) not in the sense of being separate or abstracted from, but rather in the closest

---

12. Lowrie, *A Short Life of Kierkegaard*, p. 171.

subjective relation to the background from which he emerges. Lowrie cautions: 'It is important to note the specific meaning of 'existence' and 'existential' in S.K.'s philosophy, as well as in the so-called Existential Philosophy of Jaspers and Heidegger which confessedly is derived from it.'[13]

The crucial stress here hinges on Kierkegaard's insistence that it is impossible for an individual to exist without *passion*. So that he rejects Heidegger's cool indication of what is implied by existence as *Da-sein* ('thereness') and *in-der-Welt-sein* ('being in the world'), strenuously overwriting these definitions with utilisation of the word 'interest' (*inter-est*) to denote the profoundly involving passional interaction we experience with the objective world, and which prevents our settling for a disinterestedly objective view of truth. Kierkegaard's meticulous etymological definition of his terms, in 'exist' and 'interest', take us to the core of his brilliance as writer and thinker and dispense with any doubt as to the originality and uniqueness of his insight. No subsequent 'philosophy' has been faithfully devolved from it. Central to Kierkegaard is the paradox; *knowing* and *faith* are inimical. The movement from the ethical into the religious sphere is a leap into the absurd involving all faculties, taking nothing with it but the will: a radical migration into the (as far as the ordinary consciousness is concerned paradoxically) religious sphere Kierkegaard described as lying out over a depth of 70,000 fathoms of water while still keeping faith. There can be no *proof* of faith, no compulsion, but motivations for faith are innumerable, both intellectual and passional: 'The paradoxical is S.K.'s careful and precise development of a thought which the Greeks dimly shadowed forth as the divine folly or madness (Plato's *phaedrus*).'[14] He arrives here from a position of despair. Without subjective (as opposed to abstract intellectual) doubt/despair there is no risk, without risk no faith.

When in January of the new year Kierkegaard notes delivery to the printer in mid-December 1845 of the completed manuscript of *Postscript*, some new religious epiphany seems to dawn, heralding not only disengagement from philosophy but also the demise of his

---

13. Ibid., pp. 171-172.
14. Ibid., p. 175, quoting S.K. scholar and translator, Professor David F. Swenson, 'Existential Dialectic' in *Something About Kierkegaard*, (Minneapolis: Augsburg Publishing House, 1945).

career as dreamer-up of authorial conceits. Just before Christmas an 'aesthetic annual', entitled *Gaea*, appeared in Copenhagen, a New Year's offering from P. L. Møller. Peder Ludvig Møller was an old drinking companion of Andersen and Kierkegaard's 'Unholy Alliance' student days, now a carefully anonymous editor and contributor to *Corsair*, the satirical magazine owned and edited by Meïr Aron Goldschmidt. Møller's new publication carried a sly and silly review of the *Stages*, including a passage aimed directly as personal insult at its author. On 27 December Kierkegaard responded with a vitriolic article for *The Fatherland*, entitled *The Activity of a Peripatetic Aesthete and How He Paid for the Banquet* which, referencing a legendary feast shared in the dim and distant past by the Unholy Alliance, pilloried Møller, exposing his duplicitous literary character and effectively ruining his career. Kierkegaard had recently had a brush or two with Goldschmidt, a man for whom he had a personal liking, including one earlier in the year when amidst fulsome praise for Kierkegaard Goldschmidt had declared 'Victor Eremita' of *Either/Or* to be 'deathless'. Kierkegaard, unappreciative of having his pseudonymous editor lauded in the pages of the *Corsair*, and thus primed for confrontation, now published under his own name a satirical *Prayer for the Corsair* in which he lamented never having had the honour of getting into the magazine. How hard it was to be singled out in Danish literature as the only one (given all the pseudonyms were one) who was not abused there!... and yet he had indeed already been included, for *ubi spiritus, ibi ecclesia* [where the spirit is, there is the church]– *ubi P.L. Møller, ibi the Corsair*.

Association with *Corsair* was taboo among the lettered of Copenhagen. Dirt digging made for delicious coffeeshop reading, of course, but its authors needed to mind their Ps&Qs to avoid serious censure among the higher echelons of Copenhagen society. Every writer for *Corsair* knew the risks and scrupulously guarded their own reputation. Møller, for one, had a lot to lose. He had long nurtured an ambition to succeed Oehlenschläger as professor of aesthetics at the University of Copenhagen, and with a single blow Kierkegaard had now vanquished his hopes. Møller knew his foe of old, and that he was no match for him. Goldschmidt, a huge admirer of Kierkegaard, was soon informing him that Møller had been 'annihilated'. The only route left open to the discredited was a dignified exit, and Møller took it, writing a letter to *The Fatherland* described by Kierkegaard as 'deferential', and duly vanishing from the scene: 'I do not know whither he went,' remarked Kierkegaard witheringly, 'but from that moment, according to the report of my barber, there was a busy time on the dance-floor of literary despicableness in the office of the *Corsair*.'[15]

The spat continued in Møller's absence but in just as unedifying a tone, with Goldschmidt approaching Kierkegaard in the hope that the latter might plead for a halt to it all. Alien as it was to Kierkegaard to go on bended knee before any but his God, he instead continued for the whole two months preceding publication of the *Postscript* to deny any connection with the pseudonyms and so distance himself from the jibes. Instead, he replied to Goldschmidt in a piece for *The Fatherland* 'by Father Taciturnus', one of his 'authors' from *Stages* and the *Postscript*. This tired but sustained pretence resulted in a *Corsair* article headlined, 'How the Peripatetic Philosopher Found the Peripatetic Virtual Editor of the Corsair', which was accompanied by a couple of cartoon caricatures, but otherwise not unduly offensive. Goldschmidt's vanity as well as his reverence for Kierkegaard required him to maintain their discourse. The editor was alone among the distinguished men of Copenhagen in never having treated Kierkegaard with condescension. Kierkegaard had, on the other hand, been encouraged by many prominent figures to challenge and bring down the *Corsair* on the grounds that he was the only one independent enough to succeed. All voiced outrage at the magazine, whose editors paid exorbitant slush money to domestic staff willing to betray the secrets of grand households, while hiding from libel law behind various literary devices and disguises. Every cultured man in Copenhagen publicly frowned on the *Corsair* whilst privately sniggering at it behind their newspaper; Goldschmidt had built a huge circulation and preened himself on championing the ordinary man at the cost of the mighty.

The '*Corsair* affair' was drawing to a close as infamously as it had begun, with neither Goldschmidt or Kierkegaard capable of capitulating or making an honest approach to the other, and it has gone down in Danish literary history as its shabbiest and most divisive episode. Meanwhile, Kierkegaard proofread *Postscript* and faced finally casting off his aliases, publishing under his own name a review of an anonymous novel, *Two Ages*, only later revealed to have

---

15. Ibid., p. 177.

been written by Thomasine Christine Gyllembourg-Ehrensvärd.[16] This review, of which he later professed himself inordinately proud (as further proof that preoccupation with the religious need not preclude involvement with the aesthetic), provided opportunity for Kierkegaard to deliver an excoriating critique of the passionless society in which he found himself; a modern age in which the individual counted for nothing and must be levelled and lost in the crowd, where no individualised human quality mattered which could not be numerically analysed and where the very standard of truth had become the mathematical. Most presciently, he noted: 'In the end physics will displace ethics just as metaphysics displaced theology. This modern statistical view of ethics contributes towards that.'[17] Such preoccupation with counting and prioritising the populous ran completely counter to Kierkegaard's insistence on the category of paradox. He wanted the world to understand that there was a limit to 'understanding'. Pitting himself against the whole of Enlightenment thinking, he tried to point out the failing of human understanding to appreciate paradox; how vulgarly the intellect had occupied itself with nothing but understanding, whereas had it only taken the trouble to understand itself it would simply have had to posit the paradox. The paradox, he stated, was not a concession but a category, 'an ontological definition which expresses the relation between an existing cognitive spirit and eternal truth.'[18]

With publication of the *Postscript* on 27 February and pseudonyms publicly forsworn, Kierkegaard continued to absorb the consequences of the hideous privilege he had invoked by asking to appear in the *Corsair*. He persevered in withstanding much of the ensuing abuse, but Goldschmidt did not know when to stop. His campaign of persecution would continue in successive editions for almost a year, while his insinuations of Kierkegaard's contempt for the poorer classes were so far from true as to be ludicrous. Kierkegaard had always scrupulously avoided reclusion and the ivory-tower, knowing that to withdraw into a small clique, as Hegel and others did, was to become thought of as 'something'. He knew his inner yearning towards the good made him elitist, a sort of moral aristocrat, but equally he did not wish in

---

16. Unbeknownst to Kierkegaard, Gyllembourg-Ehrensvärd was mother of the critic Johan Ludvig Heiberg.
17. Kierkegaard, *Journals*, p. 151.
18. Ibid., p. 194.

any way to elevate himself above others, or insinuate that aspiration. He had always felt most at home in the street, where 'there is danger and opposition. I refuse to live in a cowardly, soft and superior way.'[19] So now as ever Kierkegaard hid his wounds and begged for more, believing public vilification in *Corsair* served his own cause. He waited in vain for the editors of *The Fatherland* to come to his defence, as they, ironically, in turn awaited his advice on how to give it. He had scribbled A First and Last Explanation on a page of the original manuscript of *Postscript* and sent it to the printer at the very last moment to prevent it from lying about the printer's office looking as though it had been written during actual typesetting. Excruciatingly aware of all the present gossip and vulgarity surrounding his every move, he wanted truth on his side, while another voice in his head rehearsed the futility of trying to counteract public opinion.

At no other point in this sad history does so acute a sense of the perversity of small-town society impress itself upon the reader. In his desperate attempt to retain control of his own narrative Kierkegaard agonised over the timing of his revelation. By 7 February he had decided to abandon authorship altogether and prepare himself for holy orders. In this, as in all things, Kierkegaard was true to himself; authorship was for him entirely and absolutely, or not at all. So rather than begin on a new project, his usual habit, while proofreading *Postscript* he confined extramural activities to writing the book review. Meanwhile, Goldschmidt made sure that almost every edition of his magazine carried taunts and ridicule of Kierkegaard, from his books to his gait and the cut of his trousers. Encountering his prey on the street the editor would engage him in amicable conversation, complimenting Kierkegaard on the influence he had had on him, his skill in comic composition etc. Shortly after publication of *Postscript* and acknowledgment of the pseudonyms, however, Goldschmidt reported how Kierkegaard passed him by with a proud and furious glance, not wishing to greet or be greeted. Shocked into submission, the editor confessed that the effect of that glance was to reveal the moral superiority of Kierkegaard's position, which Goldschmidt had been neither able or willing to admit, despite having suspected it. Now, feeling accused and crushed, he saw that while *Corsair* may have triumphed, his personal victory had been Pyrrhic. The realisation

---

19. Ibid., p. 175.

recalibrated reality, reinstating Goldschmidt's innate dignity and pride. Before he had completed his walk home the decision was all but made to resign his editorship; on 2 October 1846 he did so, and the *Corsair* folded.

It was too late for Kierkegaard; the damage was already done. He had become a laughing stock and there was no escaping the humiliation. Copenhagen was full of street urchins smirking at the asymmetry of his trouser legs or running after his carriage with taunts. He found himself the butt of a student comedy production lampooning him, while the author protested that no one should take personal offence and Kierkegaard agreed, so long as the audience remained students. Of course, it did not, the piece was soon touring the provinces and further afield. In Norway, a newspaper openly called the character representing him 'Søren Kierkegaard', so that his Christian name became a source of hilarity throughout Scandinavia and no one would call their newborn son "Søren". The situation became so intolerable that even self-parody failed him, metamorphosing into pathos on the page: how wrong he had been ever to think that he might do something for an individual through his literary efforts – the sheer conceit of it! – obviously, the only thing they wanted from him was his trousers and all that was required of him was that he should wear them and at some point bequeath them to the city… he found himself brought to the brink once more, fearing for his sanity.

Only in extremis did Kierkegaard ever consult his doctor. Now he asked the physician whether he considered that in his case it might be possible for there to be resolution of the split between physical and psychological so that his patient might realise the universal. The doctor doubted it. Kierkegaard enquired whether force of will (his own, the scope of which the doctor had some idea) might persuade the mind to reform and realign the disproportion? The doctor thought probably not and advised strongly against any such effort for fear of creating even more mental disorder. So Kierkegaard knew where he stood. He made his decision. Having always interpreted his terrible suffering as his 'thorn in the flesh', his limitation and the cross he had to bear, he would regard it as the price he owed the Almighty for intellectual power unequalled in his generation. This was no cause for pride. He knew himself already ground to dust; his gift had become a bitter enough pill, and a daily humiliation. His 'gift' was a capacity for perception, nothing more. No revelation had led to it, nothing of the kind. He was simply tasked with stressing the universal in an age which wanted none of it; of making the universal clear and accessible to all others capable of realising it but who are led astray by the age to chase after 'the unusual and extraordinary'.[20]

In early May, Kierkegaard left for a fourth stay in Berlin. Here he acquired books by Adolph Peter Adler, a theologian and pastor on the Danish Island of Bornholm with whom he had been close friends at school in Copenhagen some twenty years before. His current interest in Adler stemmed from the pastor's ideas on revelation, personally experienced, expounded and then disavowed, and from his old schoolfriend's confusion over the categories of inspiration and genius. This reading would feed into Kierkegaard's writing *The Book on Adler*, left unfinished at his death and published posthumously in 1872. Far from marking a farewell to Kierkegaard's authorship, publication of the *Postscript* was proving a turning point and precursor to a whole new flowering of literary effort and output. He was back in charge of himself:

> Andersen can tell the story of *The Shoes of Fortune* [sic; also published as *The Galoshes of Fortune*] – but I can tell the story of the shoes that pinch, or rather I could tell it, but just because I will not tell it but treasure it in silence, I can tell a very different story.[21]

* * *

In the late summer of 1844 Andersen travelled from Föhr to Augustenborg Castle for a three-week stay with Duke Christian August. Here he befriended both the duke and his brother, Prince Frederik of Nør. Politically insouciant as ever, the storyteller was turning a deaf ear to anti-Danish feeling already surfacing four years in advance of the 1848 Schleswig-Holstein insurrection which would result in Danish loss of those territories and in which his new friends would play a prominent part. Once back in Copenhagen in September 1844 he finalised in time for pre-Christmas publication the second instalment of *New Fairy Tales*, to include his two new masterpieces, *The Fir Tree* and *The Snow Queen*. A third instalment of *Tales* would appear in April the following year. *The Snow Queen*

---

20. Kierkegaard, *Journals*, p. 170.
21. Ibid., p. 199. The story referred to is the one in which S.K. appears caricatured as the parrot.

was written quickly and without his usual agonising. The plot is complex, featuring Andersen's usual theme of Manichean polarity, but deepening its darkness with the image of the Devil himself casting down to earth a mirror the shattered shards of which taint beauty wherever they fall. A splinter becomes implanted in the eye of little Kay, a boy-child hero drawn in Andersen's idealised childhood self-image. The cruel tale features bewitchment by a beautiful seductive older woman who imprisons the boy body and soul, subjecting him to hideous psychological trial until he is eventually rescued by his childhood sweetheart, Gerda. This redemptive act is closely associated with innocence in a rooftop garden modelled on that which Andersen's mother planted with pots of herbs and flowers at their Odense cottage.

This fairy tale shows childhood love once more triumphing over adult perversity, sentiment over emotional realism; tortured defencelessness is the central theme. The narrative flows effortlessly, peerless, haunting, archetypal, and in ethos disturbingly predictive of our present-day secular technocracy: the Snow Queen a remorseless rationalist who challenges Kay to form letters of ice into the word 'Eternity' to buy his freedom and a new pair of skates. Hour after hour he devises every kind of ingenious code, figures of increasing complexity and sophistication which strike him as highly significant – but try as he may, he cannot formulate the desired word. *The Fir Tree* is another, more modest self-portrait by Andersen, a depiction of the individual for whom the grass is always greener on the other side of the fence. As it happened, Andersen's restlessness and wanderlust was somewhat subdued by 1845, when he was riding the crest of a wave both at home and abroad. The king increased his allowance, so that he felt more financially secure, and his safely long-distance involvements with Stampe and Jenny felt like sound emotional ground beneath his feet.

At the end of October 1845 he set off for his third major European tour. Jenny had reappeared in Copenhagen the month before, herself buoyed up on professional success. Her presence and celebrity worked like an aphrodisiac on Andersen, who followed her about, dancing attendance right up until her departure for Berlin, whereupon he left home on his usual circuitous route for the same destination. He arrived on 19 December in the hope of a reunion with her at Christmas. As their itineraries intersected and Andersen stalked her, appearing at concerts and visiting her apartment, so Jenny's attitude towards him cooled. On Christmas Eve Andersen saw Jacob Grimm, who on first meeting had offended the Danish writer by failing to recognise him. Next day, however, he was reading his fairy tales at a party attended by Jacob's brother Wilhelm, whom he was pleased to find a far more attentive and likable person. By New Year's Eve Andersen was back in Jenny's orbit, helping her choose ribbons for her unaccompanied attendance at the British ambassador's Ball. Then, still shadowing his muse, he made his way from Berlin to Weimar, looking forward to meeting her again when she arrived there at the end of the month. Once in Weimar Andersen surrendered to the mutual attraction between himself and the young Hereditary Grand Duke, who the previous year had welcomed him to court like a reincarnated Goethe. It was a highly charged reunion. Andersen was swept off his feet by the weepy, effeminate Carl Alexander, whose unashamedly physical demonstrations of affection were completely impossible to rebuff. The couple were soon seeking out quiet corners for cosy *tête-à-têtes* and openly cuddling in public. The gentle young hereditary duke was unpretentious and childlike in his intellectual curiosity as in his enthusiasm for the welfare of Weimar: a perfect emotional match for Andersen. It was the sort of reciprocity of which he had been starved, and such a heady change in his relationships with men that it moderated his feelings for Jenny. In any case, the pair were unabashed in assimilating their respective female loves into the circle of their own, and Jenny's arrival at the end of January was another occasion for rapturous celebration, her singing earning her a storm of hugs and kisses from the Hereditary Grand Duchess Sophie.

As his time in Weimar wore on, however, even Andersen became aware of the extreme fragility of the world he had discovered there and that the idyll could not last. On 14 September, as the drums began to sound, he wrote apprehensively to Carl Alexander that he would do everything to be worthy of him. Within months, Prussia and Denmark were at war, a conflict from which Andersen's Weimar would never recover. His loyalties now came under unbearable strain. In January he had been proudly knighted by Friedrich Wilhelm IV, King of Prussia, and in the wake of another visit to Weimar in 1847 he would again write nervously to Carl Alexander that he loved him as a man could love only the noblest and the best. Setting off from the city in February 1846 he embarked on nothing less than a triumphal tour of German-speaking Europe, passing through Jena on his way to Leipzig, the city of bookselling. Here he discovered his reputation had preceded him and, whereas German translations of his works had all previously been pirated, publishers were now queuing up to print them. Having signed with Danish-born Carl Berendt Lorck on 19 February for a collected edition with accompanying autobiographical sketch, he immediately began to fret over what to include in the new volume. His worst worry of all was knowing that the autobiography would have to be a good deal better than any attempt he had made at it so far. His contract for the collected edition was 300 Prussian *thaler*, plus another 200 *thaler* for the autobiography, a most serious commission.

Andersen had written only one story, *The Little Match Girl*, since October and despite his preference for not writing while travelling he knew he now needed to work urgently on the new project. The frontispiece for the collected edition was to be a portrait by the German painter and miniaturist August Grahl, for which Andersen began sitting in Dresden. The painting, Grahl's most famous work, now hangs at the Andersen Museum in Odense and shows the subject at forty, an elusive chimera of a man escaping the world with an enigmatic sidelong glance. It is an extraordinarily tranquil canvas: rather than the large nose, Andersen's high forehead dominates the oval face, once again in portraiture conveying the writer's intelligence. The expression in the eyes is abstracted, gentle. A soft smile plays around the lips, we see a charmingly cleft chin. Grahl has captured the childlike quality of his subject, as well as bequeathing to future generations an enchanting portrayal of masculine femininity. Andersen wears his hair bobbed, tucked behind his ears; a loosely knotted black silk cravat at the rounded wing collar of his shirt. His smile is distant, otherworldly but placatory, that of the quintessential Romantic poet.

Adulation followed him everywhere: in Leipzig Mendelssohn had teased and fussed over him; in Dresden he read to the king of Saxony; in Vienna to Archduchess Sophia and her son, the future emperor, Franz Joseph. The limelight was a drug; the minute it dimmed Andersen's mood sank into despondency and chagrin. To Edvard he wrote from his Dresden hotel room of his triumphs, whinging that such appreciation never surrounded him at home. Edvard, again suffering terrible grief at having lost a second child, this time at only four years old, replied that the Danes were probably more honest in their liking for Andersen's fairy tales than the Germans, and Andersen's mood was simply due to missing Weimar and imagining a distorted picture of home. By now Edvard took no nonsense from his friend but offered generosity as best he could in the light of his own personal circumstances and familiarity with

Andersen's personality. Extreme self-absorption and complexity demanded too much of even the most faithful and long-term of Andersen's friendships, and even Jonas Collin nowadays shrugged off his ward's overblown namedropping and whines, enquiring when he was actually going to write something. His diary reveals a certain degree of insight on Andersen's part regarding the lonely place he now occupied in the world, but this modicum of self-awareness, which might help mitigate such a plight, continued to be outweighed and negated by chronic insecurity. Bored by a Rome modernised since his previous visit thirteen years before, and suffering from stomach cramps and infantile self-pity he wrote back to Edvard on 26 April bitchily recalling their long-ago contretemps over mode of address: 'One day when I am made *Etatsraad* [councillor of state] and have a son, he shall refuse to say "Du" to your son Jonas if you are still only a *Justitsraad* [councillor of Justice].'[22] He stuck it out in Rome for two months and on 1 May left for Naples.

Andersen wanted a far more polished autobiographical account for his German publisher Lorck than was his first attempt at memoir, *The Book of My Life*. He had begun to examine his own chameleon-like behaviour and make acceptable sense of it for himself. The result is the saccharine synthesis of fact and fantasy constituting what he considered the definitive iteration of his autobiography, *The Fairy Tale of My Life*. Memoir always meant navigating perilous territory. Andersen loved Naples, which was associated for him with creativity and sensuality, but now the city was hit by a heatwave, temperatures reaching as high as a hundred degrees Fahrenheit, and he was pretty much confined to his lodgings. Isolated and unwell, on 9 June he began a macabre new tale with the working title, 'The Story of My Shadow'. Although he had begun venturing out on his familiar round of visits and museums, he could hardly cope with the exertion. The heat was intolerable, encouraging his hypochondria, and then one evening at dinner someone said there was cholera in Naples, panicking Andersen with the thought of quarantine... although he later recorded having eaten extraordinarily well! He had managed to read *The Ugly Duckling* to the assembled company but felt his strength ebbing and dreaded being asked for another story. Back at his lodgings and on the point of fainting, he immediately retired to bed with the balcony doors open and just a sheet over him. By mid-June it was 79 degrees Fahrenheit.

---

22. Wullschläger, *Hans Christian Andersen*, pp. 274.

He managed to deliver his new autobiographical sketch to Lorck on 19 June and prepared for departure, worrying about a debilitating pain in his 'rear end', which threatened to delay and lose him the ticket money he had paid for the steamer to Marseilles. Jonna Drewson and Henrik Stampe – he heard from home – had celebrated their wedding. Abandoning plans for onward travel through the heatwave to Spain, he headed home via France, Switzerland and Germany. But Naples, with its nightmarish temperatures, cacophony, fever and enervation, had worked subterraneously on Andersen to generate the most mature and psychologically sophisticated of his stories so far. Ten years before the birth of Freud and nearly three decades in advance of Carl Jung, an afflicted Andersen had abandoned himself to his unconscious to shape *The Shadow*:

> ...it was to the hot countries that a learned man out of the cold regions had come. He thought he could roam about there just as he had been accustomed to do at home; but he soon altered his opinion. He and all sensible people had to remain at home, where the window-shutters and doors were shut all day long, and it looked as if all the inmates were asleep or had gone out. The narrow street with its high houses in which he lived was, however, built in such a way that it was exposed to the sun from morning till night; it was simply unbearable! – The learned man from the cold countries, who was young and clever, felt as if he were sitting in a white-hot oven. This exhausted him and he became quite thin; even his shadow shrank and became much smaller than it was at home. Not until evening when the sun had set did these two begin to recover. It was a real pleasure to see. As soon as the candle was brought into the room, the shadow stretched itself up the wall, and even along the ceiling, getting taller and taller until it regained its strength.[23]

Going out onto the balcony, the learned man sees the street alive with people enjoying the cool of evening beneath new-born stars.

---

23. Hans Christian Andersen, *It's Perfectly True! and Other Stories*, trans. by Paul Leyssac, original illustrations by Vilhelm Pedersen (London: Macmillan & Co. Ltd, 1937), pp. 222-223.

Only the house opposite his shows no sign of life. Yet flowers bloom on that balcony, and through the open door comes the sound of piano music. One night he sees radiance emanating from there and standing among the shining flowers a beautiful slender maiden. When his shadow stretches that way, he asks it to go inside the apartment and report back on what it finds. Next day in the late morning when he goes out his shadow is gone, and he recalls with misgiving an old story about a man without a shadow. After a few days he is relieved to notice that it has appeared again; the shadow's root has evidently remained. Once back home he writes books about what is true in the world, what is good, and what is beautiful. Many years pass, and one evening there is a tapping at the door and the learned man finds there an extraordinarily thin person, very well-dressed, important and distinguished looking. Thus the old shadow keeps returning and takes more and more control of its former master. It tells him that in the house opposite theirs in Naples it had discovered the Muse of Poetry! After three weeks in her company the shadow had read all that had ever been written in poetry or prose; it had seen everything and now knew everything: 'And, moreover, I learnt to understand my innermost nature, my ego.'[24] The learned man, confounded, outwitted and more and more compliant, allows the shadow to overpower him, retaining only his intellect, which the shadow knows how to exploit. Their roles are now completely reversed. At last, during their travels in a foreign land, the masterful shadow convinces a princess to marry it, which she agrees to do, given what an asset to the throne will be a man with such a brilliant shadow; at this the learned man finally rebels, threatening the shadow with telling her the truth, but people now believe only what the shadow says, for it is about the marry the princess. The learned man is condemned. The wedding day dawns and with jubilation the newly married couple step out onto the balcony: 'But the learned man heard nothing of all this, for he had already been put out of the way.'[25]

It was a spinechilling finale to the most consummate of all its author's attempts at autobiography.

---

24. In use by 1707 in metaphysics, 'the self; that which feels, acts, or thinks', from the Latin *ego*, 'I' (cognate with Old English *ic*); its use is implied in 'egoity': https://www.etymonline.com/word/egoist.
25. Andersen, *It's Perfectly True! and Other Stories*, p. 240.

Chapter 9

Esquisse

Geopolitical events of the years 1845 to 1848 would shape the final form of both these men's lives and seal their respective fate just as certainly as Leonardo's many anatomical studies and cartoons culminated in *Mona Lisa*'s definitive smile. In May 1847 Kierkegaard was beset with practical worries, all trumped by his astonishment at having survived so long. His entire life having been overshadowed by the macabre superstition of premature death, so often substantiated in the family, he now found himself outliving all his siblings but one, Peter the priest. The youngest Kierkegaard had never enjoyed robust health, always expected to die young and lived accordingly. What money he had he spent freely in support of his writing life. The older he got, the harder he worked, and even as resources ran out it did not occur to him to pull in his horns. It is hard, perhaps, to imagine the impoverished aestheticism of this life led by a privileged citizen of one of the wealthiest lands of nineteenth-century Europe. Kierkegaard was never poor in a monetary sense, but rather in the monastic – a man utterly devoted to his vocation but living without shelter of the monastery and not even deserving as medicant of public alms. Exposed to the point of self-immolation in his insistence on remaining out in the world, even his vital need to keep body and soul together with good food and wine became a target for those accusing him of self-indulgence. Kierkegaard had always understood the gravity of life, the light and weight that must be borne; known his life, however long, would feel too short for its task and that so intense an existence demanded sustenance. He could not work at the pace he did and live in hunger and squalor, so made sure to secure the necessities. For him money meant next to nothing, it simply served an end. Often exhausted to the point of collapse, everyday practicalities defeated him, and he depended on keeping a secretary and a servant. Carriage rides out into the country were expensive, but they were his only spiritual consolation. It was a minimal existence facilitating an extraordinarily sustained regime of self-disciple and literary output. In the end some strange grace intervened, and he was returning home from the bank with the last of his money when he fell on the street and was carried, paralysed, to the hospital to die.

Writing to Peter on 5 May, the younger brother in a tone of cautious celebration at his thirty-fifth birthday had belatedly expressed how amazed he had been at his brother having managed to reach the age of thirty-four, the age beyond which no Kierkegaard could live. He proceeded to outline his plans for selling the house at Nytorv 2, asking his brother to agree to this and meet soon to finalise arrangements. It was Kierkegaard's plan to start living on his share of the proceeds, minus the third he still owed his brother in mortgage, and for the rest subsist on book sales. As things turned out, much of the considerable profit made on the eventual house sale was lost due to wartime inflation. In August 1847 he sold the rights on all his outstanding works to his publisher, Reitzel, and henceforth lived on royalties. He wanted a second edition of *Either/Or* but failed to get the price he was asking, so this was delayed for another year when, to his embarrassment, shortage of money forced him to accept a smaller sum. It was an uncomfortable transaction in any case, as his focus was by now on religious writing and republication of aesthetic work felt to him anachronistic. Then, at the very moment when he had to move house and most needed help, his faithful servant Anders was called up for military service.

Once more he was faced with the sort of social and domestic crisis for which he was least fitted, and so unequivocally reacquainted with the fact. Having failed repeatedly to meet the basic criteria for social adaptation or cope in any way with 'normal' life, he had also proved incapable of choosing the only career for which he was trained. The debate he had conducted with himself for years regarding 'a country living' continued. The priesthood was the only paid occupation for which he was qualified, and the notion of life spent in service to a rural parish appealed on several levels, not least the prospect it offered of peace and quiet. The idea of becoming a nobody where nobody knew him was attractive, but not the thought of possible humiliation and disgrace should his shameful secret past be discovered. He remembered how often he had approached Bishop Mynster in vain about the availability of a vacant rural parish, convinced the cleric would be glad to get rid of him. How he had dropped hints about teaching at the Pastoral Seminary and been repeatedly ignored or rebuffed. On these occasions Mynster had proved himself a master of evasion and even cruelty, once sarcastically suggesting Kierkegaard found a seminary of his own. So, time and again, consideration of an alternative to writing had resulted in his return to it. On 2 August he finished *Works of Love*, fair copy and all, having contemplated and discarded the idea of another distracting trip to Berlin. Now he was glad he had resisted temptation, for he felt something within him which might mean metamorphosis and to go away now would be 'to procure an abortion.'[1] He wanted to *'really think out the idea of my melancholy together with God here and now.*[2] He realised that he had been using his intellectual work to shield himself against melancholy, and now there dawned in him a conviction that God forgot in forgiveness whatever guilt there was, so that he had himself to try to forget it. Not in distraction, not at a distance, but in God. He must therefore teach himself in thinking about God to think his guilt forgotten, and so dare to himself forget it in forgiveness.

At this moment Kierkegaard was sidetracked by learning in conversation with a friend who was also an ardent reader of Hamann that the Lutheran post-Kantian philosopher had never married his 'wife' but had dared to live with her without sacrament as his concubine. This revelation, which would once have been of huge significance to Kierkegaard, now produced the realisation that although he had thought of the same thing at the time it would not have been a solution for his own situation with Regine. In their case, he felt, the redundancy of any actual marriage ceremony was clear from the outset. Their 'marriage' had never depended on church sanction; it existed eternally in the realm of the religious. This later construction contradicts his concern for the supremacy of truth-telling in relation to 'the solemn vow' required by the wedding sacrament, the reason he gave at the time for his inability to marry (or pursue ordination). Had a marriage ceremony been truly immaterial to him then, and

---

1. Kierkegaard, *Journals*, p.128.
2. Ibid.

had Regine agreed, there would appear to have been no objection but social stigma to their unwed cohabitation; apart, that is, from the overarching moral censure pronounced by his religious conscience on *any* duplicity in *any* relations with Regine.

It was a moment of profound reflection and realignment, and meanwhile the unresolved practicalities of his situation remained taxing. He did, though, allow himself the small distraction of a visit to the king. While Andersen revelled in such familiarity, Kierkegaard was extremely circumspect, not even recording such visits until several years later. He had no intention of currying royal favour, but such contact provided welcome respite from the scorn, vulgarity and treachery of aristocratic detractors who were thus given a little something of substance to chew on along with their smirking at his sartorial shortcomings. He found the king bright, well-informed, but butterfly brained. Christian VIII, for his part, loved Kierkegaard's company and tried to persuade him to visit more often. The latter resisted, protective of his independence and afraid the king would try to 'own' or favour him with the offer of a stipend in recognition of support for the monarchy. Kierkegaard did not indulge in flattery. He had no compunction in telling the king that he was in service to a higher power and was very frank and relaxed in his company. On one occasion he shared with Christian VIII some blunt reflections on what befitted a monarch: in the first instance, he had better be ugly, deaf and blind, or at least pretend to be, as this curtails a lot of difficulties. For example, intemperate or rash speechifying inflated by the fact of it being addressed to the King, might best be dealt with by an "Excuse me?" indicating that His Majesty has not quite heard.

Less amusing diversion was provided by Kierkegaard's current intellectual preoccupation with Adolph Peter Adler (1812-1869), the Danish clergyman whose works he had procured in Berlin and been reading and exploring since the previous year. He admired the deposed clergyman as a confused genius and perhaps also in his plight as an outcast from the Church. Kierkegaard and Adler had been at the same elite Copenhagen secondary school for four years, and Kierkegaard now found himself deeply in sympathy with his former classmate's radical rejection of 'mediation', or the imposition of intellectualisation on contemplation of the relationship between the individual and God. Adler's thesis basically stated 'not thought but spirit, not objectivity but subjectivity', very much in accord with Kierkegaard. In 1842 Adler claimed to have experienced 'a vision of light' in which Christ instructed him to burn his own books and stick to the Bible. Bishop Mynster had suspended him the same year and two years later he was deposed. Adler then recanted on his 'vision' but went on to write books in which he insisted that his 'revelation' had in fact been evidence of genius. Kierkegaard listened as Adler read him his work, his voice mutating from normal speech to strange high-pitched monotone, and recognised the man was deranged. Nevertheless, Kierkegaard remained fascinated by what he saw as his confusion between genius and inspiration; an uncertainty which echoed his own.

In Adler too he sought in vain for some clarification of his own position in relation to feelings arising from the persecutions of the *Corsair*. This Purgatory had imprinted in Kierkegaard more deeply than ever the dichotomy between a sense of his singularity and a suffering awareness of himself as an exception in the good sense: drawn apart from others in the feeling that he was chosen or 'called' to some mission. He often thought that had he been a different personality he might well have found himself like his erstwhile schoolfriend experiencing this fervency as Adler had done in the guise of a supernatural event. At such moments he wondered how he had not ended up as the kind of zealot who has 'seen the Light'. He finally decided it was his dialecticism which had saved him from such a fate and instead helped him find and adhere to his category of 'without authority'. While his big book on Adler was abandoned unfinished, from it he distilled *Two Minor Ethico-Religious Treatises* published in 1849 and translated with *The Present Age* in 1940 by Walter Lowrie and Alexander Dru. The reflections on Adler led him to consider whether he might have been singled out to bear witness to the truth as a martyr, and the two 'minor' treatises interrogate the right of an individual to sacrifice himself for the sake of truth. At this point he thought not, but his view would change when he launched his attack on the Established Church, for which he expected to pay the ultimate price.

* * *

With *The Shadow* Andersen arrives at his zenith as a writer, demonstrating supreme demonic mastery over his material, throwing aside the veil of sweetness and light with which he had so often cloaked his alter egos to reveal his tenuous hold on his self-identity. Also incidentally on display is a new and ferocious degree of adaptation to the wounding received in his early relationship with Edvard Collin. Now he could deploy the 'Du'/'De' episode in an exchange of almost comical charm between 'the learned man' and 'the shadow'; but the deepest suffering of the author's soul is expressible only in the story's finale, a terrifying act of annihilation with which Andersen quietly and decisively exposes the moral bankruptcy of the worldly and successful in their treatment of interiority and creativity. In a letter of 1855 he would describe how open and impressionable he had always been, like water, in which everything is reflected. He supposed this was part of his nature as a poet and confessed to enjoying the experience as often as suffering its torment. In an earlier attempted autobiography he had claimed to be able to clearly recall the face of anyone he had seen or spoken to on even a single occasion: 'I have their mirror image within me; however, I cannot recall my own features, although God knows I look at myself in the mirror often enough.'[3] *The Shadow* also served as overdue rebarbative for the literary belittling he had undergone in Denmark. A striking characteristic of some minority European cultures is the poise with which their literati idealise and/or dismiss fellow writers of underprivileged or undereducated background as 'naïve' (in Danish *naturtalent*, Dutch and Frisian *natuurtalent*), thus putting the primitives firmly in their place. However, this story forced the later Danish critic, Georg Brandes (1842-1927) to concede that:

> This tale about the shadow is a little world of its own. I do not hesitate to call it one of the greatest masterpieces in the whole of our literature… It is also one of the few works in which the poet, despite his soft optimism, has dared to let the ugly truth appear in all its nakedness.[4]

The 'tale' was to mark a seminal shift in Andersen's confidence and literary aspiration. By August he was homeward bound but still working on the new autobiography, sending it home chapter by chapter to Edvard for correction; far from resenting this arduous but

---

3. Wullschläger, *Hans Christian Andersen*, p. 283.
4. Georg Brandes, 'H.C. Andersen som Æventyrdigter' ('Hans Christian Andersen as an Author of Tales'), the first part of his tripartite treatise on Andersen's fairy tales, *Illustreret Tidende*, 11 July 1869; see https://andersen.sdu.dk/forskning/anmeldelser/kritik_e.html. Accessed 7 November 2024.

Esquisse

most necessary work on Andersen's behalf, his underappreciated friend even offered to make a fair copy for the German translator. For once, Andersen was a little chastened, it was almost as if Edvard had fleetingly become his double and he wrote to him of how deeply moved he was, how filled with shame at the thought of Edvard copying out his biography: He would never forget this testimony to… 'your fraternal soul, it is an embrace, a kiss – a toast to our becoming Dus, you know what I mean.'[5] Sanctimonious he remained. September brought news that he had at last been honoured at home with the Danish Order of the Dannebrog and on 14 October he stepped off the steamship in Copenhagen. He had been away a year but found himself feeling far from happy reinstated at the Hôtel du Nord among his fellow Danes, and at once began planning new escape. He set his sights not farther afield than usual, but more particularly on furthering his career. He had won over Europe and America, now he set his sights on London, literary London, and shared his ambition with his German translator. Autumn 1846 brought an invitation to visit England from William Jerdan, editor of the *Literary Gazette* and a friend of Charles Dickens. Richard Bentley had just published an English translation of *The Poet's Bazaar* and wrote to Andersen of the pleasure it had been to have this honour. Andersen had his reply translated for the British publisher: it was 'a singular feeling to see the children of my soul and spirit in such a richly garb',[6] and he promised he was about to begin learning english [sic.] so as to be able, on his visit the following year, to express his 'thanks and affections'.[7]

Little progress was made on the language front, but Andersen was busy throughout winter getting new and old work into print. His collected poems came out in December; in January and February 1847 the first volumes appeared of Lorck's German collected edition of the works, accompanied by the memoir written to accompany it, *The Fairy Tale of My Life*, and in April a French translation of *The Improvisatore* arrived, along with a new volume of tales, including *The Shadow*. Foreign publishers forwarded copies of translations direct to the Danish monarch, and King Christian VIII invited the storyteller to dine at court. The king, recognising how Andersen's standing as cultural figure now fitted him for ambassadorial duty, offered to

---

5. Wullschläger, *Hans Christian Andersen*, p. 284.
6. Ibid., p. 285.
7. Ibid.

subsidise his trip to Britain, but for once and for some unknown reason Andersen on this occasion refused royal sponsorship. Perhaps he was finally feeling more assertive and self-reliant in his standing as a writer of international acclaim. He had recalled in his new autobiography his early reading of Walter Scott and named him along with German novelists as a formative influence. Now he longed to meet British writers, especially Dickens, with whom he felt a special affinity; both writers specialised in deploying their sentimental imagination to depict childhood, the poor and underprivileged in a new and ruthlessly utilitarian age. Neither shied away from realism in characterising its sufferings.

May 1847 saw Andersen embarking by steamship from Rotterdam for London. His first impression of Britain was Turneresque:

> The Thames bears witness to the fact that England rules the oceans. From here its servants sally forth. Whole hosts of ships. Every minute a courier (steamer) arrives; the others have decked out their stovepipe hats: that one over there had a long smokecrepe with red fire-flower peeping out. The long white wake trails behind them... They come running under full sail, pluming themselves like swans. Thousands of fishboats, like a teeming marketplace, like a brood of chicks, like confetti. Steamer after steamer, like rockets in a great fireworks display. At Gravesend it looked like a big marsh fire, and it was smoke from the steamers! The pleasure yachts of rich young gentlemen. A splendid thunderstorm; lightning struck several times to the north, and a railway train raced along with its blue smoke against the black clouds...'[8]

These were images he preferred to the sooty edifices that loomed over the opposite bank of the great River Thames. When an Englishmen told him that everyone knew he had arrived and bid him welcome, the famous storyteller murmured that the Lord himself knew, and had made it thunder!

Fairytale first impressions were one thing; Englishness, he would soon discover, was another. It wore many faces. Having found his hotel on Leicester Square he drove out of town to visit Count Eduard

---

8. Andersen, *Diaries*, pp. 164-165.

Reventlow, Danish Ambassador to England, who regaled the new arrival with cautionary tales of his own about England and the English: they did not pay compliments; they said what they meant. The ambassador passed on a letter from Lorck, Andersen took an omnibus home and drove straight back out again to Marlborough House. Here he was admitted to a royal reception suite, soon to be kissed and embraced by Carl Alexander from Weimar, whom he was delighted to find visiting London at the same time. The duke too was graphic in his description of cultural difference: he felt extremely constrained in England, he wasn't at leisure to meet certain literary figures he should have liked to see. One dared not even mention the scandalous Lady Blessington.[9] Everything here was cliques. Dickens had blemished his own reputation by writing for *Punch*, so you couldn't speak to him either. According to Carl Alexander, they'd die here of etiquette. Not even the queen herself escaped it: two breakfasts and dinner at eight in the evening. They had been out enjoying a walk in the parks, but she had to leave to be home by eight. Etiquette prevented her from enjoying life the way they did in Germany. But, Andersen protested, she is queen, she can do as she wishes! Yes, answered Carl Alexander, he had said the very same thing, but the queen replied that it wouldn't do, the whole land would take exception. 'This is the land of freedom where you die from etiquette',[10] he insisted.

Jenny Lind was also in London, and a letter from her awaited Andersen at his hotel after a long day plodding the streets sightseeing. He was impressed by Nelson, regal atop his column in Trafalgar Square, and then by finding his own picture[11] in the window of a shop selling *Howitt's Journal*, which he promptly purchased. Street music delighted him, along with the sight of a dancing girl-child... it reminded him of Naples, lively, but without the heat and cacophony, perhaps more like Paris. Andersen began to relax. His

---

9. Lady Marguerite Blessington (1789-1849), English author and socialite, hostess of glittering salons, vilified for sexual indiscretions and for her book *Conversations of Lord Byron with the Countess of Blessington* (1834) chronicling her encounters with the poet in Genoa.
10. Andersen, *Diaries*, p. 167.
11. Ibid., p. 168. Etching published on 26 June 1847 in *Howitt's Journal*, the progressive weekly political periodical, jointly edited by husband and wife William and Mary Howitt, which ran for only eighteen months from January 1847 to June 1848.

money worries were relieved when Reventlow told him that day to stop fretting about his letter of credit, the ambassador would advance him anything needed. Another compatriot willing and able to ease the traveller's penury was Danish banker, Joseph Hambro, who owned a fine house but a long drive out of town. Jenny Lind was staying out beyond the city centre too, but Andersen drove to find her anyway, very comfortably settled in lodgings with a lovely lawned and flowery garden. She promised to secure him a ticket for the opera to spare the usual enormous expense of a seat. Wherever he found himself, Andersen's itinerary was always basically the same. So too in London, although tired, disorientated and suffering from the heat, he embarked on his usual social round of the aristocracy, discovering no hint among the lords and ladies of the diffidence and difficulties he had been warned of by his hereditary grand duke. All the ladies he met knew his work and the Duchess of Suffolk congratulated him on *The Improvisatore*, describing it as the *first* book about Italy! If the English were delighted with the Dane, the feeling was mutual, and he congratulated himself on it all. In conversation with his friends he denied the common view that the English aristocracy excluded artists from their circle and enthused about his own universally warm welcome. It was flattering beyond belief. He'd heard that even Dickens and D'Israeli were shunned by salons and company where he found himself recognised and accepted.

Sunday, 28 June proved an especially pleasant day. Andersen sat for the painter Jens Peter Møller, a *protégé* of Christian VIII, before driving out to see Hambro, who treated him to a tour of the surrounding countryside in his own carriage. It was a joy and a huge relief to get out of the metropolis, and after its smoke and grime Andersen revelled in the fresh air, bright sunshine and verdancy, cattle and horses peacefully grazing the meadows while in the distance a railway track fled towards the smoke-swathed city. Hambro's residence was equally refreshing, elegant, generously proportioned and, most welcome of all, everyone there spoke Danish. It was generally costing Andersen very great effort to communicate with his few ill-pronounced words in English, and this added to the exhaustion of heat and busyness. He had also to contend with the many small but excruciating embarrassments of being a foreigner in a foreign country, such as being made aware that his hotel was in the 'wrong' part of town. This forced him to abandon his default unnuanced delight for a nod to British snobbery; apparently, he complained to his diary, telling anyone you stayed in Leicester Square was tantamount to admitting in Copenhagen you lived in Peter Madsen's Alley, where all the prostitutes plied their trade. Revelow had done his best to point out the *faux pas*, advising Andersen just to say he was staying at the embassy. Andersen was scathing. Leicester Square bordered on an elite London location, and indeed had up until only a few years ago been part of it. The square was a lovely spacious, grassed and leafy park, with a statue of Leicester... what on earth were these English talking about!

Despite the language barrier, he imbibed a great deal of high society gossip along with the hospitality, sat for more sketches and met the magazine editor and English language translator Mary Howitt, who made him an offer for his book rights, soon overruled by Hambro, who promised to get more for him. The banker had been tipped off by his son, who lived in Edinburgh, that Andersen's world fame outshone that of Thorvaldsen, and if he went up north everyone would want to see him. The idea of more travel did not much appeal to Andersen, who was still enjoying exploring London, catching a glimpse of Queen Victoria and Prince Albert processing in the state carriage at close of Parliament, and much moved by Westminster Abbey. He nevertheless felt the pressure and was unable to refuse when at the beginning of July Hambro invited him to join him on a trip to Scotland. That evening he felt sick at the opera, for which Jenny had got him a ticket, and had to leave in the third act. He did not enjoy the performance so much here as in Copenhagen and Weimar, although the Grand Duke was also in the London audience. The thought of a long journey north sweetened London considerably and next morning, under an already burning summer sun, Andersen waxed lyrical over the city in all its greenery, like nothing less than a large English garden. As for its hospitality, the exiled Hambro was proving the most generous, enabling and confiding of welcomers. The banker had aroused all his guest's sympathy by explaining how he had been virtually forced to leave Copenhagen because as a Jew he was not eligible for public office there. Nevertheless, Hambro added with dignity, King Carl Johan of Norway and Sweden had once embraced him.

One evening in murderous heat they drove out for dinner at Lord Castlereagh's, and next day much enjoyed calling on the daring Lady Blessington. Even figures whom Andersen had been led to believe were pariahs of literary London threw open their salon doors to him. At Lord and Lady Palmerston's Andersen conversed with Benjamin

D'Israeli (1804-1881), whom he referred to as a poet. He was fascinated by D'Israeli, nicknamed Dizzy, the well-travelled, handsome charmer who was pursuing a somewhat erratic early career as scandalous socialite and political radical. He was a writer whose novels were poorly received but whose chequered history would culminate in his earning the title of Earl of Beaconsfield and Queen Victoria's favourite prime minister. As Andersen continued on his round, introduced to one after another exalted member of English society, it felt to him as though the land lay at his feet, and his romantic love of Scotland was reignited when Walter Scott's son-in-law invited him to breakfast and showed him Scott's diaries. The very last line read ominously: Slept well last night, but tomorrow... Andersen must have shuddered at this echoing of his own fearful nature. He retired early whenever he could and wrote copious letters to Jonas and Edvard Collin and other friends at home.

A Covent Garden bookseller who had ordered all his works told Andersen that they had been listed in *The Athenaeum* magazine, and he was sure he was the first Danish author to have had this happen. On 16 July, at Lady Blessington's, he was sitting writing in *The True Story of My Life* when Charles Dickens arrived. The two writers shook hands, 'looked into each other's eyes, spoke, understood each other'[12] and as they talked outside on the veranda Andersen felt their communion bring tears to his eyes. That same evening after dinner Dickens invited Andersen to come and stay at his home at the beginning of August. The meeting was momentous for Andersen, and next day he left his hotel to drive out of town for some rest and fresh air with Hambro. Not only was the banker witty and congenial company, he would go off to town leaving his beautiful home and estate for his guest to roam and make his own. Such cosseted freedom was heaven for Andersen, and even conducive to work. Whilst there he drafted the first chapter of a new novel, and on 20 July the portrait painter came out and finished his work; no more posing! Despite all this bucolic rejuvenation, the storyteller's habitual restlessness was creeping up on him again, he was suffering from toothache and had begun to miss the city. Back in his old room in Leicester Square on 22 July he was soon moaning about having been billed for getting his laundry done by Hambro's maid, as well as blaming Denmark for not making enough of him. Somehow, he could not settle back into city

---

12. Ibid., p. 183.

life, and two days later decided to accept Hambro's offer of Scotland. The decision itself was enervating. He wandered the streets in lacklustre mood, seeing nothing but misery: an impoverished father and his five motherless children selling matchsticks on a street corner, iron gratings over grime-glazed basements, beggarly demands for penny tips… and playing forever at the back of his mind Howlitt's by now constant whining and haranguing. London had lost its charm and Andersen was more than ready for a change.

Meanwhile, he discovered temporary refuge behind the graceful Attic façade of the Athenaeum on Pall Mall. It was Dicken's favoured gentlemen's club, founded some twenty years before, with magnificent floor-to-ceiling library shelves of books and leatherbound armchairs. Here, among the intellectuals and literary men of London, Andersen read in *The Examiner* a review of his own new autobiography: 'Childhood written by a man, manhood written by a child.'[13] Retreating to the crimson-velvet draped dining-room, he was again taken aback, this time by being charged three shillings for a lone pork chop and half a glass of seltzer, but it was nice to have it served on silver plate. What was more, the waiters wore silk stockings, he later reported to Jenny Lind, who observed that he would most certainly have consumed them along with the meal. He was again posing for an artist, this time Joseph Durham (1814-1877), a sculptor who had not yet made his name but who in 1856 would have his bust of Queen Victoria presented to the Guildhall. The new commission was a companion piece for a bust already completed of Jenny Lind, and after the sitting she and Andersen drove out to see Hambro, who was charmed by her, although Andersen reported that most of the conversation revolved around money. Dickens having planned to call on Andersen that day, Andersen had regretted having to put him off, but got home to find the novelist had stopped by in Leicester Square anyway and left a beautifully bound set of his complete works inscribed: 'To H.C.A. from his friend and admirer, C.D.'

At last, on 11 August he and Hambro set off for Scotland, by carriage to Newcastle, and on northwards to Berwick by train. The railway tracks were rackety, the carriages of wood and extremely uncomfortable. By the time they reached their destination they'd had nothing to eat since York and arrived at Waverley Station tired and starving. What a pleasure to see young Carl Joachim Hambro on

---

13. Ibid., p. 186.

the platform, ready with the warmest of welcomes as they alighted from the train! It was the sign of things to come. Like his father, Carl would prove the most attentive of hosts, meeting Andersen's every need throughout his Scottish stay. Emerging from the dingy vale of railway tracks up onto Princes Street at about 10 p.m., they discovered Edinburgh drowsing beneath the castle in all her silvery summer evening splendour and made their way to the waiting carriage for the drive to Trinity in the north of the city. Plenty of post awaited Andersen at Carl Hambro's fine residence, and the guest bedroom was perfect. After reading and rereading his letters, it began joyfully to dawn on the Danish storyteller that he was indeed in Scotland, the land of Walter Scott, and he retired happily and gratefully, thanking his God.

Once out and about in Edinburgh, he was doubly delighted to discover himself hailed as 'the Danish Walter Scott' and was soon taking in the sights under the well-informed guidance of the younger Hambro. Halfway down the High Street between the castle and Holyrood House he was shown the tall, narrow, lightless looking dwelling in which John Knox had lived. Andersen was shocked. In fact, the whole of the Old Town made a very unfavourable impression on him, with its darkly dank 'closes' overhung by grim six-storey tenements that seemed to topple towards the street. Through heavy doors on the pavement, he glimpsed worn stone stairs spiralling upwards between black iron bannisters. Glassless grimy windows festooned with rags reminded Andersen of the most wretched towns in Italy. However, the city redeemed itself 'on the most beautiful street of the New Town'[14] where he found the statue of Scott, with his dog Maida at his side.

In Kirkcaldy, Carl Hambro mistook the ruin of Ravenscraig for Ravenswood, the setting for Scott's *The Bride of Lammermoor*, which Andersen had dramatised in his opera libretto, *Bruden fra Lammermoor* (1832), but a fisherman reassured them that Scott had made up the name and there were no shifting sands at Ravenscraig. Back in Edinburgh sightseeing continued despite Andersen feeling sometimes on edge and unwell, and he was never too tired to admire the railway, rushing along its green bed beneath and between the Old and New Town districts. He drove up to the castle – spellbound by its stupendous views from the battlements, a city panorama sweeping

---

14. Ibid., p. 197.

down to the far pale waters of the Firth of Forth in the north, and southwards to the lower end of the Royal Mile. At Holyrood House, standing resplendent in its park under the lee of Salisbury Crags, he saw the long banqueting room full of 'bad' portraits and a lot of 'boring rooms' in which Charles X had stayed, but his patience paid off in Mary Stuart's bedroom where beside the bed hung a textile depicting Phaethon's Fall which he at once interpreted as a prophesy of her own. Shopping for souvenirs, he modestly refused the young Hambro's offer of an expensive plaid and instead bought himself a cap, a paper knife and a book of Scottish melodies. The same evening at a big dinner party in his honour he was seated next to a poetess, Miss Crowe, who read aloud *The Ugly Duckling* and *The Top and the Ball*. He was still not quite freed by new distractions from his habitual worries, however, noting: '(A thorn from a thistle in my penis.)'.[15]

The relentless tourist trail continued, the Hambros doing their utmost to please their guest. On the eve of their early departure on the morning of 19 August for a round trip of more rural picturesque spots, Andersen received a letter from the Duke of Weimar and Gebhard Moltke-Hvitfeldt inviting him to join them on their outing to Loch Laggan, Queen Victoria's royal estate in the Highlands. From another source he learnt the same day of telegraph reports of the death of Louis-Philippe of France, which threw him into miserable confusion thinking that the invitation to Loch Laggan would now be cancelled. The weather was very hot and Mrs Hambro, who was in poor health, felt unwell. Andersen's continuing uncertainty regarding a sojourn on the royal estate made him write to an advisor, hoping for a reply to reach him when he got back to Glasgow. Meanwhile the group proceeded homeward by way of Stirling, where he received welcome reassurance that the reports about the death of Louis-Philippe had been false. In Stirling they visited the castle and church where Mary Stuart had stayed, and Darnley's house nearby, before discovering the site of the battle between Edward and the Bruce. Andersen found the locals keen to relate their history to the foreign visitor, not omitting how James III had been stabbed to death by his priest-confessor; a woman showed them the site of the murder, in her very own bedroom. Callander was full of gentlemen fishers and small shops beneath grey-tiled roofs and a bitter cold wind; 'we were running around in our

---

15. Ibid., p. 198.

plaids'.[16] Andersen was generally as struck by the wild character of the Scots (they are Celts! he reminded himself) as by their weather, landscape, and fiercely skirted men, to say nothing of Edinburgh's eerily deserted Sunday streets. Via Loch Katrine, Loch Lomond and Balloch they drove to Dumbarton, where Hambro, after ascertaining the bookseller stocked work by Hans Christian Andersen, pointed to Andersen the man and his portrait in *Howitt's* Journal and asked the bookseller if it was a good likeness. So the great writer earned yet another thrilled and awestruck handshake.

Next day was the last of their sightseeing tour, Andersen due to leave half an hour after the Hambros, and everyone was very sad at the parting. Reaching Glasgow on 23 August Andersen found no advice awaiting him regarding the royal invitation to Loch Laggan, and next morning he boarded the train to brood on the problem while braving the two long, dark tunnels between here and Edinburgh. Once settled in the North British Hotel on Princes Street, an exhausted and depleted Andersen was recognised at dinner and duly feted with raised glasses all round. He had signed so many autographs, dined, admired everything and been endlessly celebrated, and now it was the end of the road. He would set off tomorrow for London without further fretting over Loch Laggan – or so he determined. In the event, overcome with tiredness and relapsing into hysterical ennui, he agonised on and on, struggling with the decision "I can; I will" and finding himself bound intractably in a Kierkegaardian knot. He had reached the farthest frontier of his freedom, he scribbled despairingly in his diary, 'the limits set by God.'[17] Standing at his window gazing down on the gaslit city he tried to calm himself, taking in the tiered lit windows of the Old Town tenements, the steam-dimmed dome of Waverley Station beneath which plaited tracks ran north and south, and down on the street he saw a dancing, singing child. All the hours of indecision resulted finally on 25 August in his boarding the new North British Railway train headed south, only to be confronted with Edinburgh newspaper reports of his travelling to Loch Laggan at the invitation of Prince Albert. Paralysed with renewed panic, he sat on an omnibus high above the River Tweed as it crossed the border into England at North Berwick, and by the time they reached York was still on the verge of changing trains and returning to Scotland.

---

16. Ibid., p. 200.
17. Ibid, p. 203.

Steaming south from York, well-meaning fellow travellers again relayed Scottish reports of his visit to the queen.

It is hard to imagine anything more punishing for Andersen than repeated confrontation with so contradictory a self-image as that of himself in contempt of the royal household. Faced head-on with the full extent of his solipsism, he lost his hold on the fragile ego he'd nurtured since leaving boyhood behind in Odense. He did not know this man, a friendless foreigner alone on a steam train. Defence mechanisms crumbled and were gone. No longer was he fighting fear, not even that of the train; disaster would be welcome, anything to fend off this sense of inner void and uncertainty. How fragile life was, how it hung by a thread! His journey south was long, his mood not quickly banished. On and on he wrestled with the blind impotence of the human condition, the dread of each decision; how we hovered on every threshold, not knowing once through the door whether to turn to the left or right, only that whatever choice we made might lead to death or to fresh life. On and on the carriage swayed and shuddered, while imprisoned in his clattering wooden cell Andersen suffered the antithesis of the liberating escapism usually afforded him by travel. As the engine drew into London, he silently blessed the sight of blackened warehouses, the station's brightly brass-buffered sidings, its shrill whistles, billowing steam and smoke-stained glass, and disembarking fell weeping into the arms of Ambassador Revelow. Back in Leicester Square his old hotel welcomed him warmly home with a proper suite, complete with bedroom and his own sitting room.

His last night in Britain was spent glorying in Dickens and his family at Broadstairs, the many Dickens children introducing themselves by turn, singing and dancing around him. Next morning he boarded the steamship for Ostend, waving farewell to Dickens, who had walked from Broadstairs to Ramsgate docks to say goodbye. Proudly Andersen describes the celebrated novelist with a dash of cultural confusion as, 'dressed in green Scottish dress coat and colourful shirt – exceedingly, elegantly English,'[18] the last to shake his hand in England. He had promised everyone he would be back. In Copenhagen, meanwhile, news had spread of Andersen's celebrity status as 'the Lion of London' and the *Corsair* satirised him with four cheeky cartoons and a feature on his triumphant conquest of Britannia. So that poor Andersen, just home and standing at his

---

18. Wullschläger, *Hans Christian Andersen*, p. 307.

window, overheard two well-dressed gentlemen passers-by observe, 'See, there stands our orang-outang so famous abroad!'[19] He realised he had left England without even saying goodbye to Jenny.

In Leipzig on his way back he had discussed a second edition of his collected works. Once settled home, he wrote five stories dedicated to Dickens and completed the epic dramatic poem, *Ahasuerus*, on which he had been working since 1840. This much cherished but doomed project was rejected on publication by critic Heiberg for its lack of cohesive structure or any seriously addressed underpinning premise.

* * *

Just as his later stories had been quickly recognised in Denmark and Germany as having been written for the adults who read them out loud as well as for their listening young, Britain viewed the same work through the prism of Victorian sentimentality and morality. This dogged insistence on infantilisation has persisted until the present day, when Andersen continues to be viewed as a children's writer rather than the serious literary figure he became in the aftermath of *The Shadow*. Henceforth his stories would be darker, more subliminal, more subtly emphatic in moral messaging, and less and less read by an adult audience here. This despite the 1937 edition of Andersen's stories translated into quirky Andersenian English by Paul Leyssac (1881-1946), the Danish writer, stage and film actor whose mother had known Andersen personally.[20] The edition was provided with a foreword by Hugh Seymour Walpole:

> I will confess at once that I am a little prejudiced in favour of these translations, because I am sure that nobody yet reads (writes, or acts, whatever word you please) the Andersen stories as Leyssac reads them. If anyone wants to know just what these stories really are, let them go and listen to the wireless or watch Leyssac on the television and he will perhaps for the first time understand. ... You ought to hear the voice, not exactly of Andersen himself, but of some old, friendly, and rather sardonic story-teller, who holds you as

---

19. Ibid.
20. Storytelling had been introduced into BBC children's television in 1937 under the umbrella title *For The Children*. Paul Leyssac read tales from Hans Christian Anderson as part of the series.

the Ancient Mariner did the Wedding Guest, with fierce insistence. ... It's just the tone of voice that Leyssac gets so beautifully in these stories. They *must* be read aloud: don't say to yourself that everyone has read them already.

Hans Andersen was not, I would say, exactly a charming person. He was ugly, conceited, sensitive, quick-tempered and elusive. As the hero of a novel he would annoy many readers. He would seem feckless and ungrateful and a bit of a muff. And yet he is part of all of us. If you feel the pathetic and humorous and lonely uniqueness of human beings, you must know that only the very unperceptive and heavy-minded are irritated by him; and out of that strange personality he produced these wonderful fairy stories, wonderful because they are filled through and through with that sense of oddity and loneliness that gives human beings so much beauty.[21]

* * *

Works of Love, the book for which Kierkegaard had resisted the distractions of Berlin, is in two parts, comprising a total of fifteen 'Christian Reflections in the Form of Discourses'. It represents the author's newly conceived key concept of the centrality of God's love in anchoring the personality and life of the individual, and emphasises a personal, inward form of love which is nonetheless objective and outwardly expressed in *acts* or *works*. This inner state cannot be reached until the individual has set aside guilt and the perception of his sins in the complete conviction of divine forgiveness; only then does he exist fully in God's love. Crucially, this concept is defined as *indicative*, neither instructive nor endowed with authority, or shrouded in any 'Christian' or philosophical ethics. In Kierkegaard's careful exposition the idea is that the thought of God no longer reminds the individual of his sin, neither does the memory of all he has done wrong, but rather how forgiven he is; at this point he 'rests in the forgiveness of sin.'[22] There is no attempt on Kierkegaard's part to list innumerable potential works of love, he simply outlines some

---

21. Andersen, *It's Perfectly True! and Other Stories*, pp. vii–ix.
22. Søren Kierkegaard, *Works of Love: Some Christian Reflections in the Form of Discourses*, trans. Howard and Edna Hong (New York, NY: Harper Torchbook, 1964), p. 52.

directions indicative of the overall weave and weft of 'works', such as the *duty* of love: *Only when it is a duty to love, only then is love made eternally free in blessed independence.*[23] The differentiation made here is between spontaneous love which is not bound by dependence on divine imperative but on self-love and is therefore cowardice (the *wish* to love), and love's eternal intrinsic imperative. Spontaneous love frees in one moment and in the next renders man dependent. The latter form of love, having undergone transformation of the eternal by becoming *duty*, grounds the law of its existence in the relationship of love itself to the eternal: it *shall* love, and only duty makes for genuine freedom.

Kierkegaard was still pondering a trip to Berlin on 14 August when a potential buyer turned up for his house, so he dared not leave town and instead set aside all distraction to devote himself to resting from work and productivity. He wanted to approach God more nearly, to 'be renewed inwardly', and jotted in his journal *A Note about myself*, reflecting on his 'poetic' condition as one who reminds the world of the requirements [of Christianity] while guarding vigilantly against acquiring followers. The task depended upon the poetic imagination and a solitary state, the imagination (always secondary to the dialectical) pointing to the myriad ways in which deflection from true might and does occur. Yet while Kierkegaard advocated solitude, he was far from immune to the universal human need for companionship. Deep within everyone, he wrote, lay the dread of being alone in the world, forgotten by God and the 'tremendous household of millions upon millions.' Reminders of the nearness of family and friends may mitigate this dread, but it remains nevertheless, and one hardly dares think of what might happen were 'all the rest taken away.'[24]

Three days later he delivered the manuscript of *Works of Love* to the printer; and it appeared on 29 September.

On 9 November 1847 Regine Olsen married Fritz Schlegel.

---

23. Ibid., p. 52.
24. Kierkegaard, *Journals*, p. 220.

Chapter 10

To Will One Thing

When on 4 November 1847 Kierkegaard called on Bishop Mynster, the cleric said he was extremely busy, so that Kierkegaard left again at once, struck by the coldness of the bishop's tone. Back home and at his journal, Kierkegaard reasoned that he must have shocked and estranged Mynster with his latest book, *Works of Love*. He had always recoiled from writing anything that might offend the bishop, and now he had done so. Perhaps he was misinterpreting the situation, but of one thing he did not feel mistaken, and that was the calm which descended upon him now that things had come to a head. This encounter was precursor to the final decisive transformation in the life and writings. Silently, stealthily and finally, that 'calm' released Kierkegaard from the spell cast upon him by his father's priest and granted him permission to challenge Mynster in his fundamental integrity as a Christian. It was another great epiphany. Kierkegaard would go on to write exclusively religious works with the avowed intent of describing true Christianity and bringing down the Established Church in Denmark by revealing its superficiality and mendacity. His new appreciation of Mynster's feet of clay verified and vindicated his previous intimations about the man. The bishop was, avowed Kierkegaard, the only man in his time who had claimed his true attention, but Mynster was concerned with dominating others in the belief that this served the truth; he had no real concern for truth, even if it fell on its knees in agony before him. The bishop understood only that the truth should and must rule supreme, and not that it's very mark was suffering. For Kierkegaard this was a painful parting of the ways; not only did he cherish the memory of his father associated with the bishop, he loved the man for himself. Kierkegaard swore he had honoured no one, not another living soul but Bishop Mynster. He was also aware that if anyone could appreciate the difficulties and criticism Mynster had faced, it was he. Yet Kierkegaard wanted it known that what he had to say need in no way harm the bishop – '*if only he does not make a false move.*'[1]

These reflections led on to consideration of what, in this context, Kierkegaard expected of himself. It seemed that the world had no more use for the genius; there had been geniuses enough. What the world needed was a martyr, a man who, in order to teach obedience, would himself be obedient to the enth degree. A man whom men would put to death and in their loss come to fear themselves. What the age needed was awakening. He reiterated his conviction that this burden must be borne not by the masses, but by the individual. It was not realistic to imagine any Christian reformation emerging or ever having emerged from a movement against its religious leadership: that was too worldly an approach. For Christianity at root decreed that every individual undergo reformation: to be reformed was the project facing each of us. The populous, he now declared, was the 'most ungodly of all unchristian categories, and actively subversive.'[2] Yet if what was needed was an individual as martyr, Kierkegaard must again confront a dilemma he had already examined and forsworn.

It was at this moment, in the wake of publication of the *Postscript* and his persecution by *Corsair*, that Kierkegaard most mourned the way his works had been received: 'With my right hand I held out the *Edifying Discourses*, with my left the aesthetic works – and all grasped with the right hand what I held in my left.'[3] These circumspect, non-didactic pieces delineating the essence of Christianity were written between 1843 and 1855. There are some 86 in all, many named after interludes in the New Testament (e.g. *The Lilies of the Field and the Birds of the Air*); all enshrine Kierkegaard's humanism, his wide view, his erudition and grounding in Greek and Roman thought, the Old Testament and early Judaeo-Christian writings. He fastidiously avoided describing these pieces as 'sermons', hoping they would be grasped by the right hand. The hope was not entirely in vain. Georg

---

1. Kierkegaard, *Journals*, p. 224.
2. Ibid., 226.
3. Lowrie, A Short Life of Kierkegaard, pp. 196-197.

To Will One Thing

Brandes, 'free-thinking Jew as he was',[4] quoting Judge Williams' stated aversion to edifying works and sermons in *Either/Or*, went on to say that however much one agreed with him one could read Kierkegaard's Edifying Discourses with nothing but respect: a noble spirit of moderation prevailed in them. Brandes was amazed that so masterful an interpreter of the wildest passions could equally well counsel the world using words of the utmost care and compassion, so offering the best comfort for life's journey.

As always, the writings run in exact concord with their author's spiritual development. The discourses chart Kierkegaard's progress in his own understanding and growing humility in relation to his central tenet. He always insisted that he himself was the most avid and needy pupil of his own works, and he never claimed to 'be' a Christian, only ever of 'becoming one' – up until, as Lowrie professes, 'he died for his faith.'[5] His literary trajectory traces the personal path, stressing the duty of the individual to differentiate himself from 'the mass' (never meant sociologically, but rather numerically), to discover in himself his own religious reality epitomised in the 1846 'Edifying Address', *Purity of Heart Is To Will One Thing*. Having set a precedent for the discourses of authorial non-authority, however, Kierkegaard in 1848 ventured to offer the later *Christian Discourses* under the 'higher category'; indeed, he had already characterised *Works of Love* as 'Christian Reflections'. By the time he arrived at the 1849 '*Lilies of the Fields*' he was classing these writings as 'Godly Discourses'… and so he charted his own religious apprenticeship. But he remained circumspect, and even the final discourses he cited only as examples of religiousness 'A': immanence, distinctively Christian but not yet exponents of the peculiarly paradoxical nature of transcendent Christianity. At no point did he claim to have reached his destination.

* * *

Kierkegaard's most cryptic commentary is always reserved for the absolutely agonising moments. Towards the end of 1847 comes:

> The girl has given me trouble enough. And now she is – not dead – but happily and comfortably married.[6]

---

4. Ibid. p. 198.
5. Ibid., p. 200.
6. Kierkegaard, *Journals*, p. 225.

He described himself now as 'an ironical individuality'.⁷ Wryly he recollected having prophesied this very outcome for Regine on exactly the same day six years before and been condemned as the lowest of the low for it. A man such as himself, he reflected, could never be understood by another who was full of longing, one who is always thinking if only... [I could have my wish]. An individuality full of hopes and wishes could never be ironical; irony lay in the opposite, in experiencing pain where others had longings. It was not ironical to love and lose the beloved. Being able all too easily to possess her, to be begged by the beloved herself to be possessed, and then to be unable to have her – that was true irony. In this instance the individuality is prevented from love by some secret, melancholy or tragic knowledge, and this secrecy also prevents him from being understood. Irony, said Kierkegaard, was 'a kind of hypersthenia'⁸ which could, as everyone knew, prove fatal. The existential isolation of such a psyche is heartrending. Cure, he wrote, consisted in the loathsome meanness of his contemporaries towards him, for such betrayal led to infinite melancholy, and in his melancholy he loved the world. He felt 'weaned'. Perhaps all would, after all, be well.

Four years earlier, in *Fear and Trembling*, his extraordinary exposition of a woman attracted to 'the interesting' and so fated to end up in the arms of a merman, Kierkegaard had painted the demoniacal scenario at the heart of both *Agnete and the Merman* and his own self-characterisation. Kierkegaard places the 'merman' at the intersection of the aesthetic and the ethical, and with her glance of absolute trust Agnete destroys the seducer in him. Now he must choose whether to confess or conceal his secret. Here Kierkegaard, in the guise of 'Johannes de Silentio', simultaneously exposes our incapacity for compassion in the absence of 'understanding' of the other [refusal of the paradox] and its resultant mutual suffering. For when guilt leads the individual to stray beyond the universal, he can return to it only by coming as individual 'into absolute relationship with the absolute'.⁹

---

7. Ibid., p. 230.
8. Hypersthenia: morbid hypersensitivity to all sensual stimuli, associated with autoimmune response, allergy etc.
9. Søren Kierkegaard, *Fear and Trembling*, intro and trans. by Walter Lowrie (Princeton, NJ: Princeton University Press, 1974), p. 108.

At the end of December 1847, he sold the house on Nytorv. He was 35 and for the first time facing money troubles and homelessness. A pensive journal entry rehearses his response to a confluence of woes in *My farewell speech at death,* ironically petitioning his contemporaries to be sure solemnly to declaim whilst decorating his grave: "had he lived in our own time he would not have been thus treated".[10] Michael Pedersen Kierkegaard had always warned his youngest son that he would come to nothing so long as he had money; the father could not have been more wrong. Finding himself suddenly threatened with the end of financial security and the opposition of the world was more than Kierkegaard felt he could bear, yet the war and division erupting on the Continent in 1848 introduced fresh perspective and with it his inner impetus shifted from personal difficulty to fresh productivity. Mortified at the petty-mindedness of the 'little war' Denmark had entered into with Germany over its southern territories, and the bloodless revolution which deposed absolute monarchy, Kierkegaard perceived the futility of acting out political ideologies and predicted hegemony as the only result. In Danish fear of Germany he recognised simply a new attempt on the part of one nation to puff itself up at the expense of another, or worse, some more ephemeral diversion, a game. He had always been aware of the national tendency to embrace the provincial, while open-mindedness had allowed him to shrug it off as largely superficial.

Now his attitude hardened; the internecine fighting looked to him like punishment come upon a people who lacked true fear of God. A people whose shared consciousness was small-town gossip, demoralised to the point of idolising being nothing; a people who envied each other, spitefully scorning everyone who was anything more. In this reduced state they sensed some strength in Germany which made them fear and want to fight its people. All without an iota of self-scrutiny. He saw his own as a people who should want to follow a fine leader yet showed no ambition for betterment, only impertinent rebellion, daily proving their contempt for discipline and lack of public morality – a people who could only be saved by 'a tyrant or a few martyrs.'[11] In 1849 he would record of the preceding year's turbulence that while in one sense it 'potentiated' him, in another it 'broke' him religiously or, as he put it to himself: 'God had run me

---

10. Kierkegaard, *Journals,* p. 209.
11. Ibid., p. 230.

to a standstill.[12] However, his decision of the previous year to stay at home after completing *Works of Love* and take a sabbatical from productivity to contemplate his melancholy now produced late fruit. Arrival at the astounding conviction that God not only forgives but *forgets* our guilt swept away the last of his scruples regarding this suffering, along with any tattered remnants of self-doubt concerning his life's task. It was seismic, revolutionary, liberating; on Wednesday 19 April 1848 he joyously proclaimed in his journal under a double *'note bene'*, the complete transformation in his being. Reserve and self-isolation gone – he must now speak out. As he wrote these words his doctor happened to arrive, presenting an immediate opportunity to test his thesis. But it was too soon, Kierkegaard could not bring himself to confide in the man, although the instant the opportunity was past he reaffirmed his decision. This momentous movement of his soul was followed by holy days providing rest for reflection on the connection between his doomed love for Regine Olsen and the present sense of liberation. Mourning the fact that he had been unable until now to break the silence of his melancholy, he nevertheless attributed essentially to her, to his melancholy and his money the fact that he had become an author. Now he intended to become himself, and thereafter, with Christ's help, a priest.

Yet 24 April 1848, Easter Monday, brought recantation, for he was becoming aware that the attempt to overcome his natural reserve was counterproductive. The more he thought of relinquishing his introversion, the more embedded within him it became. He had managed at last to speak to his doctor, which consoled him greatly. Not that the medical man had had anything useful to say, but in confiding in him Kierkegaard felt he had disproved any pride in himself at the idea of sharing his thoughts with another, and so respected the human relationship. His change of heart brought fresh joy. He was able to rest in the present, feeling such satisfaction in his intellectual work that being able to pursue it outweighed all else that came his way. This context allowed him to accept his life: if by writing out of his own impenetrable suffering he could bring consolation and joy to others, then he had no grounds for complaint against his circumstances, but must simply cherish the treasure of his spiritual endeavour. So he gave thanks and turned to face the material difficulties and self-isolation which he now understood to be

---

12. Lowrie, *A Short Life of Kierkegaard*, p. 201.

his unavoidable lot. He was thus also coincidentally furnished with an ultimate objection to his taking up the priesthood. If he accepted the impossibility of avoiding the 'painful memory' of past sins, he still drew from his new understanding of divine forgiveness the strength to submit as penitent to isolation. If God willed the reserve gone, He would in some way bring this about. For the present, rest and recreation were needed after the past seven years of labour, and perhaps even travel.

However, as there was now nowhere to go in warring Europe, Kierkegaard found himself working on a new book, *The Sickness unto Death*. In July he made a small detour from religious writing in the form of a piece for *The Fatherland* about the actress Johanne Luise Heiberg entitled *The Crisis and a Crisis in the Life of an Actress*. His aim was to illustrate transition from the aesthetic to the ethical in her life, from performing onstage as a beautiful young thing to practising the serious artistic capabilities of a mature woman. It was another chance to dispel the notion that a person such as himself, 'suffering' from religiosity, was no longer capable of aesthetic enjoyment. Inwardly, the Easter experience had been a radical metamorphosis. He understood now that in the forgiveness of sins was implied a 'must' and an 'I can'. He would do what he must do. Never again does he resort to 'indirect communication' or his previous use of pseudonyms. He had always spoken directly in his *Edifying Discourses*; plain speech becomes increasingly evident in the five books written during 1848, including the greatest of these, *The Sickness unto Death*, *The Point of View for My Life as an Author* and culminating in *Training in Christianity*. He was dissatisfied with *The Sickness unto Death*, finding it too rigidly dialectical, he could not think it stirring enough: he had gone about the book the wrong way. The thing was to perfect fluency in the dialectical, he realised, and only then begin to employ rhetoric. He would concentrate on correcting the fault. He was honing his polemic for the final onslaught. Three years must pass while alone and out on the deep he awaited further orders. Meanwhile he received the volume of new fairy stories with its tender note from Andersen offering the gift 'without Fear and Trembling, which is something'. This must, despite everything, have made Kierkegaard smile.

* * *

The years 1848 to 1851 gave Andersen opportunity to display his energetic interest and excitement in chronicling battleground events, military manoeuvres, heroism and death. He followed every campaign, noting in his diary at the same time some pitifully split loyalties thanks to his love for Hereditary Grand Duke Carl Alexander of Weimar, along with other German friends, admirers and allegiances. These were political events both literally and figuratively too close to home for him to ignore. Miserably he accepted the impossibility of corresponding with the enemy and, *en route* to Funen to visit Count Moltke-Hvitfeldt's country estate at Glorup after the battle of Schleswig on 23 April, found the action uncomfortably but irresistibly near at hand. He could not tear his mind away from the conflict while German troops occupied the southern part of Jutland, and hardly a lurid detail escaped description in his diary: men shot in the chest or head lay as though asleep, whereas those hit in the abdomen were unrecognisable due to pain having convulsed the face, and one lay literally biting the dust, hands clutching at the turf. He listened avidly to the eyewitness reports of officers who had seen action and were visiting the Moltke estate, and physicians attending the military on whom he could call as neighbours. The aristocracy were playing their patriotic part in the hostilities by supporting the troops, and one serving soldier, a Volunteer Hansen, came to dinner and told his story: 'he had lain with a fever in the camp hospital at Augustenborg in the duchess's bed (the dowager duchess's [sic]). There they were served asparagus and capon.'[13] As for Andersen, he was thriving, far from the pressures and people of Copenhagen, taking peaceful, beautiful forest walks and feeling wonderfully free to be 'a better person' among others, and to banish low spirits and express a little more enthusiasm in life. War, he saw, could have a privately beneficial effect on both friend and foe. Everyone was asking each other the crucial question: "When are the Swedes coming?" The General told the company at Moltke that 'the Prussian soldiers at Snoghøj had sent a man to the Misses Riegels with a white flag and some flowers from the ladies' garden, so that they could enjoy some of their own beautiful flowers; they enclosed a poem.'[14] For the rest, His Excellency had brought a gift of the first strawberries.

And nothing, neither war nor pestilence could disturb Andersen's drawing-room story-reading routine. He also found time to read Walter Scott's *The Heart of Midlothian* and began work on a new novel

---

13. Andersen, *Diaries*, p. 211.
14. Ibid.

to be entitled *The Two Baronesses* and published at the end of the year. The summer of 1848 finds him escaping for a three-month visit to Sweden, where he is received by King Oscar I and the royal family, honoured with a dinner by the Literary Association in Stockholm, and recognised and lauded everywhere. Out of this trip came *Pictures of Sweden*, a book of landscapes, sketches, legends and stories – the sort of travelogue at which he excelled and which perfectly expressed his lasting wish to escape fraught reality for a whimsical fantasy world. Here we learn of Andersen's interlude in a small town in Dalecarlia, delighting a small granddaughter with his paper-cuts and designing impossibly complicated shapes for her bewildered grandmother to experiment with in her traditional home-baking. He was in his element; with his scissors he snipped wonderfully intricate paper shapes, nutcrackers in riding-boots, windmills in slippers with arms and a door in the belly, and dancing girls 'pointing one leg at the Pleiades'.[15] He even dreamt up a new route to immortality, writing delightedly to Jette Wulff on 24 June 1849 of how, while Europe was busy reshaping itself, he was doing his bit sitting here in Dalecarlia redesigning… gingernuts… he hoped his name would live on in them! Autumn brought the Copenhagen stage premier of his comedy *More Than Pearls and Gold* and he published the first illustrated collected edition of his tales with the help of the painter and illustrator Vilhelm Pedersen.

Apart from, or perhaps because of Andersen's fascination with the glamour and eroticism of military uniform, it was also poignantly associated with his beloved lost father. The sights and sounds of masculine combat evoked arousal melded with old pain and loss. In Andersen's fairy tales the soldier figure recurs, often as victim and martyr. He could not help being morbidly drawn to the gore, thrill and grief of the three-year war, but his enjoyment was compromised. In Copenhagen he was wounded and incensed by people questioning his allegiance. He reports intrusive, puerile insults aimed at him by 'friends' such as Countess Sophie Scheel querying whether his handkerchief does not originate from Schleswig-Holstein? and another acquaintance cross-questioning him about his corresponding with the Duke of Weimar. Andersen swears he has never felt more Danish, and they dared speak like that to him while plenty were simply playing the role of Danish gentlemen! It was all very sensitive

---

15. Wullschläger, *Hans Christian Andersen*, pp. 322-323.

and sensitising, and he felt the need to thank the king for his noble friendship. The king replied that he wished their relations to remain entirely unpolluted by politics and wholly preserved throughout the current hostilities. Andersen's response was a highly-charged, romanticised affirmation, referencing parent storks as symbols of peace who had stayed with their young despite shells falling on the island of Als. The king wrote back with gushing praise for his poetic imagery.

* * *

Having expected to die after finishing writing *Point of View*, completed effortlessly and within a month, Kierkegaard deferred publication, and it was in fact only sent to press four years after his death by his brother Peter. Instead, he wrote an alternative short piece, *On My Work as an Author*, which appeared accompanied by *Two Discourses at the Communion on Fridays*. Similarly motivated by facilitating the posthumous understanding and reception of his works, he cultivated Rasmus Nielsen, professor of philosophy at Copenhagen University, inviting him to accompany him and discuss philosophy on his daily walks and so confirming his suspicion that 'a disciple is the greatest of all calamities'.[16] It later transpired not to have been such a bad move after all, as Nielsen was able after Kierkegaard's death to help a bewildered public understand his sudden turning upon the Church. As for the *Point of View*, the underlying reason for his postponing publication was complex, associated with deep diffidence concerning the right a man has to let people know how good he is; it was the same scruple that delayed publication of *Training in Christianity*, given that this work insisted upon the imitation of Christ. Kierkegaard had grown used to scornfully rooting out of his mind the sort of cynical notion that he might circumvent the dilemma by getting himself ensconced in a parish or professorship at the Pastoral Seminary before putting out these polemical works; he knew just how inventive he was in devising shrewd moves. There were another two practical components to his hesitation: penury, and fear of the retribution of the world for his assault on the Church. A further reason for vacillation was as surprising as it was central: his abiding hope for rapprochement with Regine.

---

16. Lowrie, *A Short Life of Kierkegaard*, p. 212.

The vow to speak out inevitably brought back awareness that had he been able to do so before he would never have lost her. He longed for reconciliation but was convinced her marriage hinged on his discretion: should he give her certainty as to how much she had been and remained loved she would regret her marriage. His construction was that however much she had once seen in him she must remain convinced of his meanness as this belief was the liberating feature upon which her marriage rested. He had judged her 'not religious enough to stand by herself with an unhappy love'[17] and had never dared offer her direct help. So audacious an assumption of her spiritual poverty and inability to cope with real life could only arise from the integrity of Kierkegaard's despair at his own sense of inadequacy. He knew he could not protect her from pain. Again and again, he had recoiled religiously from intervening in her life, feeling their relationship too sacred for any crude attempt at 'help'.

The weakness in his reasoning lies in its comprehensive exclusion of any possibility of equally valid (femininely formulated and expressed) religiously motivated rejection on her part of such an offer, i.e. Regine neither wishing nor needing to be so 'helped'. It was as though, while recognising their parity, Kierkegaard was prevented from *realising* it; clearly as he perceived the foreign nature and profundity of her female religiosity, fear precluded him from fully engaging with and exploring it, so he could form no sound conception of her as his spiritual equal. Instead, he had continued to place naïve faith in his own writings, hoping that association with these would bring her joy and renown. Now he saw that the new direction taken by his religious work might produce an opposite effect, possibly involving them both in notoriety. For a long time, Kierkegaard had regarded Regine's father's opposition as the main obstacle to a reconciliation, but during the night of 25-26 June 1849 Councillor Olsen died. It happened that on 25 June Kierkegaard had again tried and failed to see Bishop Mynster about a living and reacted furiously to the latest snub by opting to publish *The Sickness unto Death* at once and under his own name. Learning of Olsen's death on 27 June, he had sent the manuscript off to the printer, having ascribed it to 'Anti-Climacus' with his own name remaining on the title page as editor.

'Anti-Climacus' did not now, as former pseudonyms, indicate distancing of the author but was meant to reinforce his reformatory

---

17. Kierkegaard, *Journals*, p. 246.

message concerning the perception of Christianity. The pseudonym was an afterthought, probably due to reproachment with Regine being uppermost in his mind, and it would become the only exception to his new determination to publish under his own name; he had immediately regretted the lapse and run to the printers to try to get the pseudonym deleted, but he was too late to stop the press and the book appeared with it *in situ* on 30 July the same year. The death of Regine's father coupled with this publication threw Kierkegaard into confusion over a possible reconciliation. On the one hand, an objection was removed, on the other, the new book might complicate his plans. After a strangely haunted night of prophetic hallucinations, he had decided not to withdraw the book. He waited five months and then made his move, on 19 November 1849 writing a short note seeking Regine's friendship and sealing this with a covering letter to her husband asking him to pass on the enclosed should he think fit. Two days later he received the note back, unopened, with a curtly indignant refusal from Fritz Schlegel. The same month Kierkegaard drafted his final instructions 'concerning "'Her'". It was his unalterable will that his writings, after his death, be dedicated to her and to his late father. She must belong to history.

* * *

The start of the year ushered in the end of one era and advent of a new, with the death on 20 January of Christian VIII. He had been suffering from kidney cancer, and some conclude that his foreknowledge of this had prompted him to secure Andersen's welfare in 1844. In any case, Andersen was so upset on hearing of the king's deathbed that he walked from Hotel du Nord to the Amelienborg Palace in the bitter cold evening snow to stand vigil beneath the royal bedroom window. Extraordinarily, Andersen left no immediate record on paper of this singularly personal loss. Perhaps it was simply too overwhelming, freighted, ambiguous, or even forbidden for any such public response on his part. Later he would record how, on the news of the king's death at 10.15p.m. he returned home and 'wept bitterly and tenderly for him, whom I had loved unspeakably.'[18]

The end of Christian VIII's reign would reverberate widely, marking as it did the demise of benign absolutist rule and a shift from energetic royal patronage of the arts to the rise of politics as

---

18. Wullschläger, *The Life of a Storyteller*, p. 314.

predominant social preoccupation. Literally overnight, the cultural climate of Denmark underwent irrevocable transformation. Ever hungry for artistic and intellectual company, Christian VIII had deliberately drawn both Andersen and Kierkegaard to him, and the latter, while hardly referring to this publicly during the King's lifetime, would retrospectively describe their encounters in copious journal entries. He had found their conversations 'well worth noting down.'[19] His first audience culminated in Kierkegaard parrying with the monarch about his, Kierkegaard's, preference for any future meetings to be held in private, and in assessing the intelligence with which he would have to deal (he found it not wanting). He thought he had approached the king physically far too closely in his 'fear and trembling', disorientated as he was by the etiquette of bowing, not bowing, or whether to get in on hands or feet; the king took a step back and caught his eye. The second time they met, Christian VIII made clear he wished not to speak but to listen, and his visitor discovered talking to him most stimulating. He had never seen an older man so animated. Such predatory enthusiasm roused Kierkegaard's suspicions: it was oppressive, possessive. He recognised in the king a 'spiritual and intellectual voluptuary',[20] a danger, the sort of man to keep at a distance. From now on Kierkegaard avoided visiting the palace as often as invited, using the excuse that he was unwell. While he relished the monarch's company, he did not wish to become over-appreciated. On his third visit, hoping to dispel the king's reported inability to understand his ideas, Kierkegaard presented him with a copy of *Works of Love*. Entering the royal presence, he handed the king the book and waited while he briefly scanned its pages, noticing the arrangement of the first section ('thou *shalt* love, *thou* shalt love thy neighbour, thou shalt love thy *neighbour*') and instantly grasped the sense... 'he was really very gifted.'[21] Christian VIII was, according to Kierkegaard, quite brilliant but run to seed, lacking commensurate moral backbone. Had he lived in a southern country, Kierkegaard could imagine such a personality falling prey to a cunning priest, but no woman would ever have got the better of him, partly because he was too intelligent, but mainly due to his embracing the manly superstition that a man is more intelligent than a woman. On the other

---

19. Kierkegaard, *Journals*, p. 283.
20. Kierkegaard, *Journals*, p. 284.
21. Ibid., p. 286.

hand, the king would have been unable to resist a Jesuit, especially one well-versed in the *interesting*, for that was what he was most hungry for. As far as it went, though, Kierkegaard found Christian VIII a captivating character, subtle and unusually alert to ways of pleasing the individual with whom he was interacting.

Kierkegaard had other, more penetrating, less flattering insights. He deduced that the king's inflated notion of his own cleverness had a limiting effect on his actual intelligence, making him easily threatened by a superior mind. He saw how the king's life had left its mark on a nervous disposition and vacillatory intellect. The monarch lacked moral attitude, religion touched him only aesthetically, so he compensated with cleverness: the imbalance had a weakening effect on character and exposed an individual to fraud. There was a weakness in Christian VIII, Kierkegaard noted, that elicited a domineering attitude when he found himself in the presence of real character; faced with strength of personality the king took refuge in avoidance techniques, distancing himself from the other. Overall, though, Kierkegaard considered Christian VIII had enriched him with a number of psychological observations and recommended psychologists pay some attention to monarchs, particularly absolute monarchs, 'for the more free a man is, the less he is bound by the cares of everyday, the better one can know him.'[22]

* * *

Peace restored, in early 1851 Andersen wrote to Weimar in the hope of visiting Carl Alexander and was stunned and mystified to receive the cold shoulder from the latter's historian and diplomat, Andersen's erstwhile friend Baron Karl Olivier von Beaulieu-Marconnay. Andersen had suffered a miserable winter, punctuated only by the publication of some patriotic poems to welcome home the troops in February. It was almost exactly a year since he had lost Oehlenschläger, and two years previously the king. In March, within a week of one another, death claimed two more of his oldest friends: Hans Christian Ørsted, who had been first to recognise the significance of Andersen's fairy stories, and Emma Hartmann, wife of the composer, J.P.E. Hartmann, and a composer in her own right. Emma was dearly loved by Andersen as the warm, witty mistress of the household upon which he had based his story *The Old House*. To

---

22. Ibid., p. 290.

his shock and distress, her death was followed a couple of days later by that of her six-year-old daughter, Maria, and this hit Andersen like a sledgehammer. Maria had been the model for the laughing, singing child in his story, and in his sentimentality it seemed to Andersen as though in the hour of her death the mother had prayed for this comfort and taken the child with her.

Kierkegaard's world was full of children, several motherless due to the early deaths of his sisters. His nieces and nephews adored him, and he spoiled them whenever possible. Two had visited him and Regine at the Olsen's one day, while they were together, and recalled the fun and joy of it. Another recorded visiting their uncle after the engagement was broken off, how sombre and sad he was, and how unhappy they felt at seeing their uncle in so unusual a mood. His niece Henriette Lund remembered many of his visits to her home, and how much he loved to see her mother, his favourite sister; she recalled her father coming home from work to find her uncle and mother play-fighting as though they were still children. Hearing his step, a short, suppressed laugh and seeing the slight figure appear, Henriette would shrink at the thought of his teasing and how her peace was at an end, only the next moment to be happily reminded of the tenderness and hidden affection in her uncle's character.

She and the other children did not know about their uncle's broken engagement, but one day soon after Uncle Peter's marriage they had visited the old house at Nytorv to be met by his new wife, delighted that they had come to visit on their own initiative. At the same moment Uncle Søren appeared to fetch them to his room, looking very sombre and moved. Instead of all his usual jokes, he kissed his twelve-year-old niece very gently on her head and seemed to want to talk to them but instead broke down in tears. So surprised and confused were they by this that the children began to weep as well, and soon they were all crying together as though some terrible catastrophe had befallen them all. When Uncle Søren could control his tears, he told them he was going to Berlin for a while, and asked if they would all please write to him there, and of course they promised to do so. On his return, he invited the children back for an unforgettable celebratory reunion at his rooms in Nørregade 43, into which he had moved on 18 April 1850. Henriette and her cousin were presented with bunches of lily of the valley and her uncle distributed beautiful gifts to everyone, then took them all out on a surprise carriage tour of the city's special sights, places unfamiliar to them. Henriette remembered having seen a seal, whose sad, human eyes made a great impression on her. Back at the house there were games, then dinner with marzipan cake decorated with flowers, and champagne. She recalled how her parents had disapproved of the lavishness of this occasion. She spoke too of the influence her Uncle Søren had later had upon her, encouraging her in embroidery and reading Shakespeare. And how once he had made sure that she was included in a trip her older brother and cousin were making to Paris and London.

A year after this happy occasion, his nephew Carl Lund was writing to tell Uncle Peter of Uncle Søren's move out of town and into the country, where he had found a big second-floor apartment with wonderful views down over the lake and park, to which he now also had access. Kierkegaard was to occupy his six-room apartment in this stately villa in the park from April 1851 until October 1852, where in the harbour and pier district of Copenhagen the statue now stands of Andersen's Little Mermaid. It was from here that Kierkegaard took his daily walks with a little more ambition than mere exercise. In the entry dated May 1852, a section in his journal announces itself *'About her'*, and describes how Regine met him in the lakeside park every day during the latter part of 1851, passing on the same path, the Lange Linie, at precisely ten in the morning. Their exact trajectories are outlined, between Lange Linie and the Lime Kiln. How they managed these silent assignments, and kept their regularity is a mystery, but they were a cause of anxiety for Kierkegaard, who was too well-known in the city and noticed the attention of other regular walkers who knew them both. He decided to alter the habit, both for his own sake and for hers; it was exhausting, anyway, to pursue the same pattern day after day. So on New Year's Day 1852 he altered his course, and after one encounter he began varying it, and they met no more for a while. Then she met him at eight in the morning on his new route into the city, and thereafter they often passed either on this road or on his path along the ramparts… 'Perhaps,' he wrote with rare timidity, 'it is coincidence, perhaps.'[23] He speculates on her change of direction being due to the east wind, but she also came by when the wind was from the west. They continue to see each other at exactly the same time in the morning, and on Sunday in church. Then came his birthday. Normally he went out, but this year felt unwell and stayed at home apart from a visit to the doctor in town. Leaving the

---

23. Kierkegaard, *Journals*, p. 458.

house, he found her almost on his doorstep and couldn't suppress a smile – 'oh how important she has become!'[24] She smiled back and bowed to him. He doffed his hat and moved on.

The following Sunday at church a strange incident occurs, disconcerting them both. The officiating priest, Pauli, preaches not as expected on the Gospel but on the epistle: 'Every good gift and every perfect gift etc.' (James 1:17). At this, Regine turned her head and sent Kierkegaard what he thought was a heartfelt look; he remained staring straight ahead, shaken to the core by the sudden sound on the air of words they had shared, those he had always laid stress upon. It was the text they had read together in their earliest religious interludes and exchanges. He could not imagine how or why Pauli had chosen it, and could hardly credit that she remembered it too, but he had heard on good authority that she had read his *Two Addresses* of 1843 in which he had used the text. As Pauli began his sermon: 'these words are "implanted in your souls"… 'if these words should be torn out of your soul would not life have lost its value' etc.[25] Kierkegaard felt Regine's shock pass simultaneously through him, and knowing the violence of her reactions, he was frightened for her. It seemed to him a higher power was telling her what he could not, dared not, had not been able to say. Serendipity means much to lovers. It must have been known to each that the walkway on which they met every day was called the 'Marriage Path', an irony surely lost on neither, especially not arch-ironist Kierkegaard. Fit for a new dissertation! However, he was not now producing books. His mode of attack on the Church was ripening in the 'Gathering Storm' and he published nothing between 1852 and 1854, when he finally launched his attack on 'Official Christianity'. Meanwhile the journal expands exponentially with aphorisms, formulations, new concepts and consolidation as though, at rest from his usual sustained literary effort, his mind prepared another lifetime of the same.

* * *

Following his cancelled trip to post-war Weimar, Andersen set off in May 1851 for Paris instead. He travelled in his usual leisurely fashion via Germany and Prague, accompanied this time by another of Jonas Collin's ungrateful grandsons, this time Viggo Drewsen.

---

24. Ibid., p. 459.
25. Ibid.

It was a depressing journey. Schleswig-Holstein lay in ruins, with burnt-out buildings, bare scorched earth and rows of graves which led Andersen to describe Flensburg as a garden of death. Anti-Danish feeling was rife; Andersen encountered it everywhere they went and felt he could breathe freely again only once Holstein and Hamburg too were behind him. To make things worse, Viggo proved a dismal companion and Andersen was again plagued with toothache. The company of a Collin grandson on his travels during the 1850s and 1860s was a mixed blessing for Andersen; each as thankless and ungracious as the last, they at least allowed him to share the experience with a young man, so alleviating to some extent his incapacitating loneliness. As the grandsons could not otherwise have afforded to travel and Andersen was at last financially secure, it was also a way of repaying the Collins for all their many years of kindness and generosity. On his return to Nyhavn Andersen was gratified to be appointed an honorary professor and soon settled into writing a new and innovative collection of stories. Entitled *Historier* (*Stories*) rather than *Eventyr* (*Tales*), these pieces came out in two volumes, the first in spring 1852 and the second in November, and were far more adult in tone than his previous work, closer to short stories in form and content. From now on Andersen no longer considered himself a writer for children. The fabular quality of his early work was abandoned and he began to produce works in which myth and magic are absent and even the archetype is missing. It would take a decade for him to refine this new approach. In speculating as to the genesis and reason for this, Wullschläger refers to *The Shadow*, but also to new world order and vanished certainties. Whatever else was working on the author's consciousness, Andersen was also surely much more indebted to and influenced by Dickens than is generally acknowledged in embracing the exhilarating possibilities of the modern industrialised age alongside a clear view and exposure of its misfortunes.

Certainly, the literary migration is dramatic, away from *The Ugly Duckling* and *The Snow Queen* to Andersen's 1852 two-page narrative *Thousands of Years from Now,* in which young Americans fly to the old homeland of memory and romance, Europe! Here, just fifteen years after the advent of the first steam train, Andersen is accurately depicting future air travel and a tunnel beneath the Channel. Perhaps the war years had a sobering effect on the storyteller, dispossessing him once and for all of the pervasive innocence he had fostered for so long in his life and writings. In any case, and in contrast to all his former Luddite tendencies, some of the new stories evince brave new curiosity and excitement regarding current scientific innovation. Imaginatively and in content they are reminiscent of the French 'father of science fiction' Jules Verne (1828-1904), whose oeuvre reverberates with the same slightly surreal prescience of human ambition and innovation, including ingenious vehicles of transportation to places as yet unexplored and unmapped by man.

The tenor of much of this new work was nonetheless as introspective as the old and more exposed to adult scrutiny now that he had dropped the stylistic shield of fairy tale. In the absence of this cover or any new literary device, his main protagonists become frankly drawn from life. *She Was Good for Nothing* is a barely veiled portrait of his mother, the story of a drunken washerwoman whom no one can respect and who dies before she can be told of the legacy she has forfeited by unselfishly relinquishing a rich lover. At her graveside the son pleads, "Is it true that she was good for nothing?" He went on to write *Under the Willow Tree*, another recognisable depiction, this time of his unrequited love affair with Jenny Lind; the heroine called 'Johanne' (Jenny's real name) and his own self-portrait in the hero, 'Knud'. The narrative follows his clumsy and ineffectual attempts at courtship, proposing to the heroine having been impressed with her onstage presence, and Johanne's demoting him from suitor to brother – exactly as it happened in real life. The story ends with Knud frozen to death beneath a willow tree, a metaphor perhaps for Andersen's response on hearing of Jenny's sudden surprise marriage to the German pianist Otto Goldschmidt. All in all, the tale is a tragic reprise of the author's inability to process past experience, his entrapment in fantasy, and the often arctic emotional paralysis which pervaded his love life.

In 1852 he risked visiting Weimar anew and was again troubled by Beaulieu-Marconnay, as well as a new governess. He found the court much changed and the atmosphere edgy. It was a relief to be invited to the Villa Altenburg, gifted as music studio and creative refuge to Liszt, who had just moved to Weimar. Above the composer's piano in the elegant music room hung a fine crystal chandelier. Buzzing with Bohemian comings and goings, conviviality and creative minds, the villa was exactly to Andersen's taste, full of gracious reception rooms and endless bedrooms occupied rent-free by resident students. The imposing mansion stands there still today, on raised ground in a park of ancient trees, grandly porticoed yet welcoming and somehow homely. After his sojourn here Andersen made his way back to Denmark via Bavaria and Switzerland, stopping at Milan and looking forward to a quiet autumn in Copenhagen. Spring 1853 brought the death of Andersen's publisher, Reitzel, and this loss was followed by news that Carl Friedrich of Weimar had passed away, leaving Carl Alexander to inherit his title. Andersen had for some time been unable to close his eyes and ears to a rising tide of calamities that seemed to augur the end of an era for him, and now Copenhagen was hit by a cholera epidemic which killed nearly five thousand people in under three months, including two more members of the Collin family. The storyteller fled the city for Glorup, where silver-wedding celebrations were underway for Count Moltke-Hvitfeldt. Andersen, emotionally overcome but profoundly relieved to be so safely back on the estate, lay weeping in bed while his fellow guests danced and fireworks lit the night sky. Advised against returning to Copenhagen, he spent the summer instead in Jutland with the Drewsen family, returning to Copenhagen when the cholera outbreak abated to find theatres packed every evening and social life back in full swing. His winter routine resumed, and Christmas was spent with Jonas Collin and other friends.

May 1854 found him off on his travels once more, this time with yet another Collin grandson, Einar Drewsen. Starting off in Dresden, Andersen commenced a veritable round of old friends, finding a radiant Jenny Lind, married with her new baby in Vienna, and meeting up with Liszt in Weimar. He spent two days with the new Grand Duke Carl Alexander. Back home, he even paid a visit to Jonna and Henrik Stampe, and took his London publisher, Richard Bentley, to the Tivoli. Alongside writing a Danish version of his autobiography, Andersen was also working on a collected edition of his works in 22 volumes which would appear between November 1853 and 1855. Income from the first two of these had funded the trip with Einar Drewsen. From Reitzel's sons he received generous payment for this edition and again for a second printing of his tales illustrated by Pedersen. Publication of the collected work earned new reverence for Andersen in Denmark, helped by an important 20-page critical essay by the Icelandic author Grimùr Thomson (1820-96) in which the Danes were scolded for failing to pay Andersen due respect, especially given how seriously he was taken in England and Germany. Andersen was thrilled, and on 3 April 1855 told his dear, long-suffering hunchback friend Jette Wulff that this was the first judgement on him 'as a poet which is unconditional in its approval – beautifully composed, as well as clever, written with knowledge and with love'.[26]

The previous day, his fiftieth birthday, he had corrected the proofs of the Danish version of his autobiography, *Mit Livs Eventyr* (*The Fairy Tale of My Life*), which differed hardly at all from its German predecessor. It is a rollcall of rich and famous admirers, ending on the same heroic note: the story of his life up until now lies before him in all its glory, beauty, comfort and eventfulness. Out of evil had come good, from pain only joy. It is a poem more profound than he could possibly have penned... 'I feel that I am a child of good fortune.'[27] Not until after Andersen's death did the critic Georg Brandes observe of him that his personality was scarcely ever occupied with anything greater than itself, was never absorbed in an idea, never entirely free of the ego. As for all the obsequious name-dropping, Henriette Wulff was having none of it. She wrote to Andersen, launching her attack with her usual loving but scrupulous care for honesty. His book, she said, was a betrayal of himself. She found it inexplicable that someone like him, someone so endowed by Grace with special spiritual gifts, could consider himself honoured to be seated at the table of the King of Prussia, or some such high-ranking personage, or flattered by some decoration of the sort awarded the worst scoundrels and nobodies. Could it be true that he valued external things – title, wealth, nobility, good fortune – higher than genius, spirit, 'the gifts of the soul?'[28] Miffed as ever by her telling-off, the great man responded that perhaps he might be a touch ungrateful to his God when some prince pressed his hand in loving sympathy, but that was due simply to the poor circumstances of his birth. After all, he had suffered greatly in ascending to the present heights, and he repeated his theme song, admonishing Jette that his life was the strangest fairy tale. It was Andersen at his worst, but this cavalier treatment of a precious friendship harboured its own nemesis. Over the many years of their friendship Andersen wrote endlessly to Jette; at some level he must have perfectly well understood the depth of her feeling for him and been shamed by it. He dreamt a ghastly nightmare of her dying in a fire aboard ship, from which he awoke shaking with terror. Her father,

---

26. Wullschläger, *Hans Christian Andersen*, p. 337.
27. Andersen, *My Fairy-tale Life*, p. 515.
28. Wullschläger, *Hans Christian Andersen*, p. 338.

Admiral Peter Frederik Wulff, often offered her passage somewhere, but she did not travel as much as Andersen.

Andersen's second visit to England and the Dickens family country home at Gad's Hill in Kent in summer 1857 would go less well than the first. It was three years since his debut conquest of Britain and while his second arrival was greeted with warmth by the famous novelist, Andersen's temperament soon proved too much for the rest of the family. The first night he complained of being a little cold in bed, and no one came in the morning to pick up his clothes and shave him. The longer he stayed, the harder it became to communicate with a guest who refused to learn English. Novelist Wilkie Collins was a fellow guest, and perhaps the household felt a little too much extra strain on its resources. While Charles Dickens, exhausted from writing *Little Dorrit* and with his marriage at breaking point, remained the perfect kind and courteous host, after a month everyone else wanted Andersen gone. Formerly charming, entertaining and polite Dickens children remained decidedly Dickenses; one of the more outspoken declared his intent to kick Andersen out the window. Poor reviews of the English edition of his *To Be or Not to Be*, a new volume of stories dedicated to Dickens, left Andersen lying prone, sobbing and distraught on the lawn, from where Mrs Dickens had to rescue him. Even he noticed how the women and girls shrank from him, but each time the man of the house came home all returned to sweetness and light. A last straw must have been Wilkie Collins falling victim to Andersen's puerile love of practical jokes, when the storyteller secretly garlanded Collins' broad-brimmed hat with daisies and persuaded him to take a walk through the village, turning him into a laughingstock among the locals. One way and another, everyone was relieved to see the Dane off on 15 July.

A year later, between June and August 1858, Andersen was again on his travels, this time to Germany and Switzerland, but avoiding Weimar due to political anxiety. His travelling companion was another Collin grandson, Harald Drewsen, as contrary and awkward as his cousins. Staying with friends in Maxen on his way home, Andersen received a letter from Jette Wulff telling him of her planned voyage to New York. Sitting out a month in Hamburg awaiting passage to America, Jette lightly suggested that it was almost his duty to come and see her once more at Eisenach on his way through and give her his brotherly blessing. In fact, it is possible she had important news to impart, that she was emigrating to the United States. Afraid of offending the grand duke in Weimar by passing nearby without visiting him, Andersen demurred. Jette, knowing the duke was away at the time, wrote back begging forgiveness for her selfish request; she often forgot, she said, that he was what was called a famous man. Andersen had added the reason that the youngest Drewsen boy, his travelling companion, wanted to see the old buildings somewhere else. This excuse Jette accepted with gentle grace and dignity that barely veils her love: she had read his letter with her heart, she wrote, and she begged him please to read this, her reply, with his own. She knew his heart, that it was a safe anchor-hold and would not betray the trust she placed in it. Of this she was sure, even if things might appear differently sometimes...

Henriette Wulff, painting by Adam Müller 1827.

The wording of her note is so unwittingly pertinent and poignant as to make it unbearable retrospective reading. One more letter came from her, asking Andersen not to forget her and sending him her blessing, then she sailed for the New World. Twelve days later, on 13 September, as the SS *Austria* neared New York, fire broke out onboard and the vessel sank with the loss of 449 souls. Andersen waited to hear whether Jette was among the 93 survivors, only to learn on 7 October that she had suffocated to death in her smoke-filled cabin. Overwhelmed with grief and guilt, he was plunged into fresh nightmares, so much the more hideous for being founded in the new reality. To a friend he wrote of the ghastly vision he was experiencing day after day as he relived the scene of her death; the more he thought of it, the more vivid it all became to his imagination: Jette's little feeble form, alone and helpless, as she succumbed to her fate. Of the few who truly loved him, he knew it was she who had most appreciated and overestimated him. He would never be released from her gentle affection and rebuke; never forgive himself for failing to make the detour she had requested to see her in Germany before she embarked on her final voyage. Her memory would haunt him literally up until his own dying day.

While awaiting news of Jette, Andersen drafted a speech which bears witness to the more mature and sophisticated state of awareness in which he was now living and writing. His audience was to be the newly formed Mechanics Association of Copenhagen, and it turned out to be so huge a turnout that people were clamouring to be let into the hall through the windows. Andersen begins by describing how all ropes used by the British Royal Navy carry through them a red thread, signifying that they belong to the crown. Through the lives of men, he continues, runs a thread telling them that they belong to God. It is the poet artist who delineates this invisible thread, as from the earliest times parables and allegories have shown us the same, which finds its echo in each of us... 'So the poet's art places itself by the side of Science, and opens our eyes for the beautiful, the good and the true.'[29]

* * *

The opening entry of Kierkegaard's copious journal for 1850 provides the clue to continuing misgivings about the quality and integrity of his penitence and humility; and his fear of appearing meritorious. It is a prayer for Christ's sufferance in redeeming him, however slowly he crept along, however he strayed from the right path. He was concerned about the opacity of his writing and the possibility of its being misconstrued. He did not want people to think he was superiorly calling for a dab of pietism on their doctrine, rather than the self-scrutiny which leads to abandoning 'understanding' for humility in true pursuit of grace. Searching further for fresh truth at the core of lost love, he was at the same time querying the role of sex in society and its significance for the individual. He quoted Montaigne's remarking on how extraordinary it was that we despised that to which we all owed our existence. He was referring to bashfulness, clarified Kierkegaard, which in this case is really prudery. Many great minds, he added, had held the same view. He qualifies Montaigne's remark, adding notes to illuminate his own position: only in one respect did man owe his existence to the act of procreation. There was also the act of creation attributable to God. Kierkegaard did not see an equivalence in this respect between human beings and animals. Every animal seemed to him an example of its kind, whereas the man who realised the purpose of his life in becoming spirit so reduced propagation to merely the lowest side of human nature. No wonder, then, that there was bashfulness in relation to the procreative act! In this man is led by the lower part of his nature, at the opposite extremity of synthesis

---

29. Ibid., p. 358.

from spirit. The directional drag away from spirit, or the fact that a man is defined as spirit, Kierkegaard described as bashfulness: an animal had no bashfulness, neither had bestiality. 'The less spirit, the less bashfulness.'[30] Neither did he wish to neglect the comical side of the matter, reminding the world that Wesley had lived for a long time unmarried, and even written a book on the single state before as an older man wanting to be wed. A little uncomfortable about this, given what had gone before, and concerned about his public image, Wesley sought the advice of some religious friends in order to be encouraged to do whatever took his fancy. 'You see,' concludes Kierkegaard with glee, 'that's what friends are for, I've always said so.'[31]

These observations on the interrelatedness of bashfulness and the spirit, echoing as they do Kierkegaard's lifelong preoccupation with his 'thorn in the flesh', are significantly moderated and universalised by his references to women which illustrate his understanding of the spiritual nature of feminine 'immediacy' and the role of physical passion in awakening the spirit. Woman, he wrote, always has more than man of the ingredient that seems to cause him worldly unhappiness, but it is that from which in so many ways life derives: 'she has more heart.'[32] Despite his incapacity for intimacy, Kierkegaard writes more sympathetically of women in this regard than of men, and he aroused understanding and respect among his large female readership. His love for Regine has been regarded as a tragic narrative, but it is neither tragic nor was it new. It may be compared to that of the cloistered twelfth-century lovers Abelard and Héloïse, crucified on the Golgotha of their carnality, twinned spirits notwithstanding. Neither of these histories is 'tragic', except in the worldliest sense; rather, each is radiantly transcendent, proving that real love does not rest on tending and treats, nor does it require statement or structure or easement strategies. It does not need 'a happy ending'. As art critic and novelist Anita Brookner (1928-2016), past mistress of the minutiae of love, loss and loneliness observed, real love is a pilgrimage for which there is no strategy, and that is why it's very rare: most people are strategists. Kierkegaard knew the impossibility of love between human beings in the absence of its *a priori*, and so did Regine Olsen. An even older precursor to their story is that of the

---

30. Kierkegaard, *Journals*, p. 408.
31. Ibid.
32. Ibid.

father who took his son to a mountain there to sacrifice him to his God.[33] What, asked Kierkegaard, is hidden in this story? The father who becomes a monster; the son who sees his father with the knife and cries out to God for mercy. The unspeakable conversion at the heart of the moment. The leap of faith. Kierkegaard knew that 'she' would read his words and if her mind could not grasp the paradox, her soul surely would.

---

33. Genesis 22: 1-19.

Chapter 11

Divine Folly

It was rumoured that one bitterly cold late winter day Regine Olsen Schlegel ran out into the street from her home, where she had overseen the last of the packing; everything was in trunks and tea-chests ready for shipping. She and her statesman husband, Fritz, were leaving Denmark that 18 March 1855 for the island of Saint Croix in the Danish West Indies, where he had been posted as the new governor. His wife was at this moment in a quite ungovernable state, scouring the vicinity for Søren Kierkegaard, whom she knew would not have taken a long walk in such weather. Apparently, she caught up with him and in passing whispered, "God bless you. May all go well with you!" It is not known at what point exactly he learned of her departure. Bishop Mynster had died on 30 January the previous year, to be succeeded in April 1854 by Professor Hans Lassen Martensen (1808-84), an authority on Hegel and author of an important treatise on ethics. Martensen was consecrated on 6 June. He had taught Kierkegaard at the University of Copenhagen between 1830 and 1841. Professor Martensen was a man whom Kierkegaard disliked but had defended against detractors, citing his status as the most eminent theologian in Denmark. Kierkegaard had a very great deal more he wanted to say about Martensen, starting with his farewell eulogy for his predecessor, but several factors militated against the younger man unburdening himself.

Kierkegaard's love for Mynster had meant that despite their differences he had enjoyed close, open and honest communications with the bishop. He knew that *Training in Christianity* had enraged Mynster, who had taken it as a personal insult. Kierkegaard had been appraised of this by Pastor Pauli, the pastor's son-in-law, who had relayed Mynster's furious condemnation of the work as 'a profane game played with sacred things'[1] and the bishop's intention to tell Kierkegaard this personally the next time he saw him. By now the book had been out for three weeks without a dissenting murmur from the Church, and Mynster had even mentioned its publication in a sermon; one of his remarks had seemed to Kierkegaard conciliatory, and he had welcomed it as a possible opportunity for discussion. Next day, 22 October 1850, Kierkegaard sought out Bishop Mynster to make amends, at which point the bishop denied that the book had caused him offence... 'I have no right to reprimand. I have told you before that I have no objection to every bird singing its own song.'[2] He added that people had a perfect right to say whatever they liked about him. This remark sounded hollow to Kierkegaard and he instantly assured Mynster that he had meant no offence, begging the bishop to tell him if he had in any way distressed him by publishing such a book. Mynster then admitted he had indeed been upset; he really considered the book less than helpful. In his journal Kierkegaard expresses himself content with this response, which seemed honest, sympathetic and personal. He felt the situation had been redeemed, but by the time a second edition of *Training* appeared in the middle of his attack on the Church he had changed his mind, declaring that had this been the first edition he would have strengthened his polemic by withdrawing his Preface and the Moral which ends the first part; in retrospect he felt these sections softened the severity of the book to its detriment.

The Moral offered the essence of all that was required of a Christian: in quiet inwardness to humble oneself before God, honestly admitting how things stood with us so as to receive the grace offered the imperfect. For the rest we should simply love and rejoice in our life, in work, marriage, children and our fellow beings. Although the Law seemed terrifyingly to demand that we hold fast to God by our own power, in the language of love it is Christ who holds us fast, and if any more is required of us He will let us know exactly what. The

---

1. Kierkegaard, *Journals*, p. 409.
2. Ibid.

trouble was that becoming a Christian had been reduced to less than nothing, mere sleight of hand, idiocy. The matter was as simple and substantial as that.

In case any room was left for misunderstanding, Kierkegaard underlined his message with a note on *The Proof of Christianity* in which he ordered the clerics to keep their mouths shut on Sundays; for if scrutiny of their daily lives failed to disclose the essence outlined in his Moral, how could they be preaching Christianity? Here is the devout compassion of Kierkegaard's position, the gravity with which he balances the severity of his criticism of the way Christianity had become a sort of default position, something which everyone just *was* as matter of course. He feared posterity judging him as refractory exponent of haughty, narrow-minded religiosity while in truth he rejected all sectarianism, only ever advocating the unalloyed Christianity of the New Testament. The 'church' for which he stood was a truly broad and democratic concept based not on grandiosity but free moral choice and humility. The grandeur and hauteur of the Protestant Lutheran Church seemed to him entirely wrong-footed. From where he stood, Kierkegaard saw the demise of monastic tradition as catastrophic in effect: 'The Meaning of the Reformation is that Luther installed girls, wine and cards in their rightful place in the Christian Church... a real perfection as opposed to the imperfections: poverty, prayer and fasting.'[3]

Sharpening his quill, he lambasted the entire Protestant Reformation for its inability to substitute for Catholicism anything properly religious, including the slightest concept of renunciation. Having done away with the monastery, Reformed Christianity stumbled about directionless and worldly business thrived as never before. Every sectarian division of Lutheranism he subjected to the same critique; Calvinism he completely ignored. Kierkegaard's 'Moral' implies, according to Lowrie, reintroduction of the Catholic idea of *concilia*,[4] which discriminates between counsels of perfection and duties imperative for every Christian. Having dispensed with this distinction, Protestantism replaced it with a dilution of the more demanding maxims of the Gospel. Dislodged and discredited was the aspirational position of the saint, the martyr, the disciple and

---

3. Ibid. p. 402.
4. Lowrie, *A Short Life of Kierkegaard*, pp. 220-221.

witness, and even the monk, replaced by a watered-down version of the religion which asked only practise of the most basic Christian duties.

This summarises the fundamental premise of Kierkegaard's assault on the Established Church, especially in Denmark, and he knew that in this extreme he would be taken seriously only if supported by the most senior cleric. His demand must, even to himself, have seemed unrealistic: that the new bishop publicly admit how the current form of Christianity was a sham, no more than mild accommodation of human weakness. In holding high the ideal, Kierkegaard hoped to shine a little light, to show every individual that in their weakness they may accept grace. He believed he had offered Bishop Mynster, the man he had most loved, the one way that remained of standing up valiantly in vindication of the Church. His trust had been disastrously misplaced. On 9 November 1854 he committed to his journal the bitter depths of his disappointment; it was not that Mynster had caused him such grief by failing to live up to his hopes and needs, but rather the guile displayed by the cleric in convincing the world of his stature as a leader. In Kierkegaard's eyes Mynster was by now reduced to the status of Sunday orator, hack, a slave to public opinion, and he had told the bishop so frankly to his face in private. The trouble was that Mynster did not care what was said to him behind closed doors, 'he was afraid only of the public, for he was a coward.'[5]

Kierkegaard now mobilised his gift for satire on several fronts, not least to illuminate the character of 'The Professor' Martensen, and for this purpose he took as template the field of mathematics. A famous mathematician might sacrifice his life for the sake of his discipline, leaving teachings for others to follow. Here the essential is the teaching, the personal life of the teacher being immaterial. However, in terms of Christianity there is no teaching, the whole object is imitation of the master, and this is the essential... 'what nonsense it is therefore that instead of following Christ or the Apostles and suffering as they suffered, one should become a professor – of what?[6] The mission had become to persuade Martensen to take upon himself the mantel Kierkegaard had fashioned for his predecessor. As his diatribe gathered strength, so it grew in imaginative majesty. He returned to marine analogy, describing a passenger liner at sea. All

---

5. Kierkegaard, *Journals*, pp. 532-33.
6. Lowrie, *A Short Life of Kierkegaard*, p. 228.

is luxury, dancing, champagne, fine dining. On the bridge stands the captain, giving commands. The master mariner at last retires to his berth, opens his Bible at random and finds on the page a warning that his soul may be taken from him that night. Upstairs between decks the music and dancing gathers momentum and the captain goes back up, the life and soul of the party. A white speck has appeared on the horizon, but is noticed by just one man, a passenger, and although not a seaman he is frightened and sends word to the captain to come and look. The captain, however, is raising his glass to his own health and ignores the message. Again, the passenger tries to alert the captain, and again fails… It will be a dreadful night. It is dreadful for the noisy passengers that only the captain knows what impends, but the most important thing is that he knows, so even worse when the only other person who knows this is a passenger. As Kierkegaard interpreted things, a terrifying tempest was brewing and about to descend upon Christianity; he clearly saw the sign, but as mere layman was in no position to save the ship.

Now, like the captain in his earlier sketch of the man-o'-war, Kierkegaard was again far out on the deep and awaiting orders. From the end of January 1854, the journal pages teem with vignettes in which the writer rehearses his stance. His main target is the dissolution of Protestantism; secondarily, he takes aim at Martensen as the new commander of an impregnable stronghold who decides to build bridges over the moat… 'Charmant!' the fortress is transformed into countryseat and of course the enemy takes it. The template for Christianity is changed, and so the world appropriates it. Martensen's greatest misstep, according to Kierkegaard, was his official memorial eulogy given on the fifth Sunday of Epiphany, two days before Mynster's funeral. In this politically calculated address Martensen had pronounced the deceased an irreplaceable prelate (whom he expected to replace), a genuine witness for the truth, not only in word and profession but also in deed, and numbered the late bishop among the chain of holy witnesses stretching back to the days of the Apostles. Martensen, himself well appraised of Kierkegaard's relations with the late bishop, had used the specific wording 'witness for the truth' deliberately, and Kierkegaard had no hesitation in taking this as personal provocation. It was the word of command he had been waiting for, and he sat down at once to write an excoriating article for the daily newspaper exposing Mynster's shortcomings and asking whether 'the Professor' was himself telling the *truth*. This was the article delayed a year by two main scruples; firstly, Kierkegaard felt it unseemly to launch any kind of attack on Martensen until he had been officially appointed to the vacant See. Secondly, a popular subscription had been set up for a memorial to the late bishop and Kierkegaard waited discreetly for this to be fulfilled. Finally, on 18 December 1854 *The Fatherland* carried his article – but published with the original February date to show how long he had waited.

The piece was greeted by the public with shock and consternation. His contemporaries were dumbfounded by the violence of this sudden salvo against Church and State by a Kierkegaard they had known as conservative, a loyal supporter of the status quo. Had he lost his mind? There was certainly rumour and conjecture surrounding his physical health, he looked much frailer these days, but no outside observer could have guessed with what deliberate intellectual acuity he had prepared and was now focused on his task. His lifelong trajectory had led him here, and now the goal was in sight. The assault on Martensen's speech was merely the opening volley of his campaign; now Kierkegaard had found his moment he was to forge ahead relentlessly, speaking out in support of his one thesis, elemental as it was iconoclastic: that Christianity no longer exists. He proceeded to publish a series of twenty articles averaging one a week in *The Fatherland* in which he expanded on his theme. In a finale to the series, printed on 26 May 1855, he thundered at Martensen's cowardice in failing to react to his attack in any convincing way, enumerating the aspects in which the bishop's silence was indefensible in Christian terms, being laughable, obscurely sagacious and in more than one way contemptible.

Just before the appearance of this last article, he had issued a separate tract, *The Midnight Cry*, referring to Matthew 25:6. It was a public plea for people to stop participating in divine worship as it now was, which made God out to be a fool by pretending to be the Christianity of the New Testament, which it was not: such refusal would be one less burden of guilt on their shoulders. Kierkegaard waited in perturbation for the reaction, none came. He had completely misjudged the effect of the piece, which he had truly thought would land him in prison or put to death by the mob. What he had underestimated was in the first place how highly regarded he was among the general public, and secondly the apathy of the Church. Just in case, the Prime Minister had made clear that if anyone had the temerity to arrest an author who had crowned Denmark with so much glory he would immediately order his release. Who then was left to condemn him? Not the younger generation, who were his most ardent supporters, and not the clergy, most of whom had never read his work, had no idea what was going on, or else just let a minor squall pass for what it was. As for Bishop Martensen, lame as ever, he too found silence his best ally. 'The establishment', pronounced Kierkegaard, 'is so demoralised that one can spit in its face, and it takes care to sneak away.'[7] Perhaps he regretted the lack of a more dramatic response which may have strengthened his cause. Yet he was as much to blame as anyone for the nonplussed or lukewarm reaction to his outburst, having continued to attend church regularly until *The Midnight Cry* and missed not a single one of Mynster's sermons up until the last. Most Copenhageners who met him on the street found him a most charming and pious member of society.

After his final article in *The Fatherland*, Kierkegaard began a pamphlet he called *The Instant*, to which he invited the public to subscribe. This became more popular than *The Fatherland*, the daily newspaper he had been using all along to promulgate his views, and he could be sure it was read by people who understood the 'plea'. The pamphlet appeared fortnightly carrying seven or eight short features, all by Kierkegaard himself. The ninth number came out on 24 September, and the tenth was almost ready for the printer at the time of his death. Denying in his journal the accusation that he represented Christian severity in contrast to Christian leniency, he stated that all he wanted was mere human honesty. The point was, he wrote, that by canonising Mynster the new bishop made an indecent mockery of the church establishment. If Bishop Mynster was a witness for the truth, then so was every dog-collar in the land. What sort of man Mynster had been, however distinguished and extraordinary, was entirely irrelevant when it came to being a witness for the truth, which involved life, character, the very existence of an individual in terms of imitation. Given this, Mynster filled the bill for every priest who upheld the basic rules of civil obedience and respect for the law, which made every cleric in the land a witness for the truth, and this was obviously nonsense. Certainly, there were many clergymen, some of Kierkegaard's personal acquaintance, who were remarkably capable and respectable, but he would guarantee there wasn't one among them who, judged as a witness to the truth, would not be found plain comical.

---

7. Ibid., p. 243.

By now Kierkegaard's outbursts and projections are so urgently expressed as to sound frankly alarmist, and a catastrophic result for the author may be more easily imagined than at any previous stage in his confrontation with the Church. One of the final journal entries sketches his understanding of the future in the bleakest of terms as a 'frightful reformation' to come, compared with which the Lutheran 'will be almost a joke'. The new reformation, he prophesises, will mobilise under the banner of a universal search for faith, and will be recognisable by the fact of millions falling away from Christianity... 'for the thing is that Christianity no longer exists, and it is terrible when a generation which has been mollycoddled by a childish Christianity... has to receive the death blow of learning once again what it means to be a Christian.'[8]

* * *

On 2 October 1855, while working on the final issue of *The Instant*, Søren Kierkegaard fell to the floor unconscious. He found it difficult to walk afterwards but recovered enough to take his daily promenade. The same day he collapsed again, this time on the street. His legs were paralysed, and he was carried to Frederiks Hospital where on arrival he announced he had come there to die. His trouble was vaguely diagnosed as originating in the spine, but symptoms also involved the stomach and urinary tract; there was lower-limb neuropathy. He coughed up bloodstained sputum. In relation to the patient's physical frailty, the admitting physician took careful account of the toll taken on his physical health by superhuman commitment to his life's work. For the rest, Kierkegaard was

Frederiks Hospital, Copenhagen, where Kierkegaard died on 11 November 1855.

---

8. Kierkegaard, *Journals*, p. 547.

predictably non-compliant, countering all attempts at diagnosis and treatment with the assertion that his disease was not physical but purely psychical, and that the doctors' remedies would be useless. He was registered as a paying patient and allocated a single room furnished with soft carpets, a single bed, wardrobe, mirror, table and chair, and a bone-china tea-set in the corner cupboard. He received meals in half portions, probably in view of the alimentary symptoms. Prescribed topical turpentine for his back pain, he also received the sedative *Essensia valeriana officinalis* (valerian) for his nerves, and a calming tea of clover, chamomile and arnica morning and evening. Ten days after admission, his physician reported on the patient's insistence that he was dying. A few days earlier Hans Christian Andersen had anxiously informed Jette Wulff that Kierkegaard was very sick; it was rumoured he was paralysed in his lower body and he lay in the hospital.

His childhood friend and lifelong confidant, Pastor Emil Boesen, visited his bedside and spoke with Kierkegaard at regular intervals as life ebbed away. Confronted by mortality, Boesen did not shirk his clerical duty to interrogate the religious condition. Kierkegaard told him that like Paul he had his 'thorn in the flesh' which had debarred him from entering into the usual relations of life and led him to believe his task was the life and fate of an extraordinary messenger, and this was also what had stood in the way of his marriage with Regine Olsen. He had thought his condition might be changed, but it could not, so he had broken off his engagement. Boesen took notes as his friend elaborated on his love, expressing how extraordinary he found her husband's appointment as Governor of the Danish West Indies. Kierkegaard allowed Boesen to record his wish that this had not happened: he would have preferred everything to have gone off quietly. An enigmatic but emphatic remark that may be interpreted simply to allude to the suddenness of the Schlegel's departure from Denmark having sparked unwholesome public speculation, or far more profound personal trauma and grief of which Kierkegaard could never speak. He went on to dictate his approval of Regine having married Schlegel; it was after all Fritz to whom Regine had originally been engaged, and then he, Kierkegaard, had come along and thrown everything into confusion. His deathbed remarks on Regine are open, humble, contrite, loving, respectful and tenderly ironic: 'She suffered a good deal through me, I was afraid she would become a governess, but she did not, and yet she is one in the West Indies.'[9]

Asked if he had been angry or bitter, Kierkgaard replied he had not, but he had certainly been concerned about things and extremely indignant with, for instance, his brother Peter. Kierkegaard had by this time ejected Peter from his hospital room and forbidden him to return. The elder brother had delivered what the younger felt a detestable speech at Roskilde, the Lutheran conference, and now Kierkegaard enlarged on the sibling rivalry, describing how Peter thought himself the superior and natural leader just because he was at school while his younger brother was still having his bottom smacked. At this point Kierkegaard advised Boesen of a highly disparaging piece he had written about his brother, telling his friend it was at home in his desk. Peter, a Grundtvigian[10] had compared his passionate brother unfavourably with Martensen, whom Peter saw as an icon of sobriety while Søren personified an ecstatic monk whose ravings included swimming over seventy thousand fathoms without a lifebelt. Despicable! declared the dying man, whose epithets for Peter had demonstrated a good deal more verve and panache: the elder brother was variously a 'vapid gadabout', a 'fuddy-duddy' and 'nonsensical mediator'. A whimperer who 'specialised in literary theft' (of his younger brother's ideas), and who had eventually been promoted to pusillanimous, superficial and drivelling status as a 'figurehead of mediocrity'.[11]

When Boesen asked Kierkegaard whether he had done anything about his papers, the dying man replied no, let come of them what may, whose author was financially ruined and lay on his deathbed. He had nothing left beyond covering his funeral. His 'thorn in the flesh' had prevented him from taking on the only living open to him as a theological student, and that had led him to understand his life's task differently. Hereafter he had devoted himself to approaching God as

---

9. Ibid., p. 549.
10. Nikolai Frederik Severin Grundtvig (1783-1872) was a bishop and poet who is credited as having begun a movement named after him which revitalised the Danish Lutheran church. A social liberal, he advocated replacing current church doctrine with the living word as descended from historical revelation and passed down through the unbroken chain of sacramental tradition at baptism and communion.
11. Garff, *Kierkegaard's Muse*, p. 47.

nearly as possible, and while there were some who needed others for this purpose, there was one who needed only one. It was this one, said Kierkegaard, whose need was greatest, but who was also the least among men.

Boesen wondered whether his mind was clear or if his thoughts were confused? His friend said he was mostly lucid, but his thoughts wandered at night. Could he pray? Kierkegaard replied that he could, he prayed that his sins be forgiven and that he might know a little beforehand that death was nigh, so that it might be made pleasing to God. The same Thursday on which they had mentioned Regine the weather was so fine and Boesen found Kierkegaard looking so fresh and well, he suggested they might go out together. Kierkegaard replied that it was a great idea, the only problem being that he couldn't walk. He might, however, be carried. He had felt that he was growing angel's wings... and that was what he knew awaited him. Boesen was extremely concerned about the impression left on their world by his friend's forthright views, and now he ventured to ask whether there was anything Kierkegaard would like to moderate or change in what he had said? Gently but firmly Boesen drove his point home, protesting that Kierkegaard's statements had often been over-inflammatory and run counter to reality, his words far too severe... to which Kierkegaard retorted that had he spoken more softly no one would have taken any notice of his message. He accused Boesen of having no conception of the extent of Mynster's toxicity or how disastrously the late bishop had disseminated his corruption. It had taken mighty force to bring Mynster down and he, Kierkegaard, was now at peace. After all, he had seen Christianity from its innermost core and perceived the poverty and ungainliness of its current manifestation. As the pastor took his leave, Kierkegaard seems to have retreated a little from their contretemps, thanking him humbly and profusely for his loyalty and discretion in their friendship, and acknowledging its having been a cause of embarrassment to Boesen at times. He told his confidant how hugely grateful he was for his visits.

The next day he was on good form and gave a spirited resumé of how he had thrown his brother out of the hospital the previous evening. Boesen asked if he wanted to take Holy Communion and Kierkegaard said he did, but not from a parson; from a layman. This, responded his frocked friend, would be difficult. In that case, replied Kierkegaard, he would die without it. Boesen vehemently condemned the impropriety; Kierkegaard remained unmoved. He had made his decision and would brook no further discussion on the matter. The parsons were the King's officials, he stated, and the King's officials had nothing to do with Christianity. When his friend again objected, Kierkegaard enlarged: there were many men who looked for and found a comfortable life through Christianity, a thousand parsons, and as a result everyone was co-opted into the religion, so that now it was impossible even to die happy in the knowledge that one stood safely outside the club. Sovereignty now belonged to the clergy and God was deposed, but He must be obeyed in all things. As the dying man's voice weakened and he sank down uneasily in the bed Boesen withdrew, deeply disconcerted at their exchange. Much as he loved him, how could Kierkegaard think and say such things? it was apostasy! a layman could make anything he liked of the sacrament!

The following day his nurses had to carry the patient from bed to chair, he was almost incapable of holding up his head and asked Boesen to support it for him. Kierkegaard told him that the death-struggle had begun, and they should say their farewells. He thanked Boesen over and again for their friendship, and for causing him trouble which he would not otherwise have had. Boesen continued to visit every day, gauging his friend's deteriorating condition and sometimes staying only a few minutes. On 25 October, Kierkegaard was very weak and tremulous, rejecting a farewell sermon Boesen had brought him from someone whom he mistrusted. Another mild altercation took place between the two men when Boesen tried to assure his friend that he was in fact well regarded by people he accused of hypocrisy and betrayal; everyone had a right to self-defence, remonstrated Boesen, and goodness and blessedness existed even within the establishment Kierkegaard had so reviled. The patient replied that he could not bear to discuss it any further, he was worn out with the subject.

When the previous week Boesen had asked if there was anything Kierkegaard still wished to say, he had replied: 'No, yes, remember me to everyone, I was much attached to them all'.[12] He wanted them to know that his life had been a great suffering, incomprehensible to others. It may all have looked like pride and vanity, but it was not, and he had always maintained that he was no better than anyone else. By now he was failing fast and had been prescribed a stronger sedative in a higher dose. Boesen asked whether he had managed to achieve

---

12. Kierkegaard, *Journals*, p. 550.

all he had wanted with *The Instant* and Kierkegaard said he had; he was glad to have been able to get the pamphlet out. Faced with the choice of conserving his money and energy or continuing to work he had chosen the latter course, and then fallen, and now he was done. What a lot in your life has come out exactly right! Boesen consoled. Yes! responded Kierkegaard, that was why he was very happy and melancholy in equal measure, for he could not share his happiness with anyone. In truth, it was no stumble on the street to which he attributed his decline, but that fatal downfall hitherto admitted only in writing, and at last he spoke openly of the lack of faith which had prevented him from staying with Regine Olsen. So confidant became father confessor and the acme was articulated; in the presentation of Kierkegaard's final illness may be discerned at every level the accumulated pain, humiliation and defeat of all his life. He was dying of a broken heart.

The final exchange between the lifelong companions took place on 27 October. Finding his dear friend approaching the end of his sufferings, Boesen tried to introduce some cheer by commenting on the unusually busy street outside, to which Kierkegaard whispered of the pleasure and contentment the city's thoroughfares had once afforded him. A daily walk among his fellow citizens, the humblest of human pleasures. Lovingly, Boesen accused Kierkegaard of never having looked him up in his parish in Horsens: "No," rejoined Kierkegaard, "how should I have found the time!" On what was to be Boesen's final visit he found the dying prostrate, hardly able to speak. Recalling how Kierkegaard had prayed that he might know a little beforehand that death was approaching so that he might prepare for it, Boesen quietly withdrew, and soon afterwards, at 9 p.m. on 11 November, the end came. Søren Kierkegaard was 42. The cause of death is recorded in his medical notes tentatively as 'tubercul?' a diagnosis disputed by some, including Kierkegaard's biographer Joachim Garff, on grounds of the impossibility of the senior physician in charge, Seligmann Meyer Trier, having failed to recognise such common pathology. Instead, Garff posits ascending spinal paralysis, or Guillain-Barré syndrome, the aetiology of which is still unknown. So that the cause of death might just as well be left to the deceased, the only man who understood it. The same evening Hans Christian Andersen, in a gesture of grief-stricken love and respect identical to that he had offered the late king, came and stood desolately on the street beneath the window of Kierkegaard's room at Frederik's Hospital.

* * *

Throughout his stay there Kierkegaard had been attended by his nephew, Henrik Lund, the son of his brother-in-law, Christian. Henrik, a fervent follower and reader of all his uncle's works, was then a young intern, living and working at the hospital. Wholly respectful of his position as relative and junior clinician, he left no personal record of his uncle's final illness and deathbed. His care had been absolute, tender and the last gift of human love to be personally bestowed upon Kierkegaard by a member of his family. In common with all his nieces and nephews, Henrik had adored and been adored by him. There were many among and beyond his close circle who had greatly loved Kierkegaard, and after his death the philosopher and biographer Hans Brøchner wrote of him that he had always shown gentleness and loving sympathy, friendliness and humour for everyone, even in the smallest of matters, and his calm faith had not deserted him even through the severe trials of his deathbed. His niece, Henriette Lund, in her memoirs recalls her beloved Uncle Søren not only in happier times, but also at his life's end. On entering the sickroom, she was overwhelmed by the radiance that seemed to emanate from his face. It was something she had never seen before, as though the spirit broke free of the husk, imparting to it glory like that of 'the transfigured body on the resurrection morning.'[13]

His secretary, Israel Levin, spoke of Kierkegaard's superlative imagination and virtuosity with words, recollecting a conversation they had shared concerning Andersen one afternoon in the Frederiksberg Gardens when Kierkegaard had remarked, '"He has no idea what a fairy story is – what should he know about poetry – he has a kind heart and that is enough – it is all very innocent—but fairy stories!" and at once he conjured up six or seven stories so that I felt uncomfortable – his imagination was so vivid that it was as though he saw pictures before his eyes – as though he lived in a spiritual world and with an extraordinary impropriety and eccentricity – thus he described the Attic nights and immoralities of the Greeks, and as a contrast an anchorite in a wood suffering spiritual tribulation – and everything with a care that was indecent and demoniacal – with

---

13. Ibid., p. 561.

Divine Folly

regard to his descriptions he was of the opinion that only indecent thoughts should be avoided, not the daring expressions.'[14]

Ultimately, no words seem adequately to convey the brilliance, pathos, courage and luminosity of this life that ended in the quietest admission of defeat. Kierkegaard leaves us with his final utter surrender to failure, no attempt at excuse or mitigation. He found it quite appropriate after such an extraordinary life that death should arrive as and when it did in the public hospital. In the end he had no complaint against man or God. In his *Point of View* he had already announced his death would be a longing for eternity and, as usual, when it came to the decisive moment there was no evasion or compromise.

* * *

Peter Kierkegaard rushed to Copenhagen on the day of his brother's death. The future Bishop of Aalborg, banished from the deathbed, now faced burying his wayward sibling. Such botched funeral arrangements may or may not have been deliberate, in any case they were extraordinarily disrespectful of his brother, undignified and tactless in the extreme. Vor Frue Kirke was chosen for the ceremony: the bishop's cathedral, the church most representative of Established Protestantism in the whole of Denmark. The date, 18 November, fell on a Sunday, a day never used for burial, and the ceremony was crammed in between two services. This admixture of ineptitudes at least resulted in maximum attendance. The church was packed well in advance of the solemnities, the majority of the congregation young and among them many women. The only priests in the building were Peter Kierkegaard, due to give the address, and Dean Tryde, who was to conduct the graveside service. The atmosphere in the church was tense, awareness spreading of a certain unnamed impropriety in the situation. Slowly this sense among the mourners surfaced as barely muted anger and outrage at the way the Church had laid claim to this man who had so vehemently and publicly defied it, thus failing to respect his will. A motley group came forward and shuffled around the bier at the front of the church until disbanded by a larger contingent of students who took up positions of guard around the coffin. There was a feeling of impending free-for-all. Nevertheless,

---

14. Ibid., pp. 562-563.

Peter Kierkegaard's sermon was carefully calibrated to calm the crowd, and all went quietly in the church.

Once at the cemetery things took a very different turn. The moment everyone was gathered at the graveside Henrik Sigvard Lund stepped forward and took charge of proceedings. In a shattering defeat of protocol, the young doctor claimed the right to speak not only as Kierkegaard's nephew, but as one deeply familiar with the deceased and in sympathy with his thoughts. As no one was mentioning these and they appeared to have been immaterial to the proceedings so far, he invited the mourners now to join him in investigating their truth or untruth. It was as though his uncle rose again before the assembled company; Henrik's voice was strong, but equally calm and controlled as he inveighed against the Church and clergy for conveying Kierkegaard here in what amounted to a violation of his uncle's life and wishes. Quoting from Kierkegaard's articles in the *Fatherland* (*Fædrelandet*) and his pamphlet *The Moment*, in which he had so recently raged that even a free thinker who in the most outspoken terms had denounced the Christianity of his day as an outright lie could not avoid a Christian burial, Henrik went on to cite St. John the Divine addressing the Laodiceans on their lack of passionate commitment to God: 'I know thy works, that thou art neither cold nor hot; I would thou wert cold or hot. So then because thou art lukewarm, and neither cold nor hot, I will spue you out of my mouth.'[15] Henrik challenged all present: did this not precisely describe the situation? Was this not exactly the scenario being played out among them this very day? A poor man who had devoted his whole life, every iota of his vital energy to protesting against the individual being commandeered in this way by the 'Official Church', yet at the end committed to the earth as a beloved member of that same institution... precisely when he could no longer defend himself from it... This could not happen, declared the young doctor, within Jewish society, and never among the Turks or Mohammedans... No, such travesty was purely the preserve of official Christianity! Could this then be the true Church? It could not!

The speech was calculated to scandalise and the clerics present must have had difficulty controlling themselves. Perhaps the mood among many of the mourners was far less condemnatory; maybe it veered more towards suppressed approval, celebration, even triumphalism. A tight-lipped Dean Tryde reminded Henrik that it was not permitted for

---

15. Revelations 3:15-16.

laymen to speak at a funeral. Professor Rasmus Nielsen, philosopher and critic of Kierkegaard who had planned an address now left the scene. The whole ceremony had been a shambles, the official funeral reduced to farce. As the crowd dispersed, the coffin was lowered to rest in the family plot, but to this day no one knows precisely where Kierkegaard lies. Grass would soon cover the raw earth mound, but no attempt was made to mark the spot. Only long afterwards was Søren Kierkegaard's name inscribed on a marble slab, along with the verse he had chosen from a Danish hymn,[16] and this still leans against the pedestal of his father's monument in Copenhagen's Assistens Cemetery. The clergy immediately set about planning the penalties to be paid by Henrik Lund for daring to conduct himself in contempt of convention, including the gross offence he had committed against the Church in Copenhagen. He should be made to pay a fine and apologise to the dean and congregation for the profane impropriety and disrespect shown for the nation's most high church. Thus publicly upbraided, punished and humiliated, Lund withdrew into silence, psychological collapse, hospitalisation and breakdown.

Kierkegaard's gravestone leans against his father's in Assistens Cemetery.

Had Kierkegaard elaborated on his own funeral, even he could surely never have contrived a more faithful facsimile of his central contention. It was the perfect parody that proved his premise: faced with transparent integrity, the Established Church

---

16. In a little while / I shall have won, / Then the whole battle/ Will at once be done, / Then I may rest / In halls of roses / And unceasingly / And unceasingly / Speak to my Jesus. Possibly derived from Advent hymn by James George Deck (1802-1884), published in 1841 as *"A Little While"*: A little while – come, Saviour, come! / For thee thy church has tarried long; / Take Thy poor, wearied pilgrims home,/To sing the new eternal song. https://hymnary.org/text/a_little_while_our_lord_shall _come Accessed 22 November 2024.

conducted itself precisely as crudely and mendaciously as expected. Here was ossified objectivity faced down by impassioned subjectivity: morbid mediation challenged by a man acting in the true faith of 'immediacy after double reflection'. Henrik Lund knew Søren Kierkegaard's thought through and through; lifelong he had studied and made it his business to understand his uncle and his works, so that when the moment arrived his inspired insurrection could not miss its mark. Every facet of this final denouement would have delighted Kierkegaard, epitomising as it did the desecrated 'Christianity' he had depicted, deplored and fought to the death. The aesthetic in extremes of self-parody. The ethical entangled in internecine bickering and buckling on the lifebelt he recommended be foresworn when out over seventy thousand fathoms. The religious subsumed beneath sham. The terrible tyranny of an empowered clergy over commoner, body and soul. Above all, the nobility of suffering individuality in the struggle to know itself apart from the crowd so as to learn to love within it.

* * *

Two, small, almost identical envelopes addressed 'To Mr. Pastor Dr. Kierkegaard. To be opened after my death' were found by his brother in a desk in Søren Kierkegaard's lodgings the day after his funeral. The sealing wax on one was black, the other red. The black sealed envelope contained Kierkegaard's will, bequeathing 'unconditionally what little I leave behind' to:

> my former fiancée, Mrs. Regine Schlegel. If she herself refuses to accept it, it is offered to her on the condition that she act as trustee for its distribution to the poor.
>
> What I wish to express is that for me an engagement was and is just as binding as a *marriage*, and that therefore my estate is to revert to her in exactly the same manner as if I had been married to her.
>
> Your brother,
S. Kierkegaard[17]

---

17. 'From Søren Kierkegaard's Posthumous Papers', noted in Garff, *Kierkegaard's Muse*, p. 51. Taken from Bruce H. Kirmmse, *Encounters with Kierkegaard: A Life as Seen by His Contemporaries*, collected, ed. and annotated by Bruce H. Kirmmse and Virginia R. Laursen. (Princeton, NJ: Princeton University Press, 1996, pp. 51-52).

The request was unequivocally vetoed by Fritz Schlegel, who replied to Peter Kierkegaard in punctiliously correct civil-service-ese, including an icy statement to the effect that his wife found totally unacceptable the lines in the will referring to an engagement being as binding as a marriage. Regine acquiesced. Fritz added that his wife had requested and been allowed one or two letters and had written to Dr Henrik Lund concerning some minor items found among Kierkegaard's property which she thought had once belonged to her. Among the keepsakes she eventually took possession of was a little gold ring retrieved from the Brazilian rosewood cabinet. Penning his response to Kierkegaard's will must have afforded Schlegel some small satisfaction – before the abject humiliation that descended on him with publication of Kierkegaard's posthumous papers. Here, in response to the husband's outright rejection of permission for contact with his wife, her lover takes aim with laconic but faultless precision: he finds it truly saddening how this girl has been left languishing in the shadows; Schlegel is undoubtedly a nice enough man with whom his wife is quite happy, but she is… 'an instrument he does not know how to play. She is capable of tones that I knew how to summon forth.'[18]

* * *

After a period of recovery, Henrik Lund travelled to Saint Croix to see Regine. Her husband's permission to write to Lund asking for some things from her late lover had been an absolute blessing in that she had been able to share with his nephew at least a bare outline of her present feelings. Otherwise, the extent of her bereavement remained entirely hidden from the world. Only when her husband was mercifully delayed from returning home from government business on another island did she find a few days privacy in which to succumb to her overwhelming grief, and then fury at his authoritarianism. Fritz Schlegel was certainly deeply offended and outraged by Kierkegaard's will. He was a statesman and diplomat, a mediator and a strategist. He was devoted to his wife, verbally affectionate, solicitous during her many illnesses and extremely hard-working. That he was also long-suffering is certain, and just as certainly he would have suffered in silence. It is inconceivable, given the vitality of the city's grapevine, that he had not heard of the 'secret' assignations between his wife and

---

18. Garff, *Kierkegaard's Muse*, p. 259.

Kierkegaard in Copenhagen; and very possible that this entire history had been an expediting factor in his foreign posting.

The time spent by the couple in the tropics was testing, but Regine dutifully adjusted to colonial life. She was a good manager and official hostess, organising ceaseless dinner parties at which she tolerated the vulgarity, greed and facile gossip of fellow expatriate wives. Privately shocked at European treatment of West Indian slaves and servants, she ran her own household as compassionately and respectfully as possible. She and Fritz had no children of their own, but she cared lovingly as surrogate mother for her niece, Thilly, daughter of her widowed brother, the child whom they had brought from Copenhagen to live with them on Saint Croix. Her marriage was stable, companionable and comfortable. In less than easy moments, her little book-filled study in the governor's residence provided refuge. She was a talented artist; Kierkegaard had given her a paint set for her nineteenth birthday on 23 January 1841, and an accomplished still-life by her is reproduced in Garff's book.[19] She loved to bathe each early morning in the sea, and rode through the rainforest and along the shore, noting all that grew and flourished. Her health was not robust, and whenever she was downhearted, or fell from her horse, and when she contracted relapsing fever,[20] Fritz fussed over and nursed her. He was proud of their smooth partnership in governorship. She was a perfect wife.

* * *

Reading the letters from Denmark after his death revealed to Regine in a way his books could never do the immediacy, fidelity and depths of Kierkegaard's love and determination to take her with him into history. It was agony to realise that he had died without hearing from her own lips her answering devotion and understanding. Above all, she needed to hear his final sentiments regarding her, so that Henrik Lund's arrival in the West Indies was indescribably welcome. He was to prove the gentlest, most trustworthy conduit of this information and of reassurance, and a faithful and discreet confidant. Having taken the position of colonial physician on the small island of Saint

---

19. Ibid., p. 245.
20. A recurring febrile disease caused by Borrelia spirochetes transmitted by lice or ticks and treated with antibiotics. Symptoms are recurrent episodes of fever, headache, myalgia, and vomiting, separated by intervals of apparent recovery.

Divine Folly

John, Henrik spent time on Saint Croix whenever he could, remaining in the West Indies until Fritz's posting officially ended on 31 May 1860 and resigning his own position on the same date. That summer he made the return voyage with the Schlegel family to Copenhagen, where Fritz and Regine would resume their place in Copenhagen society, he as high-ranking public servant, she his official hostess.

Henrik's arrival in the West Indies and the information he shared, along with Kierkegaard's letters, enabled Regine privately to prepare herself for eventually speaking out openly of her relations with the man to whom she had remained spiritually faithful. She continued nonetheless to honour her marriage vows by refraining from public disclosure until after her husband's death on 8 June 1896, at the age of 79. His had been an exemplary life and civil service career, fully enabled and supported by the woman he had always loved. Lines written to Fritz from his sister-in-law Olivia Olsen late in their lives provide a glimpse of his private persona. Addressing him affectionately as her "dear sweet Fritz", she reminds him of her habit of trying to shout him down in arguments, and how in answer he would react with typical tropical cool that she was, in fact, off her head, always insisting on seeing things from such a weird angle!

By the time of Fritz Schlegel's death, nearly thirty years had passed since publication in September 1869 of the first of Kierkegaard's nine volumes of *Posthumous Papers and Journals*. Regine, knowing this moment would arrive, must have borne mute witness to her husband's response as the full extent of the eroticism and intimacy of her relationship with Kierkegaard was revealed. Perhaps harder for her to bear, as so private a woman, was the public exposure. From beyond the grave her lover's words reached the still warm ears of the world:

> And when the sun closes its searching eye, when the story is over, not only will I wrap my cloak around me, I will throw the night around me like a veil and I will come to you – I will listen as the savage listens – not for footsteps but for the beating of your heart.[21]

* * *

---

21. Garff, *Kierkegaard's Muse*, p. 253, note 9.

Letters of condolence for the loss of her husband were accompanied by direct enquiries concerning Regine's youthful relationship with Søren Kierkegaard; requests for a meeting to speak with her increased in frequency. At last, the time had come for her to tell her story. One late summer afternoon she opened the door to the librarian Julius Clausen, whom she had invited to index and catalogue her late husband's copious library of some 7,000 books. Clausen would later recall them talking of Fritz, whose many excellent qualities she praised, but he noted that the conversation always turned ultimately to Kierkegaard. Respectful of the elderly lady for whom he was working, Clausen quietly arrived at his own conclusions concerning relations between her and her late husband. When it came to mention of the sealed letter, he must have been extremely curious, secretly suspecting a direct correlation between Kierkegaard's request for contact with his wife and Schlegel's looking for a posting to the West Indies. His widow remained entirely silent on the matter.

During 1897 Regine moved in with her brother, Oluf, who still lived in the villa at Frederiksberg. Sometime in 1893 Regine had visited Kierkegaard's niece, Henriette Lund, to ask her to take custody of the letters and journal entries recording their relationship. After initial hesitation at the responsibility involved, and fully cognisant of the biographical significance of the documents, Henriette agreed, but wrote once more to Regine to clarify her motives; perhaps Regine, unable to bring herself to destroy the material, was trying in effect to offload this sad task. Regine vacillated in response, but eventually it became clear that far from avoiding responsibility she was intensely aware of her duty to the deceased and more than mindful of his stature as an author and religious thinker. Her whole aim was to leave to the world whatever could illuminate this aspect of his life. The two women managed to reinstate trust between them and Henriette called truce. In autumn 1895 Regine handed over all the rest of the material to Henriette, who supplemented it with relevant quotations from Kierkegaard's journals. When a year later she read her account to Regine the widow expressed entire satisfaction with it, and they agreed that after Regine's death the whole account would be submitted for publication in book form. In 1898, however, Regine reclaimed the entire documentation from Henriette's home, citing concern for fire or other domestic disaster, and lodged it all with the university library. Shaken at this new display of distrust, Henriette wrote asking Regine to promise not to redact any of the material and to seal the package in her presence before it was removed to the library. Henriette also requested that it remain unopened for ten years after Regine's death; after all, she added, everything the public might want to know was already in her own presentation. The now 74-year-old Regine refused to bow to any such attempt at monopoly over the history or to comply with Henriette's request for a ten-year moratorium. She wanted the story told widely and well. She took control, within the year negotiating with her contemporary, Hanne Mourier, to produce a document that could, if need be, form a counterbalancing disclaimer to any inaccuracies in the narrative stemming from Henriette and her husband's accounts and attitudes toward the person and views of Søren Kierkegaard. Mourier's document includes a short postscript dated 1 March 1902 in which Regine declares herself satisfied with the present version of her reportage. The full account is seven pages in printed length and includes a range of important information about the history of the engagement, chronological as well as biographical.

A month before the transfer of documents to the library, Regine contacted the librarian Raphael Meyer with an offer to speak to him personally on the same subject. He subsequently visited her weekly until May 1899, noting the content of all their conversations. She was most eloquent and willing to talk about Kierkegaard, and Meyer prepared the new material for publication in consultation with her and had this included in his 1904 *Kierkegaardske Papirer: Forlovelsen: Udgivne for Fru Regine Schlegel* (*Kierkegaard's Papers: The Engagement: Published for Mrs Regine Schlegel*). In the Preface he tells how, after Kierkegaard's death, a number of letters were sent to the West Indies in two sealed packages, among them some of her own which, according to her own testimony she had 'fortunately burnt'. Meyer goes on to state that she had squirreled others away to preserve them for her eyes only, until during her husband's final illness when stricken with grief and suffering from recurrent influenza she presented the letters [from Kierkegaard to herself] to S.K's niece Miss Henriette Lund. It is not known whether Meyer respected his own caveat concerning the material being opened and published only after Regine's death, but in any case, the extraordinary interest in her love story was now fully awakened and Regine, previously described by Georg Brandes as most shy of public self-disclosure, became more than prepared to talk openly about her life. Many sought her out for this purpose, discovering in her drawing-room the epitome of elderly feminine beauty and grace; a white-haired, dignified woman in black silk, ready to describe the privilege of having met in her life with the singular. By the time she was in her eighties, Julius Clausen noted, having visited her often after her move to Frederiksberg, there was no more mention of Schlegel, and she spoke only of Kierkegaard. Regine Schlegel died at the age of 82, on 18 March 1904. Her obituary in the newspaper *Politiken* cited primarily her relationship with Kierkegaard, referring only as afterthought to her marriage. She had already passed into eternity.

Diamond ring given to Regine on their engagement, returned, and refashioned by Kierkegaard into a cross which he wore until his death in 1855.

* * *

Twenty years after Kierkegaard's inglorious funeral, Hans Christian Andersen was buried in Assistens Cemetery after a ceremony at the same church on 11 August 1875. He had died in his sleep on 4 August 1875 from liver cancer at the age of 70 years. After a lifetime of loneliness he would eventually be joined in the same grave by Edvard and Henriette Collin in 1886 and 1894 respectively, but their bodies were later exhumed and reburied in the Collin family plot at Frederiksberg Cemetery, leaving the storyteller alone in perpetuity. Shortly before his death he had asked his housekeeper, Mrs Melchior, to sever his veins in case he were to be mistakenly buried alive, to which she had replied that he could leave his usual note beside his bed saying he only appeared to be dead. Her implication that his note would be there for someone else to deal with caused a small smile to cross his wan features. Among the hundreds in Vor Frue Kierke on the day of Andersen's funeral were the king and the crown prince of Denmark, but not a single blood relation of the deceased. He left his entire estate, worth about 30,000 *Rigsdalers*, to Edvard Collin, along with the rights to his works, which Reitzel bought for 20,000 *Rigsdalers*. He had requested a triple plot in the graveyard, to leave space for Edvard and Henriette.

Andersen's grave, in Assistens Cemetery.

Despite decades spent absorbing the fairy-tale adulation of the world, Andersen's otherworldly imagination persisted to the end, reminding him of more shadowy realities. On 21 July 1875, a fortnight before death overtook him, his dimming memory presented him with a vision recorded in his diary as that of a silk-clad young girl with a crooked back, who burst into his rooms at the Hôtel du Nord and whom his friends claimed was in love with him. They said she had been wandering around Copenhagen quoting indecently from his erotic play *The Mulatto*. Complimenting him on his very lovely rooms, the creature stretched herself on the sofa, inviting him to embrace her. In his hallucination, Andersen reacted with true-to-life horror and indignation, asking what on earth was wrong with the girl, didn't she have a mother, whatever would *she* have to say about such behaviour? Commanding his uninvited guest to leave at once and stop frightening him with her provocation, he sees her whole personality change before his eyes as she tells him what a disgusting person he is and how she used to love but now hates him. Shaking, he banishes her from the room, rushing to dress and run to Titular Councillor Collin's. To the surprised questioning of an elderly lady guest at Jonas's home, Andersen can only stammer, 'God, there was a female up in my rooms!'[22]

From now on his housekeeper wrote down all he said and brought him a white rose each morning, which he kissed. On 29 July

---

22. Wullschläger, *Hans Christian Andersen*, p. 426.

she recorded how he took her hand and kissed it too, pressing it repeatedly and warmly and gazing at her with a blissful smile, thanking and blessing her. Edvard Collin would publish his own memoir of Andersen in 1882, much of it cold and critical, but ending in the warmest thaw of which Edvard was capable. He wished, he wrote, to express the true essence of Andersen's character, and having looked into the depths of his subject's soul he had found it possible to excuse the contradictory excesses of his imagination and confirm that he was good. This simple affirmation, wrote Edvard, would not be misunderstood by those who really knew him. It was surely all that Andersen would have wished for as eulogy.

* * *

In considering their legacy a backward glance might be taken at Andersen and Kierkegaard through the lens of their respective treatment of the same traditional ballad, *Agnete and the Merman*. Andersen's poem and later stage play based on it, *Agnete* (1833), was a twice repeated disastrous flop; over a decade of reworking, Andersen wrote himself into both main protagonists of the famous Danish folklore ballad dating back to oral tradition, in which Agnete is an adventurous young woman who goes to live beneath the waves with a flirtatious merman and then deserts him and their seven children, tempted back onto land by the ringing of church bells. Andersen imbues her with his own simple sentimental spirit, while her mutant suitor is as feeble a failure in love as his creator. In contrast, Kierkegaard's fable 'Agnete and the Merman' in *Fear and Trembling* (1843) presents a mercilessly stereotypical romantic 'rescue' scenario of seduction involving a fair maid who tries to save the predatory merman's soul, awakening at her most loving only his violent passion. The dilemma for the merman is binary: to save them both by trust in the divine, or daemonic escape. This cautionary tale about the impossibility of saving another individual its author sent during their courtship to 'his' little Regine, along with a cruel sketch of a subaquatic damsel. The same Kierkegaard who on his premature deathbed would equally transparently and unequivocally confess his life's failure, while the so much less self-punishing Andersen lived out his remote renown into desultory old age.

In his essay *On the Relation of Analytical Psychology to Poetry*[23] Carl Jung describes the progenitor of creative work as an 'autonomous complex' which begs, borrows, and steals energy from the consciousness to unearth 'primordial' images from the unconscious, which are then activated in elaborating and shaping the archetype and incorporating it into the finished work (see Chapter One, pp. 3-10). So the archetype leads remedially back to the deepest springs of life and connects us to our collective need for healing. Via the archetype art acts as the edifying spirit of the age, identifying what is most lacking and offering a compensatory primordial image to correct any imbalance and inadequacy. This image represents the one-sidedness from which the age is suffering and raising this awareness from the unconscious, bringing it into alignment with conscious current values, renders it available and accessible to the contemporary mind. 'Just as the one-sidedness of the individual's conscious attitude is corrected by reactions from the unconscious, so art represents a process of self-regulation in the life of nations and epochs.'[24] But even such powerful symbols as archetypes may be counteracted. Because human beings and societies have the propensity and capability to 'edit out' input to the conscious, elements dissonant with currently preferred wisdom may be rejected and an archetype remain unseen or unrecognised and thus unassimilated into consciousness, both individual and collective. A dark archetype may, for example, appear anachronistic to an age whose leitmotif is radical compensatory positivity; or it may in some other way seem an affront to the *zeitgeist* and so be cast out and its regulatory effect aborted and/or annulled:

> Peoples and times, like individuals, have their own characteristic tendencies and attitudes. The very word "attitude" betrays the necessary bias that every marked tendency entails. Direction implies exclusion, and exclusion means that very many psychic elements that could play

---

23. Lecture delivered to the Society for German Language and Literature, Zurich, May 1922. First published as *Uber die Beziehungen de analytischen Psychologie zum dichterischen Kunstwerk, Wiissen und Leben* (Zurich), XV:1920 (Sept. 1922). Reproduced in C.G. Jung, *The Spirit in Man, Art and Literature*, Princeton University Press, 1972.
24. Jung, *The Spirit in Man, Art and Literature*, pp. 82-3.

their part in life are denied the right to exist because they are incompatible with the general attitude.[25]

To sentimentalise a body of work such as Andersen's phantasmagoria is to strip it of remedial potential; in banishing the negative and cleaving only to the light and positive archetypes in his mythology we emasculate the work to the point at which it can no longer fulfil its function as corrective for the age. Fantasy is not imagination; the former implies flight from reality, the latter engagement with its infinite potential. In his dialogue with the Romantic imagination Kierkegaard credits the potentising possibilities of the imagination for individual 'becoming'; passion and imagination offer myriad pathways to an authentic self. To imagine, reflect and act in the real world, so progressing from the aesthetic to the ethical and on into the religious sphere is to move towards an attitude of universal love, shedding along the way the many fragmentary aspects and shadows of the nascent personality. To approach *agape* is at last to behold the sun. If dazzled by the light we then shirk reengagement with the shades of darkness we, like Socrates' freed captives of the cave, risk forfeiting the redemptive gift endowed by art and allegory for the common good.

---

25. Ibid., p. 83.

Bibliography

Andersen, Hans Christian, *The Complete Illustrated Stories of Hans Christian Andersen*, first published by George Routledge & Sons as *Stories for the Household* (1889), facsimile edn. (London: Chancellor Press, 1987)

———, *The Diaries of Hans Christian Andersen*, selected and trans. Patricia L. Conroy and Sven H. Rossel (Seattle: University of Washington Press, 1990)

———, *Andersen's Fairy Tales: 16 plates in colour by Margaret W. Tarrant* (London and Melbourne: Ward, Lock & Co. Ltd, c. 1930s)

———, *It's Perfectly True! and Other Stories*, translated from the Danish by Paul Leyssac, with the original illustrations by Vilhelm Pedersen (London: Macmillan & Co. Ltd, 1937)

———, *My Fairy-tale Life*, trans. W. Glyn Jones (Sawtry: Dedalus, 2013)

Bowlby, John, *Child Care and the Growth of Love*, abridged and ed. Margery Fry, two new chapters by Mary D. Salter Ainsworth (London: Penguin Books, 1985)

Buber, Martin, *I and Thou*, trans. Walter Kaufman (NY: Dover Publications, 1970)

Garff, Joakim, *Kierkegaard's Muse: The Mystery of Regine Olsen*, trans. Alastair Hannay (Princeton, NJ: Princeton University Press, 2017)

Heltoft, Kjeld, *Hans Christian Andersen as an Artist* (Copenhagen: Royal Danish Ministry of Foreign Affairs, 1977)

Jung, Carl Gustav, 'On the Relation of Analytical Psychology to Poetry', a lecture first delivered to the Society for German Language and Literature, Zurich, May 1922, in C.G. Jung, *The Spirit in Man, Art, and Literature* (Collected Works of C.G. Jung, Volume 15) (Princeton, NJ: Princeton University Press, 1972)

———, *The Spirit in Man, Art, and Literature* (Collected Works of C.G. Jung, Volume 15) (Princeton, NJ: Princeton University Press, 1972)

Kierkegaard, Søren, *Af Søren Kierkegaards Efterladte Papirer*, ed. H.P. Barfod (Copenhagen: C.A. Reitzel, 1869)

―――, *Either/Or: A Fragment of Life*, ed. Victor Eremita, abridged, trans. with Notes by Alastair Hannay (London: Penguin, 1992)
―――, *The Journals of Søren Kierkegaard: A Selection*, ed. and trans. Alexander Dru (London: Oxford University Press, 1938)
―――, *Kierkegaard's Writings, XXV: Letters and Documents*, trans. Henrik Rosenmeier with Introduction and Notes (Princeton, NJ: Princeton University Press, 1978) (further details available at: https://www.jstor.org/stable/j.ctt1d2dm59)
―――, *Letters*, available online at: *SAK Journals: Letters*
_____, *Fear and Trembling*, trans. with intro. and notes by Walter Lowrie (NJ: Princeton University Press, 1974)
―――, *Repetition: An Essay in Experimental Psychology*, trans. with Introduction and Notes by Walter Lowrie (NY: Harper Torchbooks, Harper & Row Publishers, 1941)
_____, *The Sickness Unto Death*, trans. with intro. and notes by Walter Lowrie (NJ: Princeton University Press, 1974)
_____, *Purity of Heart is to Will One Thing*, trans. and intro. Douglas V. Steere (NY: Harper & Row Publishers, 1956)
―――, *Works of Love: Some Christian Reflections in the Form of Discourses*, trans. Howard and Edna Hong (NY: Harper Torchbook, Harper & Row Publishers, 1964)
―――, *Stages on Life's Way*, trans. Walter Lowrie, new intro. Paul Sponheim (NY: Schocken Books, 1967)
Lowrie, Walter, *A Short Life of Kierkegaard* (Princeton, NJ: Princeton University Press, 1974)
Lund, Henriette, *Erindringer fra Hjemmet* (*Memories from Home*) (Copenhagen: Gyldendal, 1909)
Maté, Gabor, *When the Body Says No, The Cost of Hidden Stress* (Wiley, 1 January 2011)
Meyer, Raphael, *Kierkegaardske Papirer: Forlovelsen: Udgivne for Fru Regine Schlegel* (*Kierkegaard's Papers: the Engagement: Published for Mrs Regine Schlegel*) (Copenhagen: Gyldendal, 1904)
Pattison, George, *Kierkegaard and the Crisis of Faith: An Introduction to His Thought*, repr. edn. (Eugene, OR: Wipf & Stock, 2013)
Prince, Alison, *Hans Christian Andersen: The Fan Dancer* (London: Allison & Busby, 1998)
Steiner, Henriette, *The Emergence of a Modern City: Golden Age Copenhagen 1800-1850* (Aldershot: Ashgate, 2014)
Storm, D. Anthony, *Commentary on Kierkegaard*, 'First Period, Works of Youth 1835-1842', commentary on *The Concept of Irony*; available online at sorenkierkegaard.org
Wullschläger, Jackie, *Hans Christian Andersen: The Life of a Storyteller* (London: Penguin, 2001)

Index

Adler, Adolph Peter, 170, 180–1
Andersen, Anne Marie, 32–5
Andersen, Hans Christian:
  Life & Career: childhood and family, 31–6; arrival in Copenhagen, 30–1, 37; illegitimate sister, 33; death of father, 34–5; cultivation of eminent friends, 37; attends Slagelse grammar school, 38–9; views a hanging, 38; publishes first volume of poems, 39; treatment of Christianity, 43; friendship with SK, 43, 56; death of mother, 45, 52–3; infatuation with Edvard Collin, 5, 46, 49–50, 89, 147; tours in Germany in Italy (1834), 46, 49–56; sketches in Italy, 50–1, 53–4; member of 'Unholy Alliance,' 17–18, 56; trip to Sweden (1837), 58–9; and SK's critique of his work, 59–62; fictional world of, 76–9; literary reviews, 79; papercuts, 84; attempts at theatrical career, 85; visit to Germany (1840), 94–6; attends performance by Liszt, 95; describes first train journey, 96; in Rome (1840), 96–7; travels in the Balkans, 97–100, 106–8; portrait painted by Vogelstein, 107; rumoured to be illegitimate son of the king, 127; sought out by illegitimate sister, 129; visit to Paris (1843), 144–8; relationship with Jenny Lind, 148–53, 171–2, 215; attends opening of Tivoli Gardens, 150; visit to Germany (1844), 154–5; guest of King Christian VIII, 154–5, 183; European tour (1843), 171–6; portrait by Jens Peter Møller, 186; knighted by King of Prussia, 172; portrait painted by Grahl, 173; French and German translations of his work, 183; London visit (1847), 183–9; meets Charles Dickens, 188; visit to Scotland, 189–92; English translations of his stories, 194; trip to Sweden (1848), 205; reaction to death of Christian VIII, 208; visit to Paris (1851), 213–14; publishes *Stories* (1852), 214; second visit to England, 218; travels to Germany and Switzerland, 218; reaction to SK's death, 235–6; death and funeral, 246–8
  Character & characteristics: casual treatment of women, 89; childlike persona, 11; compulsion to travel, 85, 106; desire for fame, 58, 173; disdain for the Danish people, 83–5; fascination with theatre, 34; fear of insanity, 4–5; hypochondria, 98, 174–5; lack of education, 35; odd appearance, 15–16; paranoia, 106; political naivety, 123–4, 170; poor syntax and grammar, 143–4; self-aggrandisement, 34, 76; sexuality, 130; susceptible to superior social status,

56, 124
Writings: *Agnete and the Merman*, 49–50, 147, 248; *The Dying Child*, 39; *The Fairy Tale of My Life* (autobiography), 174, 182–3, 217; *The Fir Tree*, 151; *The Ice Maiden*, 35; *The Improvisatore*, 53, 55; *The Little Mermaid*, 5, 77, 79; *The Moorish Maid*, 85, 89, 96; *More Than Pearls and Gold*, 205; *The Mulatto*, 88; *New Fairy Tales for Children* (1843), 148, 151, 170; *The Nightingale*, 17n, 149–51; *O. T.*, 77; *Only a Fiddler*, 59–61; *Pictures of Sweden*, 205; *A Poet's Bazaar* (1842), 108, 122–3; *The Shadow*, 175–6, 181–2; *She Was Good for Nothing*, 215; *The Shoes of Fortune*, 17; *The Snow Queen*, 32, 35, 151, 170–1; *The Sweethearts*, 149; *Tales Told for Children*, 108, 122; *Thousands of Years from Now*, 214; *The Tinder-Box*, 38, 56; *The Ugly Duckling*, 125–9, 151; *A Walking Tour* (1829), 44; *The Wild Swans*, 78; *Under the Willow Tree*, 215
Andersen, Hans (HCA's father), 31, 34–5

Barck, Lady Matilde, 89
Beaulieu-Marconnay, Baron Karl Olivier von, 210, 215
Bentley, Richard, 183, 216
Bettelheim, Bruno, 127
Blessington, Lady Marguerite, 185, 187
Boesen, Emil, 17, 74, 119–20, 231–5
Bournonville, August, 14, 148, 149
Bowlby, John, 24
Brandes, Georg, 182, 198–9
Brøchner, Hans, 236

Carl Alexander of Saxe-Weimar-Eisenbach, Hereditary Grand Duke, 154, 172, 185, 204, 210, 216
Caroline, Queen, 15
Carstens, Fedder, 31
Carstensen, Georg, 150
Castlereagh, Lord, 187

cholera, in the 19th century, 97–8
Christian August, Duke, 170
Christian VIII, King of Denmark: support for science and the arts, 15; invites HCA to court, 88; gift of ruby ring to HCA, 126–7; and the Tivoli Gardens, 150; audiences with HCA, 154–5; audiences with SK, 180; death, 208–9
Clausen, Julius, 244, 246
Collin, Edvard, 5, 46, 49–50, 147, 173, 182–3, 246–8
Collin, Jonas, 37–9, 52, 96, 106, 129, 147, 174
Collin, Louise, 45
Collin, Theodor, 144, 145
Collins, Wilkie, 218
Conroy, Patricia L., 143
Copenhagen: cholera epidemic (1853), 216; 'Golden Age,' 14–15, 40–3; history, architecture and culture, 12–15; Jewish pogroms (1819), 30–1, 59; literary circle, 16–17; Royal Theatre, 13–14, 31; Tivoli Gardens, 14, 149–50
Corsair (periodical), 86, 114, 123, 165–9

Danneskjold-Samsøe, Countess, 124
Denmark: 'Golden Age,' 14–15; history, 12–13; political history, 12–13, 40; Schleswig-Holstein crisis, 170, 203–4; death of Christian VIII, 208–9 *see also* Copenhagen
Dickens, Charles, 188, 189, 193, 214, 218
D'Israeli, Benjamin, 187–8
Drewsen, Elinar, 216
Drewsen, Harald, 218
Drewsen, Jonna, 152, 154, 175
Drewsen, Viggo, 213–14
Dru, Alexander, 181
Dumas, Alexandre, 144–6
Durham, Joseph, 189

Fatherland, The (periodical), 165–6, 168, 203, 228

Index

Felix, Rachel, 145–6, 147
Frederick VI, King of Denmark, 13, 88
Frederik, Prince of Nør, 170
Freud, Sigmund, 7
Friedrich Wilhelm, King of Prussia, 172

Garff, Joachim, 235
genius, and madness, 5–11
Gisselfeld, Zealand, 124–5, 128
Goldschmidt, Meir Aron, 86, 123–4, 165–9
Goldschmidt, Otto, 215
Grahl, August, 173
Grand Tour, 122–3
Grimm, Jacob, 154, 171–2
Grimm, Wilhelm, 172
Grimms' fairy tales, 55–6, 78
Grundtvig, Nikolai Frederik, 232n
Gyllembourg-Ehrensvärd, Thomasine Christine, 167

Hamann, Johann Georg, 64
Hambro, Carl Joachim, 189–91
Hambro, Joseph, 186–7, 188
Hanck, Henriette, 58, 79
Hansen, Christian Frederik (architect), 13–14
Hartmann, Emma, 210–11
Hegel, Georg Wilhelm Friedrich, 64
Heiberg, Johan Ludvig, 16, 17, 49, 85, 89, 97, 136
Heiberg, Johanne Luise (née Pätges), 16–17, 85, 88–9, 203
Heidegger, Martin, 164
Heine, Heinrich, 123, 146
Heltoft, Kjeld, 52
Hertz, Henrik, *Moods and Conditions*, 17
Hoffmann, Ernst Theodore Amadeus, 44
Holst, Hans Peter, 96
Howitt, Mary, 187
Hugo, Victor, 146
Hume, David, 64

Ingemann, Bernhard Severin, 84

Jerdan, William, 183
Jung, Carl Gustav, 3, 5–11, 249–50

Kierkegaard, Michael Pedersen, 18, 20–2, 24–7, 72–3, 75
Kierkegaard, Peter (later Bishop of Aalborg), 18, 21, 47, 73, 116, 177, 206, 232, 237–8
Kierkegaard, Søren:
Life & Career: at university, 18–19; member of 'Unholy Alliance,' 17–18; daily walks in Copenhagen, 16, 41; family bereavements, 19; influence of his father, 20–1, 24–7, 72–3; rejection of father's religiosity, 28–30; 'The Great Earthquake' crisis, 25–7, 46–9; family house in Copenhagen, 42; treatment of Christianity, 43; friendship with HCA, 43, 56; critique of HCA's work, 56–62; attempts at self-reform, 63–6; first meets Regine Olsen, 67–70; indebtedness to Paul Møller, 71–2; death of father, 75; visits to Regine Olsen at her father's house, 80–3; takes theological exams, 86, 89–90; pilgrimage to father's birthplace, 101–4; gifts and letters to Regine Olsen, 91–4; meetings and observations of Regine in Copenhagen, 102–6; proposes to Regine and then breaks off engagement, 108–13; enters the seminary, 110; study trip to Berlin (1841), 116–20; publishes *Either/Or*, 134–9; in Berlin (1843), 137–9; daily encounters with Regine, 139, 142; scorn for the Tivoli Gardens, 150; moves back into family home at Nytorv 2, 161; *Corsair* affair, 165–9; longing for reconciliation with Regina, 206–8; sale of house at Nytorv, 178, 201; audiences with King Christian, 180, 209–10; relationship with nieces and nephews, 211–12, 236; assault on

the Established Church, 225–30; illness and death, 230–6; deathbed thoughts on Regina, 231–2; funeral, 237–40; bequest to Regine Schlegel, 240–1
Character & characteristics: appearance, 16; childlike qualities, 11; difficulty in relations with women, 114–16; fear of insanity, 1–3; love of Denmark, 3; relationship with mother, 22–5, 115–16; self-loathing, 57; use of pseudonyms, 90, 118, 161, 207–8
Writings: *Agnete and the Merman*, 200, 248; *The Concept of Dread*, 49, 157–8; *The Concept of Irony*, 86; *Concluding Unscientific Postscript* (1846), 45, 71, 161–8, 163; *Edifying Discourses*, 133, 198–9; *Either/Or* (1843), 17, 57, 70, 93, 118–20, 134–6, 158, 162–3; *Fear and Trembling*, 137, 200; *Journals*, 19, 25–6, 114–15, 156–60, 220; *On My Work as an Author*, 206; *From the Papers of a Person Still Living*, 59–60, 100–1; *Philosophical Fragments* (1844), 161, 163; *The Point of View for my Life as an Author* (1848), 58, 203, 206; *Quidam's Diary*, 93; *Repetition*, 137; *The Sickness unto Death*, 203, 207; *Stages on Life's Way* (1845), 17, 93, 156–61; *Training in Christianity*, 203, 206, 224; *Two Minor Ethico-Religious Treatises* (1849), 181; *The Wild Goose: A Symbol*, 128; *Works of Love*, 179, 195–6
Koch, Robert, 98
Küchler, Albert, 51–2

Lamartine, Alphonse, 148
Leipzig, 96, 107, 154, 172–3, 194
Levin, Isabel, 236
Leyssac, Paul, 194
Lind, Jenny, 148–53, 171–2, 185–6, 215
Liszt, Franz, 95, 108, 215, 216
Lorck, Carl Berendt, 173, 174
Lowrie, Walter: translations of SK, 114–15, 181; *A Short Life of Kierkegaard*, 1, 3, 22, 58, 65, 137, 161
Lund, Ane Sørendatter (SK's mother), 21–2, 24–5
Lund, Carl, 212
Lund, Henriette, 211–12, 236, 244–5
Lund, Henrik, 236, 238–43
Lutheranism, 13

Marmier, Xavier, 58, 144
Martensen, Hans Lassen, 223, 226–8
Marx, Karl, 123
Mendelssohn, Felix, 96, 173
Meyer, Raphael, 245
Møller, Paul, 57, 71–2
Møller, Peder Ludvig, 165–6
Moltke-Hvitfeldt, Count, 107, 216
Mourier, Hanne, 245
Mynster, Bishop, 22, 110, 179, 181, 197–8, 223–4

Naples, 53, 97, 174–6
Nielsen, Rasmus, 206, 239

Odense, 30, 32–3
Oehlenschläger, Adam Gottlieb, 14, 39, 49, 153
Olsen, Regine *see* Schlegel, Regine Olsen
Ørsted, Hans Christian, 14, 37, 43, 80, 210
Overskou, Thomas, *Of My Life and My Time* (1868), 41

Pacini, Filippo, 98
Pasteur, Louis, 98
Pauck, Professor Wilhelm, 114
Pedersen, Vilhelm, 205

Reitzel (publisher), 44, 127, 151, 178, 216, 247
Reventlow, Count Edvard, 184–6
Romanticism, 14–15
Rørdam, Bolette, 67, 68–9

Sartre, Jean-Paul, 1

Index

Schall, Anna Margrethe, 36, 37
Scheel, Countess Sophie, 205
Schelling, Friedrich, 96, 116, 119
Schlegel, Fritz, 109, 140, 141, 196, 208, 241–3
Schlegel, Regine (Regina) Olsen: first meeting with SK, 67–8; SK's visits to, 80, 105; SK's letters and gifts to, 91–4; brief engagement to SK, 108–13; character and appearance, 132–3; engagement to Fritz Schlegel, 140–1; marriage to Fritz Schlegel, 196; departure for West Indies, 223; SK's bequest to, 240–1; in Saint Croix, 241–3; eagerness to talk about her relationship with SK, 244–6
Schumann, Clara, 108, 154
Scott, Walter, 188, 204
Stampe, Baron Henrik, 152, 154, 175
Steiner, Henriette, 40
Swenson, David Ferdinand, 91, 115

Swift, Jonathan, 158

Thomson, Grimùr, 216
Thorvaldsen, Bertel, 14, 50–2, 55, 152, 153–4

'Unholy Alliance, The', 17–18

Verne, Jules, 215
Vogel von Vogelstein, Carl Christian, 107
Voigt, Riborg, 45, 148

Walpole, Hugh Seymour, 194
Werliin, Christian, 39
Winther, Matthias, 78
Wulff, Admiral Peter, 37
Wulff, Henriette ('Jette'; *née* Collin), 39, 147, 217, 218–19
Wullschläger, Jackie, 44, 123, 127, 214

You may also be interested in:

A Grundtvig Anthology

Selections from the Writings of N.F.S Grundtvig (1783-1872)

edited by Niels Lyhne Jensen

A notable figure in the cultural and social history of Denmark, Nikolaj Frederik Severin Grundtvig's (1783-1872) works are still salient for us now. Highlighting his vivacious ideas and personality, *A Grundtvig Anthology* includes extracts from Grundtvig's historical, educational, theological, devotional, and poetical works. Each chapter is prefaced by insightful explanatory introductions by leading authorities on Grundtvig's monumental body of work, along with a comprehensive general introduction and illuminating annotations.

Grundtvig viewed the myths of the North as an expression of the moral values and understanding of life, and his hymn and song writing reveal the same joy of life, openness and freedom as the Norse perspective. By offering selections from across his major works, this anthology succeeds in capturing his spirit in English translation, and continuing his written legacy.

Nikolaj Frederik Severin Grundtvig (1783-1872) was a theologian, priest, poet, writer and teacher who left an indelible mark on the life and culture of Denmark. A contemporary of Hans Christian Andersen and Søren Kierkegaard, and cited as one of the greatest poets in the Danish language, he left a great legacy which is still felt in public life and cultural activities in Denmark.

Niels Lyhne Jensen (1921-2001), lecturer and amanuensis, joined the Nordisk Institute at Aarhus University in 1969, having taught Scandinavian literature at Newcastle University. He wrote numerous articles and books on literary and historical subjects.

Published 2024

Paperback ISBN: 978 0 7188 9821 2
PDF ISBN: 978 0 7188 9822 9
ePub ISBN: 978 0 7188 9820 5

You may also be interested in:

R.C. Hutchinson

The Man and His Writing

by Barry Webb

In *R.C. Hutchinson*, Barry Webb reclaims the legacy of a highly-acclaimed, yet often forgotten writer. Despite having been awarded the Sunday Times Gold medal for fiction, the W.H.Smith award for the best novelist of the year, being short-listed for the Booker Prize, and several of his 17 novels becoming best-sellers in the UK and America, Hutchinson has not withstood the test of time compared to his contemporaries. Combining Hutchinson's own reflections with insightful critical analysis, Webb traces Hutchinson's thoughtful, observational life alongside his extraordinary literary output. He draws out how Hutchinson's firmly held Christian beliefs allowed him to eschew didacticism for nuanced reflections on the nature of human suffering.

Part biography, part critical study, *R.C. Hutchinson* sheds light on this influential and gifted writer, contextualising his work and highlighting his genius. He was described by Sebastian Faulks as a novelist 'on the grand scale' and 'a mid-century master of the genre', and by Cecil Day Lewis as 'one of the very few living novelists who will be read fifty – even a hundred years hence'. Webb offers readers the opportunity to re-discover this exceptional writer.

Barry Webb is a former Fellow and Tutor in English at St. Peter's College, Oxford, and has now realised his long-held ambition of writing a book on R.C. Hutchinson. He is also the official biographer of the poet and scholar, Edmund Blunden. He now lives in retirement in Oxford. He enjoys reading poetry, listening to Schubert, solving crosswords and watching cricket.

Published 2024

Hardback ISBN: 978 0 7188 9800 7
Paperback ISBN: 978 0 7188 9799 4
PDF ISBN: 978 0 7188 9802 1
ePub ISBN: 978 0 7188 9801 4

You may also be interested in:

Katherine Briggs

Story-Teller

by H.R. Ellis Davidson

Katharine Briggs made an indelible mark on the world of folklore with her compilation of the Dictionary of British Folktales in the English Languages, while her subsequent Dictionary of Fairies confirmed her already distinguished place among British Folklorists. Briggs's initial academic interest while at Oxford University was in seventeenth-century literature and the Civil War. Upon leaving Oxford she pursued amateur dramatics and worked for the Guide Movement, and during the Second World War she served in the Women's Auxiliary Air Force. It was here, perhaps, that her personality fully matured; among other activities she delighted her fellows with her remarkable gift for story-telling.

After the war, her career as a folklorist began to blossom. As if to make up for lost time, she spent the last twenty years of her life writing and lecturing almost continually. As well as her books on folklore, she gained renown for her children's books Kate Crackernuts and Hobberdy Dick. She was responsible for revitalising the Folklore Society and as its President, she laid the foundations of the Society as it is today. Hilda Davidson's biography brings to life a remarkable woman whose combination of academic excellence and natural gift for narrative found her friends all over the world.

Hilda R. Ellis Davidson (1914-2006) was President of the Folklore Society. She published a number of books, including many on Norse and Anglo-Saxon mythology. Dr Davidson was a Lecturer and formerly Vice-President of Lucy Cavendish College, Cambridge, and was the general editor of Mistletoe Books, published by the Folklore Society.

Published 2024

Paperback ISBN: 978 0 7188 9748 2
PDF ISBN: 978 0 7188 9749 9
ePub ISBN: 978 0 7188 9750 5

You may also be interested in:

Science and Sensibility

From the Heavens Above to the Earth Below
by David Howe

In an outer arm of the spiralling Milky Way galaxy can be seen an insignificant speck. This is our home, planet Earth. Its skies, clouds, lands and seas, and indeed life itself have long drawn the interest of scientists and artists alike. Our cultural and scientific history is evidence enough that curiosity and wonder are the twin drivers of both scientific and artistic imaginations. In *Science and Sensibility*, David Howe unveils the stories of the scientists who helped to make sense of the stars, clouds, life, rocks, and the elements, and weaves their tales with the thoughts and feelings of artists who found meaning as they experienced nature's beauty, grandeur and mystery.

Scientific greats such as James Hutton, Charles Darwin, Dmitri Mendeleev, Gregor Mendel and Annie Jump Cannon all the way up to today's leading scientists are complemented by the literary insights of people such as William Wordsworth, Jorge Luis Borges and Iris Murdoch. Readers are encouraged to embrace what the sciences and the arts can reveal together. In doing so, the earth below and the heavens above become brighter and richer. The wonder and curiosity embodied in *Science and Sensibility* could perhaps take us a step closer to holding 'Infinity in the palm of your hand / and Eternity in an hour'.

David Howe is Emeritus Professor at the University of East Anglia. He has published other non-fiction titles, most recently *Extraction to Extinction: Rethinking Our Relationship with Earth's Natural Resources* (2021), alongside *Rocks and Rain, Reason and Romance* (2019), and *Wandering in Norfolk: Time Lines and Crossing Places* (2016) which was short-listed for the East Anglian Book Awards.

Published 2025

Paperback ISBN: 978 0 7188 9809 0
PDF ISBN: 978 0 7188 9810 6
ePub ISBN: 978 0 7188 9811 3